Introduction to

# HEALTH BEHAVIOR THEORY

SECOND EDITION

## Joanna Hayden, PhD, CHES
Professor, Department of Public Health
William Paterson University
Wayne, NJ

JONES & BARTLETT
LEARNING

*World Headquarters*
Jones & Bartlett Learning
5 Wall Street
Burlington, MA 01803
978-443-5000
info@jblearning.com
www.jblearning.com

Jones & Bartlett Learning books and products are available through most bookstores and online booksellers. To contact Jones & Bartlett Learning directly, call 800-832-0034, fax 978-443-8000, or visit our website, www.jblearning.com.

Substantial discounts on bulk quantities of Jones & Bartlett Learning publications are available to corporations professional associations and other qualified organizations. For details and specific discount information contact the special sales department at Jones & Bartlett Learning via the above contact information or send an email to specialsales@jblearning.com.

**Production Credits:**
Executive Publisher: William Brottmiller
Publisher: Michael Brown
Senior Managing Editor: Maro Gartside
Editorial Assistant: Chloe Falivene
Production Assistant: Alyssa Lawrence
Senior Marketing Manager: Sophie Fleck Teague
Manufacturing and Inventory Control Supervisor:
  Amy Bacus
Composition: Laserwords Private Limited, Chennai, India
Cover and Title Page Design: Kristin E. Parker
Cover and Title Page Image: © R.T. Wohlstadter/
  ShutterStock, Inc.; © cluckva/ShutterStock, Inc.
Printing and Binding: Edwards Brothers Malloy
Cover Printing: Edwards Brothers Malloy

**Library of Congress Cataloging-in-Publication Data**
Hayden, Joanna.
  Introduction to health behavior theory / Joanna Hayden.—2nd ed.
    p. ; cm.
  Includes bibliographical references and index.
  ISBN 978-1-4496-8974-2 (pbk.)—ISBN 1-4496-8974-4 (pbk.)
  I. Title.
  [DNLM: 1. Health Behavior. 2. Attitude to Health. 3. Behavioral Research. 4. Health Promotion. W 85]
  RA776.9
  613—dc23
                                                                                            2013008470

6048
Printed in the United States of America
17  16  15     10  9  8  7  6  5

# Contents

# Acknowledgments

This book certainly would not have been written if it were not for all of my former students who struggled to understand theory. They were the reason I stopped trying to find the right book for them, and decided to write it myself.

I must thank my editorial assistant, Chloe Falivene, and my editor, Michael Brown, at Jones & Bartlett Learning for their immeasurable support throughout this entire process, and for being so available to answer "just one more question." They have the patience of saints. A huge thank you also goes to the many reviewers who provided me with wonderful suggestions that guided the writing of this second edition.

Finally, I'd like to thank my husband, Roger, for his understanding of the time I spent in "Qup's garage" completing this edition, and Salty Dog for keeping my lap warm the whole time.

# Introduction to Theory

The idea of studying theory can be a bit daunting. But understanding and being able to use theories is essential because they provide the foundation for professional practice. They help us develop approaches to solving problems and formulating interventions to best provide the services we offer. In fact, having a theoretical foundation upon which practice is based is among several criteria that have been identified as differentiating a profession from an occupation (Upton, 1970).

# WHAT IS THEORY?

So, what is theory? A theory is "a set of statements or principles devised to explain a group of facts or phenomena, especially one that has been repeatedly tested or is widely accepted and can be used to make predictions about natural phenomena" (*American Heritage Dictionary of the English Language*, 2011). "A theory is a set of interrelated concepts, definitions, and propositions that present a systematic view of events or situations by specifying relations among variables in order to *explain* and *predict* events or situations" (Glanz, Rimer, & Viswanath, 2008, p. 26).

From a health promotion and disease prevention perspective, "the term *theory* is used to represent an interrelated set of propositions that serve to explain health behavior or provide a systematic method of guiding health promotion practice" (DiClemente, Crosby, & Kegler, 2002, p. 8). "Theory, then, provides a framework for explaining phenomena and may serve as the basis for further research as well as practice application" (Baumgartner, Strong, & Hansley, 2002, p. 18). Simply put, theories *explain* behavior and thus can suggest ways to achieve behavior change (Glanz, Rimer, & Viswanath, 2008). By understanding why people engage in unhealthy behaviors, we can better develop interventions that will enable them to change their behavior, if they choose, and adopt healthier lifestyles.

In addition to theories, there are also *models*. A model is a composite, a mixture of ideas or concepts taken from any number of theories and used together. Models help us understand a specific problem in a particular setting (Glanz, Rimer, & Viswanath, 2008), which perhaps one theory alone can't do.

Theories and models help us explain, predict, and understand health behavior. Understanding the determinants of health behavior and the process of health behavior change provides the basis upon which interventions can be developed to improve the public's health and their effectiveness evaluated (Noar & Zimmerman, 2005).

Theory is also the driving force behind research. It guides the variables to be studied, how they should be measured, and how they might be combined (Noar & Zimmerman, 2005).

# TYPES OF THEORIES

Theories and models can be separated into three different levels of influence: intrapersonal, interpersonal, and community. Theories at each of these levels attempt to explain behavior by looking at how different factors at these different levels influence what we do and why we do it.

## Intrapersonal Theories

At the intrapersonal or individual level, theories focus on factors within the person that influence behavior, such as knowledge, attitudes, beliefs, motivation, self-concept, developmental history, past experience, and skills (National Cancer Institute [NCI], 2005). These theories and models include, among others, the Health Belief Model, Theory of Reasoned Action, Self-Efficacy Theory, Attribution Theory, and the Transtheoretical Model.

## Interpersonal Theories

Theories addressing factors at the interpersonal level operate on the assumption that other people influence our behavior. Other people affect behavior by sharing their thoughts, advice, and feelings and by the emotional support and assistance they provide. These other people may be family, friends, peers, health care providers, or co-workers (NCI, 2005). Social Cognitive Theory is a very commonly used theory addressing behavior at this level.

## Community-Level Theories

Community-level models and theories focus on factors within social systems (communities, organizations, institutions, and public policies), such as rules, regulations, legislation, norms, and policies. These theories and models suggest strategies and initiatives that can be used to change these factors (Cottrell, Girvam, & McKenzie, 2009; NCI, 2005). These are change theories more than explanatory theories. Changing a social system from one that maintains and supports *un*healthy behaviors to one that supports healthy behaviors ultimately supports individual behavior change (McLeroy et al., 1988). A commonly used community-level theory is Diffusion of Innovation. More recent additions to this category are ecological models and Social Capital Theory.

In health promotion, theories and models are used to explain why people behave, or don't behave, in certain ways relative to their health. They help us plan interventions to support the public's adoption of healthier behaviors. However, in order to understand how theories help explain health behavior and support behavior change, it is important to understand where theories come from in the first place.

# WHERE DO THEORIES COME FROM?

Theories are born from the need to solve a problem or to find an explanation that would account for some repeatedly observed occurrence. The development of a theory in this manner begins with inductive reasoning and qualitative methods (Mullen & Iverson, 1982; Thomas, 1992).

If you recall, inductive reasoning starts with specific observations or evidence and moves to a conclusion.

For example, using inductive reasoning we observe that HIV is transmitted through sexual activity and we observe that condoms prevent the transmission of diseases through sexual activity. Therefore, we conclude that condoms prevent the transmission of HIV.

In deductive reasoning we start with the conclusion—condoms prevent the transmission of HIV—and seek the observations to support the conclusion—condoms prevent transmission of diseases through sexual activity. HIV is transmitted through sexual activity

With this as the basis, let's look at visits to the student health service on campus. Suppose every year it is observed that the number of students needing treatment for alcohol overdose is greater during the month of September than any other time of the academic year. Suppose it is also observed that all of the students needing treatment are freshmen. Through inductive reasoning it might be concluded that risky behavior (drinking) occurs when environmental controls (parents) are absent. This is a reasonable conclusion based on the observations or evidence. However, this may or may not be true, which means the conclusion drawn from the observations needs to be verified, that is, tested to find out how accurate it is in predicting or explaining the behavior. Can risk-taking behavior be explained by the lack of external controls? To further develop this theory, research would be done to determine what happens, why, and under what conditions (Mullen & Iverson, 1982).

Observation, inductive reasoning, and qualitative research methods are what led to the development of the Health Belief Model. The Health Belief Model was developed by researchers at the U.S. Public Health Service in the late 1950s as a means to understand why so few people were being screened for TB. Triggered by the observation of poor screening utilization, possible reasons why people might or might not utilize these screenings were identified and research conducted to determine if the reasons proposed did in fact explain the behavior (Hochbaum, 1958; Rosenstock, 1960). They did explain the behavior and the outcome was the Health Belief Model, one of the most widely used theories in health education and health promotion (Glanz, Rimer, & Viswanath, 2008).

New theories are also developed when existing ones are revised in some way, as is the case with the Theory of Reasoned Action. This theory was not very useful in predicting or explaining behaviors that were not under a person's volitional (willful) control. To make the theory more useful for these types of behaviors, the perception of behavioral control (ease or difficulty of doing something) was added and the Theory of Reasoned Action became the Theory of Planned Behavior.

# HEALTH BEHAVIOR

Health behavior includes all of those things we do that influence our physical, mental, emotional, psychological, and spiritual selves. These behaviors range from the daily brushing of our teeth to having unprotected sex; from practicing yoga for stress management to smoking for weight management. A myriad of factors influences the type of behavior in which we engage, whether it is helpful or harmful to our health. Some of these factors are socioeconomic status, skills, culture, beliefs, attitude, values, religion, and gender.

## SOCIOECONOMIC STATUS

Socioeconomic status (SES) makes a significant contribution to health since it encompasses education, income, and occupation. Of the SES factors, education level seems to be the best predictor of good health (Winkleby et al., 1992). The higher the education level, the greater the employment opportunities, income, and, ultimately, health status. With knowledge, people can make informed decisions about their health and, as a result, are more likely to engage in health-enhancing behaviors.

However, behavior is driven by more than just knowledge. For example, it is common knowledge that unprotected sex increases the risk of contracting the human immunodeficiency virus (HIV). It is also common knowledge that condoms decrease the risk of contracting HIV. If knowledge were the only factor contributing to behavior, then every sexually active person at risk of contracting HIV would be using condoms. We know this is not the case, but why?

## SKILLS

In the grand scheme of things, it is relatively easy to teach people new information, thereby increasing their knowledge. But without the skill or ability to use that knowledge, it is almost useless. So, behavior is influenced by having both knowledge and skill. Going back to the condom example, unless people know how to use condoms, all the knowledge in the world about their HIV risk-reducing benefits is not going to make a difference.

We find a perfect example of this with child safety seats. Parents know the importance of using child safety seats. What they don't know is how to use them correctly. In fact, a study conducted by the National Highway Traffic Safety Administration found that 72.6% of them are *not* used correctly (Decina, Lococo, & Block, 2005).

## CULTURE

Sometimes, even armed with the information and the skills, people still don't use what they know and do what they know how to do. That's because behavior is significantly influenced by culture. In every culture there are norms, or expected, accepted practices, values, and beliefs that are the foundation for behavior.

Think about some of the American cultural norms that dictated what you did this morning in preparing for the day. In our culture, people typically shower on a daily basis and follow it with a daily application of deodorant. These behaviors are not necessarily based on knowledge because bathing every day is actually not the best thing for our skin, and using deodorant has no health benefit and in fact can cause problems for people who are allergic to the ingredients.

Looking at this scenario, why do we bathe every day? Other cultures bathe much less frequently and don't use deodorant. So, there must be something else that underlies these behaviors—that something else is our culture. Bathing every day and using deodorant is culturally expected if we are mainstream Americans.

Imagine, if you will, that there was a movement underway that sought to change these behaviors to the more health-enhancing ones of bathing less frequently and not using deodorant. Imagine that this campaign was based on the factual information that daily bathing is bad for the skin and that deodorants and antiperspirants inhibit a natural bodily process. Would you adopt these new behaviors? Would you simply stop taking that morning shower and stop rolling on that deodorant? Why not?

## BELIEFS

Beliefs are intimately woven with culture. Beliefs are one's own perception of what is true, although they might not be viewed as being true by others. A very common health belief is that going outside with a wet head causes pneumonia. Certainly, knowledge, based on our Western medicine, tells us pneumonia has many causes, but a wet head is not one of them. However, if one's belief is that a wet head causes pneumonia, then the behavior it supports is not going out of the house with a wet head. This seems like a very innocuous behavior on the surface. But take it one step further: an elderly woman with this belief would not get a pneumonia vaccine, believing instead that staying indoors until her hair is dry is all that is needed to avoid "catching pneumonia."

## ATTITUDE

When there are a series of beliefs, you have an attitude. Add to the previous belief about a wet head causing pneumonia the belief that wet socks also lead to pneumonia, as does "getting a chill." This results in an attitude that pneumonia can be easily avoided by drying your hair, quickly changing your wet socks, and keeping warm.

## VALUES

Along with attitudes are values. Values are what people hold in high regard, things that are important to them, such as nature, truth, honesty, beauty, education, integrity, friendship, and family. What we value influences the types of behaviors we adopt. For example, if someone values nature, she might be more likely to recycle, use organic fertilizers, feed the birds, and plant trees. If someone values health, he might be more likely to exercise, maintain a normal weight, and drink in moderation.

## RELIGION

Values and beliefs are often reflective not only of a culture, but of a religion. Religion is another enormously important factor in health behavior. Take, for example, the practice of male circumcision. There is no question in Judaism that a male infant will be circumcised, or, in the Muslim faith, that followers will fast from sunrise to sunset during Ramadan. Religion dictates diet, as in Hinduism, whose followers adhere to a strict vegan diet, or Orthodox Judaism, whose followers adhere to strict kosher laws. Religion influences the way we handle stress, such as by prayer or meditation, and our family planning—whether or not we use contraception.

## GENDER

Gender is another important determinant of health behavior. Research consistently shows that men engage in fewer health-promoting behaviors and have less healthy lifestyles than women. A review of national data and hundreds of large studies has revealed that men of all ages are more likely than women to engage in more than 30 controllable behaviors conclusively linked with a greater risk of disease, injury, and death. Men eat more fat and less fiber, sleep less, and are more often overweight than women (Courtenay, 1998).

# PUTTING IT ALL TOGETHER: CONCEPTS, CONSTRUCTS, AND VARIABLES

The factors we have been discussing not only influence health behavior, they are also the concepts of the theories we use to explain behavior. For example, we saw that beliefs influence health behavior. Beliefs form the concept (or idea) of the Self-Efficacy Theory and Health Belief Model, while attitudes are the basis of the Theory of Reasoned Action and the Theory of Planned Behavior. As the concept of a theory develops and evolves, as it becomes less nebulous and more concrete, constructs emerge. *Constructs* are the ways concepts are used in each specific theory (Kerlinger, 1986).

Each theory, then, has at least one concept at its heart, and a series of constructs that indicate how the concept is used in that theory. To use an analogy here, if a theory is a house, the concepts are the bricks and the constructs are the way the bricks are used in the house (see **Figure 1–1**). In one house, the bricks are used for the front steps; in another house, the bricks are used for the façade.

A *variable* is the operationalized concept, or how the concept is going to be measured (Glanz, Rimer, & Viswanath, 2008). Going back to the house analogy, the bricks can be measured (operationalized) by square footage, number, size, or weight.

**FIGURE 1–1** Theories, concepts, and constructs. How the concepts (bricks) used in each theory (house) are the constructs (steps, walkway), and how they are measured (number, color, size) are the variables.

## SUMMARY

Theories and models help us understand why people behave the way they do. They are based on concepts and take into account the many factors influencing health behavior. They enable us to focus on these factors from three different levels: intrapersonal, interpersonal, and community. In addition to providing an explanation for behavior, theories and models provide direction and justification for health education and health promotion program planning activities.

Although many theories and models are used to explain health behavior, unfortunately it is beyond the scope of this text to include them all. Rather, this text provides an introduction to the ones most commonly used for health promotion interventions.

## CHAPTER REFERENCES

*American Heritage Dictionary of the English Language* (2011). Retrieved July 23, 2012, from http://ahdictionary.com

Baumgartner, T., Strong, C.H., & Hansley, L.D. (2002). *Conducting and Reading Research in Health and Human Performance.* New York: McGraw-Hill.

Cottrell, R.R., Girvam, J.T., & McKenzie, J.F. (2009). *Principles & Foundations of Health Promotion and Education* (4th ed). San Francisco: Pearson/Benjamin Cummings.

Courtenay, W.H. (1998). College men's health: An overview and call to action. *Journal of American College Health, 46*(6).

Decina, L.E., Lococo, K.H., & Block, A.W. (2005). *Misuse of Child Restraints: Results of a Workshop to Review Field Data Results* (DOT HS 809 851).

DiClemente, R.J., Crosby, R.A., & Kegler, M.C. (2002). *Emerging Theories in Health Promotion Practice and Research.* San Francisco: Jossey-Bass.

Glanz, K., Rimer, B.K., & Viswanath, K. (Eds.) (2008). *Health Behavior and Health Education* (4th ed.). San Francisco: Jossey-Bass.

Hochbaum, G.M. (1958). *Participation in Medical Screening Programs: A Socio-psychological Study* (Public Health Service Publication No. 572). Washington, DC: U.S. Government Printing Office.

Kerlinger, F.N. (1986). *Foundations of Behavioral Research* (3rd ed). New York: Holt, Rinehart & Winston.

McLeroy, K.R., Bibeau, D., Steckler, A., & Glanz, K. (1988). An ecological perspective on health promotion programs. *Health Education Quarterly, 15,* 351–377.

Mullen, P.D., & Iverson, D. (1982). Qualitative methods for evaluative research in health education programs. *Health Education, 13,* 11–18.

National Cancer Institute (2005). *Theory at a Glance: A Guide for Health Promotion Practice* (2nd ed.) Washington, DC: U.S. Department of Health and Human Services. Retrieved January 25, 2013 from http://www.cancer.gov/cancertopics/cancerlibrary /theory.pdf.

Noar, S.M., & Zimmerman, R.S. (2005). Health behavior theory and cumulative knowledge regarding health behaviors: Are we moving in the right direction? *Health Education Research, 20*(3), 275–290.

Thomas, B.L. (1992). Theory development. In J.L. Brooking, S.A. Ritter, & B.L. Thomas (Eds.), *Textbook of Psychiatric & Mental Health Nursing.* New York: Churchill-Livingstone.

Rosenstock, I.M. (1960). What research in motivation suggests for public health. *American Journal of Public Health, 50,* 295–301.

Upton, L.A. (1970). *A Study of Secondary School Counselors' Perception of School Counseling as a Profession and Their Desire for Professionalization of School Counseling.* Doctoral dissertation, State University of New York, Buffalo, New York.

Winkleby, M.A., Jatulis, D.E., Frank, E., & Fortmann, S.P. (1992). Socioeconomic status and health: How education, income, and occupation contribute to risk factors for cardiovascular disease. *American Journal of Public Health, 82*(6), 816–820.

# Self-Efficacy Theory

## STUDENT LEARNING OUTCOMES

After reading this chapter the student will be able to:

- Explain the concept of Self-Efficacy Theory.
- Identify the constructs of Self-Efficacy Theory.
- Explain how vicarious experience influences self-efficacy.
- Describe the influence of mastery experience on self-efficacy.
- Demonstrate how verbal persuasion impacts self-efficacy.
- Explain how the somatic and emotional states affect self-efficacy.
- Use Self-Efficacy Theory to explain one health behavior.

## THEORY ESSENCE SENTENCE

People will only try to do what they think they can do, and won't try what they think they can't do.

---

### Self-Efficacy Constructs Chart

**Mastery experience:**
Prior success at having accomplished something that is similar to the new behavior

**Vicarious experience:**
Learning by watching someone similar to self be successful

**Verbal persuasion:**
Encouragement by others

**Somatic and emotional states:**
The physical and emotional states caused by thinking about undertaking the new behavior

---

# IN THE BEGINNING

For eons of time, we have been trying to understand and explain why people do what they do. Early on, the theories used to explain behavior had a psychodynamic basis and shared three characteristics—that behavior is regulated psychically at a sub-conscience level; that behaviors diverging from the prevailing norm are a symptom of a disease or disorder; and that behavior changes as a result of gaining self-insight through analysis with a therapist (Bandura, 2004). These theories formed the foundation of the "lie on the couch" approach of talk therapy thought to be the magic bullet of behavior change. Unfortunately, research on the outcome of talk therapy showed that although people did gain insight into their behavior, their behavior usually didn't change (Bandura, 2004).

In the 1960s an alternative behaviorist approach to the explanation of human behavior was introduced. This new approach viewed behavior as the result of an interplay between personal, behavioral, and environmental factors rather an unconscious process with psychodynamic roots, and it did not consider deviant behavior a disease symptom (Bandura, 2004).

A shift in treatment also occurred at this time in terms of content, location, and (behavior) change agent. Treatment content became action oriented and focused on changing the actual deviant behavior rather than on trying to find the psychological origins of the behavior. Mastery experiences were used to give people the skills and belief in themselves to adopt healthier behavior. Treatment occurred in the settings where the behavior occurred—at home, school, workplace, and community rather than in a therapist's office. And this new approach did not limit treatment change agents to being mental health professionals only. For example, teachers were trained to assist in reducing problem behaviors in the school setting and peers or role models who had overcome the problem behavior themselves were also change agents (Bandura, 2004).

Although both approaches were very different, research done on phobias showed that both were equally as effective. Since both approaches worked, it was apparent there was some underlying mechanism connecting them. It was Albert Bandura in the late 1970s who proposed Self-Efficacy Theory as the unifying mechanism (Bandura, 1977, 2004).

## THEORETICAL CONCEPT

If you were given the opportunity to fund your college education by swimming 10 laps in a pool, you surely would give it a try, assuming you can swim. Now imagine you were given the same opportunity to raise tuition money, but had to swim the English Channel instead. Would you still go for it? If your swimming ability is like the average person's, there's no way you'd even attempt it. Why the difference? In the first case, you believe you can swim the 10 laps. In the second, you don't believe you can swim the English Channel, and so you won't even try. Think back to your childhood and the book *The Little Engine That Could*: "I think I can. I think I can." This is the concept of self-efficacy.

Self-efficacy is the belief in one's own ability to successfully accomplish something. It is a theory by itself, as well as being a construct of Social Cognitive Theory. Self-Efficacy Theory tells us that people generally will only attempt things they believe they can accomplish and won't attempt things they believe they will fail. Makes sense—why would you try something you don't think you can do? However, people with a strong sense of efficacy believe they can accomplish even difficult tasks. They see these as challenges to be mastered, rather than threats to be avoided (Bandura, 1994).

Efficacious people set challenging goals and maintain strong commitment to them. In the face of impending failure, they increase and sustain their efforts to be successful. They approach difficult or threatening situations with confidence that they have control over them. Having this type of outlook reduces stress and lowers the risk of depression (Bandura, 1994).

Conversely, people who doubt their ability to accomplish difficult tasks see these tasks as threats. They avoid them based on their own personal weaknesses or on the obstacles preventing them from being successful. They give up quickly in the face of difficulties or failure, and it doesn't take much for them to lose faith in their capabilities. An outlook like this increases stress and the risk of depression (Bandura, 1994).

# THEORETICAL CONSTRUCTS

The theory introduces the idea that the perception of efficacy is influenced by four factors: mastery experience, vicarious experience, verbal persuasion, and somatic and emotional state (Bandura, 1994, 1997; Pajares, 2002).

## MASTERY EXPERIENCE

We all have mastery experiences. These occur when we attempt to do something and are successful; that is, we have mastered something. Mastery experiences are the most effective way to boost self-efficacy because people are more likely to believe they can do something new if it is similar to something they have already done well (Bandura, 1994).

Perhaps you never thought about this, but babysitting is a significant mastery experience (**Figure 2–1**). Babysitting is among the strongest predictors of a new mom's belief in her ability to take care of her own children. Women who have experience taking care of infants prior to becoming mothers themselves are more confident in their maternal abilities, and even more so in completing infant care tasks they did frequently (Froman & Owen, 1989, 1990; Gross, Roccissano, & Roncoli, 1989). So, babysitting as a teenager pays off in many ways.

Mastery is the basis for preoperative teaching of men undergoing surgery for prostate cancer. Since this type of surgery can result in urinary incontinence, it is important for men to do pelvic exercises postoperatively to restore urine control.

© Jamie Wilson/Shutterstock, Inc.

**FIGURE 2–1**  Babysitting provides mastery experiences

If they are taught these exercises before surgery and practice them, their self-efficacy increases and they are more likely to regain urine control more quickly after surgery (Maliski, Clerkin, & Litwin, 2004).

Providing opportunities for people to gain mastery is the reason why workshops, training programs, internships, and clinical experiences are offered. These are ways people can become proficient at new skills and increase their self-efficacy. For example, training programs are one way of providing mastery experiences for people with disabilities who are entering the labor market (Strauser, 1995). Hours in the clinical practice areas provide opportunities for student nurses to master nursing skills, and internships afford health education students the chance to master the competencies needed for professional practice.

In a fall prevention program for older adults, mastery experiences in the form of practice opportunities for negotiating outdoor activities such as using public transportation, stairs, and crossing streets proved to be one of the most effective strategies of the program for increasing participants' self-efficacy (Cheal & Clemson, 2001). Falls are a major contributor to morbidity in people 65 and older, with one in three older adults falling each year. Of those who do fall, 20 to 30% have injuries severe enough to impact their ability to live independently (Centers for Disease Control and Prevention [CDC], 2012). Increasing self-efficacy through mastery experiences is one way of assisting older adults at risk of falling to gain confidence in safely participating in everyday activities (Cheal & Clemson, 2001). For personal trainers, mastery experiences are effective ways to support client exercise self-efficacy. Starting with a simple exercise program that can be successfully completed creates a mastery experience that can lead to success with more challenging programs (Jackson, 2010).

It would seem that mastering something new is relatively simple: all you have to do is practice. However, this isn't always the case. If the new tasks are always easy and similar to ones already mastered, and difficult, unfamiliar ones are avoided, then a strong sense of efficacy does not develop. To develop a strong sense of efficacy, difficult tasks also need to be attempted, and obstacles worked through (Bandura, 1994). In reality, it's great if you tried to make brownies, were successful, and now make them all the time. But you can't live on brownies alone. At some point, you need to try making a meal.

## VICARIOUS EXPERIENCE

Another factor influencing perception of self-efficacy is vicarious experience, or the observation of the successes and failures of others (models) who are similar to one's self. Watching someone like yourself successfully accomplish something you would like to attempt increases self-efficacy. Conversely, observing someone like you fail detracts or threatens self-efficacy. The extent to which vicarious experiences affect self-efficacy is related to how much like yourself you think the model is (Bandura, 1994). The more one associates with the person being watched, the greater the influence on the belief that one's self can also accomplish the behavior being observed.

This construct can be used to explain how group weight loss programs work. If an obese person sees someone just like himself or herself lose weight and keep it off by following a sensible diet and exercise, then the belief in his or her own ability to also do this is strengthened. Watching friends who have taken a nutrition course choose healthy foods at a fast food establishment may increase your belief in your ability to also choose healthy foods: "If they can do it, so can I."

Not only do workshops and training sessions increase mastery, they can also provide vicarious experiences, as well. Watching others in a training session, a class, or during role playing can provide observational experiences that enhance self-efficacy, especially if the person performing or learning the behavior is similar to the observer.

In the "Sun Protection Is Fun" program (Tripp, Herrmann, Parcel, Chamberlain, & Gritz, 2000), developed to teach children about cancer prevention, vicarious learning was used not only with the children, but with the parents and teachers as well. Within the context of the curriculum, children observed their teachers and other students demonstrating how to protect their skin by using sunscreen and wearing protective clothing. In parent and teacher videos developed for this intervention, instead of using actors as the role models in the video, families and teachers from the intervention schools were used instead.

Vicarious learning is at the core of coach/trainer–student/client instruction. The coach or trainer demonstrates the skill, the student/client then copies. This is also how you learned to tie your shoe, brush your teeth, eat with a fork. You watched, observed your parents or older siblings, then copied what they did. Think about all the things you learn, every day, by watching others and how successfully accomplishing the skill increases your self-efficacy (**Figure 2–2**).

## VERBAL PERSUASION

The third factor affecting self-efficacy is verbal or social persuasion. When people are persuaded verbally that they can achieve or master a task, they are more likely to do the task. Having others verbally support attainment or mastery of a task goes a long way in supporting a person's belief in himself or herself. Coaches

© AISPIX by Image Source/Shutterstock, Inc.

**FIGURE 2–2**  Learning by watching others

frequently use this tactic with their teams. They psyche them up, verbally, before a game or a meet (**Figure 2–3**). The coach tells the players that they are going to win, that the other team is no match for them, that they are stronger, faster, better prepared, and so on.

© Doug James/Shutterstock, Inc.

**FIGURE 2–3**  Coaches use verbal persuasion to psyche up players

If a team performs poorly, the team members' perception of ability can be negatively affected depending on the coach's reaction. For example, saying we lost the game because you are all lousy players doesn't do much for improving self-efficacy, whereas saying we lost because we need more practice does (Brown, Malouff, & Schutte, 2005).

Conversely, when people are told they do not have the skill or ability to do something, they tend to give up quickly (Bandura, 1994). Imagine the same coach telling his team that they can't possibly win against the opposition. What would the likely outcome be?

## SOMATIC AND EMOTIONAL STATES

The physical and emotional states that occur when someone contemplates doing something provide clues as to the likelihood of success or failure. Stress, anxiety, worry, and fear all negatively affect self-efficacy and can lead to a self-fulfilling prophecy of failure or inability to perform the feared tasks (Pajares, 2002). Stressful situations create emotional arousal, which in turn affects a person's perceived self-efficacy in coping with the situation (Bandura & Adams, 1977).

People new to exercising at a gym, especially it they perceive that others are watching them, may become anxious in anticipation of an exercise session. This is a negative somatic state that may be detrimental to their self-efficacy, and in turn, threaten their continued exercising. The fitness professional in this situation can minimize the negative effects by teaching relaxation techniques and positive self-talk in an effort to reduce anxiety and support self-efficacy (Jackman, 2010).

A classic example of how the emotional state affects self-efficacy and, ultimately, health behavior is fear of the dentist (**Figure 2–4**). For millions of people in this country, the mere thought of going to the dentist is associated with intense pain and anxiety. It is certainly a stressful situation. As a result, they cannot bring themselves to make appointments or keep appointments for even routine, preventive dental care. This avoidance behavior results in a situation in which dental health deteriorates, causing them to have the very pain they wanted to avoid, and the need for more extensive treatment or possible tooth loss (Rowe & Moore, 1998).

As is evident from this example, emotional arousal affects self-efficacy, and self-efficacy affects the decisions people make. If the emotional state improves—that is, emotional arousal or stress is reduced—a change in self-efficacy can be expected (Bandura & Adams, 1977).

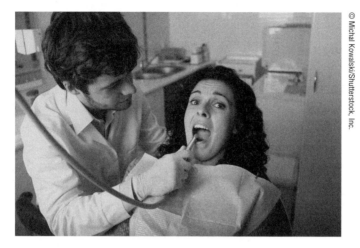

**FIGURE 2–4** Fear of the dentist can lead to avoidance behavior

While we tend to think about negative examples of how the emotional state impacts self-efficacy and health behavior, sometimes the emotional state is positive. Think about the effect of the "runner's high" on health behavior. In this case, the emotional state that results is pleasurable, rather than uncomfortable This would positively impact self-efficacy, and support continued engagement in the behavior that created it.

In summary, according to Self-Efficacy Theory, verbal persuasion, mastery experiences, vicarious experiences, and somatic and emotional states affect our self-efficacy and, therefore, our behavior (**Figure 2–5**).

## THEORY IN ACTION—CLASS ACTIVITY

In all aspects of life, sometimes we win and sometimes we lose. Learning how to cope with the losses is extremely important as loss can affect our health in many ways. In a small group, identify a "loss" situation—perhaps loss of a job, a scholarship, or a relationship. Discuss how this type of loss might affect the way people think about themselves, their mental health, and how it might affect their behavior. Brainstorm ways in which the constructs of Self-Efficacy Theory might be used to help people cope with this type of loss. Read the following article and then answer the questions at the end.

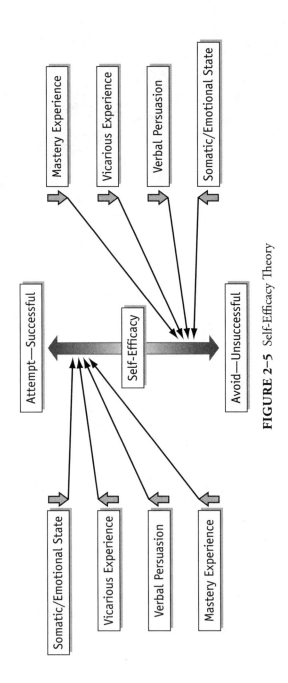

FIGURE 2-5 Self-Efficacy Theory

# Chapter 2 Article: The Effectiveness of a Self-Efficacy Intervention for Helping Adolescents Cope with Sport-Competition Loss[1]

*Brown, Lisa J; Malouff, John M; Schutte, Nicola S*

## Abstract (summary)

Building on prior intervention research with women athletes (Arathoon & Malouff, in press), this study examined the effectiveness of a self-efficacy intervention for helping adolescents cope with sport-competition loss. The study included 111 adolescent netball and soccer participants (mean age = 13.98, SD = 1.36), who completed a positive affect scale prior to competition. Defeated participants were randomly assigned to intervention or control groups. Intervention participants were asked to choose one or more of six thoughts related to self-efficacy and apply those to themselves before both groups again completed the positive affect scale. Control group participants showed a significant decline in self-reported positive affect compared to intervention participants. Observational ratings also indicated that the control group showed less positive affect after the loss than the intervention group. The results provide support for self-efficacy theory as applied to helping individuals cope with competition loss.

Winning and losing are fundamental outcomes faced by adolescents not only in the sporting arena but also within a competitive modern society. There is evidence that losing in competitive sport can instigate a decline in positive affect among adult competitors (Arathoon & Malouff, in press; Cox & Kerr, 1990; Robinson & Howe, 1978). High positive affect involves "high energy, full concentration, and pleasurable engagement" and low levels of positive affect involve "sadness and lethargy" (Watson, Clark, & Tellegen, 1988, p. 1063). It seems plausible that adolescent athletes, like adult athletes, experience a decline in positive affect as a result of competition defeat.

The consequences of a reduction in positive affect following competition defeat can be far reaching, with the perceived importance of the loss mediating

---

[1] Reproduced from Brown, L.J., Malouff, J.M., & Schutte, N.S. (2005). The effectiveness of self-efficacy intervention for helping adolescents cope with sport competition loss. *Journal of Sports Behavior, 28*(2), 136–150.

the degree of influence of the loss (Bandura, 1997). A decline in positive affect in response to competition loss tends to lead to negative cognitive and behavioral responses (Morris, 1989). Cognitive consequences of a decline in positive affect can include impaired decision making and problem solving (Isen, 1999). Behavioral consequences can include acts of frustration, anger, and aggression (Isberg, 2000; Wehlage, 1980), with the social consequence of being labeled a "poor loser."

Research has shown that affect is associated with self-efficacy (Bandura, 1997; Forgas, Bower, & Moylan, 1990; Heimpel, Wood, Marshall, & Brown, 2002). These findings raise the possibility that one way to enhance affect after a competition loss is to enhance self-efficacy.

Self-efficacy involves individuals' beliefs about their own ability to successfully engage in a task in order to obtain a desired outcome (Bandura, 1977). Self-efficacy is important because individuals with high self-efficacy for a task tend to try harder at the task and experience more positive emotions relating to the task (Bandura, 1997).

In competitive sport, desired outcomes include winning and playing well. It seems likely that when sport competitors lose, their self-efficacy in the sport decreases (Lane and Terry, 2000). Athletes saying dejectedly after a loss that "I stink" or "I don't even belong on the field" provide examples of the sort of low self-efficacy that can result from a loss and lead to lowered positive affect. If one could boost athletes' self-efficacy after a loss, their prior level of positive affect might be preserved (Bandura, 1997; Hanin, 2000).

There are various possible ways of boosting self-efficacy in young athletes following a loss. Parents, coaches, and teammates might be able to help through providing encouragement and positive evaluative feedback (Feltz & Lirgg, 1993) and prompting adaptive attributions about the loss (see Robinson & Howe, 1981; McAuley & Gross, 1983), such as that "we played poorly today because we haven't practiced enough" rather than "we played poorly because we are no good." A related possibility involves causing the athletes to think in such a way, initially through prompting, that boosts self-efficacy, e.g., by thinking about prior successes or positive aspects of their play in the just completed game (Bandura, 1997).

Prompted cognitions have successfully influenced affect and behavior in a variety of studies (Brewer, Doughtie & Lubin, 1980; Thayer, Newman & McClain, 1994). For instance, Velten (1968) used cognition prompting to decrease and then increase positive affect. Arathoon and Malouff (in press) found that asking women field hockey players to think for two minutes about their choice of six different positive or coping thoughts led to less of a decline in positive affect after losing a game. The type of thought most commonly chosen involved the individual or the team playing well at some point in the game. According to Bandura (1997), success thoughts like these, along with thoughts about encouragement or positive feedback from others, and thoughts about observing another person succeed, tend to enhance self-efficacy. Hence, the findings of the study of Arathoon and Malouff suggest that enhancing self-efficacy might be the key element of any intervention that prevents a decrease in positive affect following competition loss.

The purposes of the present study were to investigate the results of losing competitively on the positive affect level of adolescents and to examine the effectiveness of a self-efficacy intervention for helping adolescents cope with competition loss. The first hypothesis was that adolescents who experience defeat in a sport competition (and receive no intervention) would show a significant lowering of positive affect from pre to post-competition. The second hypothesis was that following competition defeat, adolescent athletes prompted to focus on thoughts suggested by self-efficacy theory would experience less decline in positive affect than athletes who received no intervention.

# METHOD

## PARTICIPANTS

The 111 participants included 53 males and 58 females who were 11 to 17 years old, with an average age of 13.98 (SD = 1.36). Participants were recruited from local netball and soccer clubs in eastern Australia as part of a convenience sample intended to include adolescent males and females and two different sports. Participants provided written assent and a parent provided written consent.

## MEASURES

**Positive Affect Self-Report Measure.** All participants completed the 10-item Positive Affect scale of the Positive and Negative Affect Schedule present-moment version (PANAS; Watson, Clark, and Tellegen, 1988) as a pre and post-competition measure of positive affect. Respondents used a 5-point response scale ranging from 1 "very slightly or not at all" to 5 "extremely" to indicate the degree to which they feel (1) interested, (2) excited, (3) strong, (4) enthusiastic, (5) proud, (6) alert, (7) inspired, (8) determined, (9) attentive and (10) active, at the present moment. Scores on the PANAS can range from 10–50, with low positive affect scores signifying sadness and lethargy, and high positive affect scores indicating enthusiasm, high energy and full concentration levels (Watson et al., 1988).

According to Watson et al. (1988), the Positive Affect scale of the PANAS has good internal consistency with a Cronbach's alpha coefficient of .89 reported when respondents focus on the present moment. Long-term stability has also been shown with a correlation of .54 over three months for measurement of the present moment (Watson et al., 1988). The Positive Affect scale of the PANAS has been shown to be a useful measure of changes in affect (Watson et al., 1988) and shares good convergent validity with other measures of positive affect (Watson et al., 1988). The scale's psychometric properties in adolescent populations were investigated by Huebner and Dew (1995), who found a coefficient alpha of .85 along with support for the independence of negative and positive affect dimensions.

The Negative Affect scale of the PANAS was not used in the study because (a) the Negative Affect scale, with items such as "tense, anxious, nervous, and jittery," has been found to be related closely to anxiety (Watson et al., 1988), an emotion that one would not expect athletes to experience after losing and that Abadie (1989) and Sanderson and Ashton (1981) found did not significantly increase after losing; and (b) the additional time needed to complete the scale might have reduced participant cooperation.

**Observational Measure of Positive Affect.** An independent observer, blind to the research hypotheses, observed the behavior of small subgroups of the experimental and control conditions following the intervention procedure in the post-competition phase, in order to determine which small group of individuals showed greater levels of positive affect. The observational rating was based on evidence that facial expressions and overt behavior tend to indicate level of positive affect (Ekman, 1999; Parrott & Hertel, 1999). So, if a team was divided into two small groups of (a) three members in the experimental condition and (b) two members in the control condition, the observer would decide after the intervention which small group as a whole appeared to have more positive affect.

## INTERVENTION

The intervention participants were asked to focus on or imagine for a minute one or more certain thoughts or images that related to three sources of self-efficacy (Bandura, 1997). The items were (1) personal mastery: (a) "Think about something you did really well during the game" and (b) "Think about winning your next game and how you will feel"; (2) verbal encouragement: (a) "Think about a time when your team-mates or coach praised you" and (b) "Think about a time when your team-mates or coach showed confidence in you"; (3) vicarious mastery: (a) "Think about a great athlete who failed at first and then succeeded" and (b) "Think about a great athlete who works harder after losing so he or she can win in the future." The paired items were randomly assigned to create two forms. To create Version 1 (1) the three pairs of items were blocked, (2) a random numbers table was used to randomly choose the order of the three pairs and (3) the randomization process was used to determine which item in each pair would be used first. To create Version 2, the order of items was reversed.

## PROCEDURE

Netball and soccer clubs were contacted and provided with written and verbal information regarding the study. Clubs then signed forms to indicate their consent for involvement. Team coaches were approached one week prior to the game, and parents or caregivers of competitors were provided with information sheets and participation consent forms to sign.

The senior author asked coaches which teams were likely to win and lose and used team won-loss records to select teams that were likely to lose an upcoming game. Competitors on these teams were requested to arrive at the field 10 minutes prior to the start of the game. During this period players anonymously completed the pre-competition Positive Affect scale. Competitors were asked to place completed measures in boxes adjacent to the field. Following competition, athletes who played on losing teams were randomly assigned to a control and an experimental condition. Individual participants were assigned to either the experimental or the control group on the basis of a coin toss done before the game.

Coaches and parents or caregivers were asked to refrain from offering any post-competition feedback to the competitors in order to control for any changes in competitors' positive affect in response to positive or negative exchanges. Participants in the control group were asked to remain separate from the experimental group and wait quietly until experimental group participants completed the self-efficacy intervention. Experimental group participants were asked to read the six-item self-efficacy intervention and visualize or focus on one or more of the statements for one minute. A randomly selected half of the intervention participants were given the first order of the six self-efficacy items; the other half received the items in the reverse order. Both groups were then requested to complete anonymously the positive affect measure again. Code words on pre and post measures allowed sets of responses for each participant to be combined. The independent observer observed and recorded the behavior of the experimental and control groups while they completed the positive affect measure postgame.

Sixteen teams in total participated in the study (six netball teams and ten soccer teams), over a period of three months. Three teams won their game. Thirteen teams were defeated in competition. Two teams experienced game delays of one week due to inclement weather conditions and forfeiting. For both these teams, new Positive Affect scales were completed prior to competition the following week.

## PILOT STUDY

A pilot study was undertaken prior to commencement of the main study in order to clarify the suitability of assessment procedures. Four female netball players aged between 12 and 14 years, whose team was defeated in competition, participated in the pilot study. The precompetition measures took approximately three minutes to complete and the post-competition measures approximately five minutes. In the post-competition phase, two players were assigned to the control condition and two to the experimental condition. The data for these players were excluded from the main study sample. The pilot test was useful in identifying that (1) language used throughout the assessment procedure was appropriate for the adolescent cohort, (2) the experimental intervention was completed by two players without difficulty, and (3) specific modifications would be likely to enhance the procedure. These modifications, which we made, included (a) requesting the coach's assistance in coordinating players participating in the study directly before and after the competition, (b) ensuring players were given clipboards to write on, (c) utilizing areas beside the court that were relatively free of distraction for the competitors, and (d) requesting that the coach refrain from offering any post-competition discussion prior to the survey.

# RESULTS

Collation of pre and post-competition scores and responses yielded 97 useable data sets, including 75 for losing competitors and 22 for winning competitors. Fourteen data sets of players were excluded from the final analyses because the players left during the game (N = 7) or after the game but before being given the post-game research materials (N = 7). Three data sets failed to reveal age details, but these sets were still included in the final analyses.

The main analyses involved a within-group t test to determine mean changes between pre and post-competition measures of positive affect for players who lost and did not receive an intervention, and an ANCOVA, as recommended by Tabachnick and Fidell (2001), to determine group differences in post-competition measures of positive affect (the dependent variable) controlling for the influence of pre-competition measures of positive affect (the covariate). Assumptions of the statistics, including normality of the data, homogeneity of variance, linearity of relationship between the pre and post-competition measures of affect, and homogeneity of regression slopes, were met. Also, the reliability of the covariate, pre-competition Positive Affect, was adequate, with Cronbach's alpha at .80.

The first hypothesis was that adolescents who experienced defeat in a sport competition and received no intervention would show a significant lowering of positive affect from pre to post-competition. A within-group t test was done to evaluate the impact of competition loss on measures of competitors' positive affect, specifically to determine whether positive affect for control group participants decreased following defeat. See **Table 1** and **Figure 1** for the group means for pre-competition and post-competition measures of positive affect. Control group participants showed a statistically significant decrease in positive affect from precompetition scores to post-competition scores, $t(36) = 5.42$, $p < .001$ two-tailed. Cohen's d was 0.61, indicating a moderate effect size in terms of the standards of Cohen (1988), who described effects of .20 as small, .50 as moderate, and .80 as large.

**Table 1** Descriptive Statistics for Pre- and Post-competition Positive Affects Scores

| | Positive Affect Scale Scores | | | |
|---|---|---|---|---|
| Groups and Times | $n$ | Mean | SD | Range |
| **Winning Teams** | | | | |
| Pre-Competition | 22 | 34.23 | 6.50 | 22–44 |
| Post-Competition | 22 | 37.82 | 11.15 | 19–50 |
| **Losing Teams** | | | | |
| **Control Group** | | | | |
| Pre-Competition | 37 | 35.54 | 4.87 | 27–48 |
| Post-Competition | 37 | 30.03 | 8.14 | 16–50 |
| **Experimental Group** | | | | |
| Pre-Competition | 38 | 33.68 | 7.81 | 16–48 |
| Post-Competition | 38 | 32.08 | 10.41 | 13–50 |

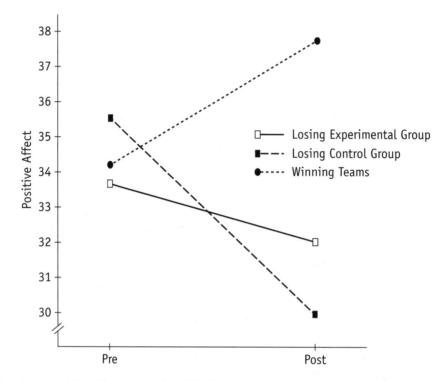

**Figure 1** The Effectiveness of a Self-Efficacy Intervention for Helping Adolescents Cope with Sport-Competition Loss

*Source:* Reproduced from Brown, L.J., Malouff, J.M., & Schutte, N.S. (2005). The effectiveness of self-efficacy intervention for helping adolescents cope with sport competition loss. *Journal of Sports Behavior, 28*(2), 136–150.

In order to obtain as much useful information as possible from the study, we conducted some supplemental, exploratory analyses relating to the first hypothesis. To determine whether declines of positive affect were different between gender groups, male and female control group participants were compared. After adjusting for pre-competition measures of positive affect, a one-way between-groups ANCOVA revealed there was no significant difference between males and females in terms of a reduction in positive affect following competition loss, F (1, 34) = 1.36, p = .25.

In order to test the unhypothesized possibility that just playing, regardless of outcome, leads to a decrease in positive affect, we analyzed whether adolescents on defeated teams decreased in positive affect more than adolescents on winning teams. For the relevant ANCOVA the assumption of homogeneity of variance was violated, so we followed the recommendation of

Tabachnik and Fidell (2001) and set alpha at .01. A comparison of the winning players and the losing control players showed a significant difference in post-game positive affect, $F(1,56) = 15.01$, $p < .001$, with the losing players decreasing in positive affect from pre-game to post and the winning players increasing from pre to post.

In order to determine whether the three groups in the study, the winning players, the losing players in the intervention, and the losing players in the control condition, varied across all three groups in post-game positive affect, we used an ANCOVA to compare the three groups. The differences in group means at post-game were statistically significant, $F(1,93) = 7.78$, $p = .001$, laying a foundation for testing the second hypothesis, which stated that following competition defeat, adolescent athletes prompted to focus on thoughts suggested by self-efficacy theory would experience less decline in positive affect than control group participants. We conducted a one-way between-groups ANCOVA comparing post-competition self-report positive affect between experimental and control group participants. After adjusting for the pre-competition positive affect scores, there was a significant difference between the control and experimental groups' post-competition measures of positive affect following the intervention procedure $F(1,72) = 4.67$, $p = .034$. The effect size of the difference in mean scores at post-game between the groups was small, with $d = 0.22$. Another way to interpret the meaningfulness of the effect is to consider what percentage of athletes in each group suffered a large decline in positive affect, for instance of more than the pooled standard deviation at pre-game (6.55). For the control group, 17 of 37 players (46%) decreased that much in positive affect; for the intervention group, only 9 of 38 players (24%) decreased that much.

In order to obtain as much useful information as possible from the study data, we conducted a supplemental, exploratory analysis to determine whether changes in self-reported positive affect were different for males and females in the comparison of the intervention group and the control group. A 2 (intervention versus control conditions) by 2 (genders) between-groups ANCOVA using scores on the pre-competition positive affect scale as a covariate showed that gender did not significantly interact with which condition the participants were in, $F(1,70) = 0.08$, $p = .78$.

In all 12 of the 12 post-intervention comparisons of small same-team subgroups of experimental and control participants, the observer rated higher the overall positive affect shown by members of the experimental subgroup. A binomial probability distribution test (Howell, 1997) indicated that this pattern showed a statistically significant difference between conditions, $p < .001$.

**Table 2** Self-efficacy Intervention Choice Frequency

| Option | Response Frequency | Response Percentage |
|---|---|---|
| **Direct experience of success** | | |
| 1. Think about something you did really well during the game. | 23 | 26.74% |
| 2. Think about winning your next game and how you will feel. | 18 | 20.93% |
| Subtotal | 41 | 47.67% |
| **Encouragement or positive feedback regarding one's performance** | | |
| 3. Think about a time when your teammates or coach praised you. | 12 | 13.95% |
| 4. Think about a time when your teammates or coach showed confidence in you. | 16 | 18.60% |
| Subtotal | 28 | 32.55% |
| **Vicarious mastery** | | |
| 5. Think about a great athlete who failed at first and then succeeded. | 7 | 8.14% |
| 6. Think about a great athlete who works harder after losing so he or she can win in the future. | 10 | 11.63% |
| Subtotal | 17 | 19.77% |

*Note.* Respondents were able to choose more than one self-efficacy option. Each pair of options relate to one of the following three factors that can influence self-efficacy: (1) direct experience of success, (2) encouragement from others, and (3) observation of another person succeeding (Bandura, 1997).

An analysis was conducted into the selection of self-efficacy options made by respondents during the intervention procedure. **Table 2** shows choice frequency. Participants in the experimental condition were randomly assigned one of two orders of the self-efficacy options in order to minimize order effects. In determining whether selection responses of participants were equally distributed across items, analysis revealed the obtained chi-square value (11.81) for the 6 categories and 86 choices exceeded the critical value (11.07), $p < .05$ (Howell, 1997). This indicates a significant difference among the options chosen by participants in the experimental condition, with more participants choosing options which related directly to personal experience of success (47.67%).

# DISCUSSION

The results provided support for the first hypothesis in that defeated competitors in the control group experiencing a significant decline in positive affect levels from pre to post-competition. Further, the defeated competitors showed a significantly greater decrease in positive affect than did winning competitors. These finding are congruent with research carried out on adult field-hockey (Arathoon & Malouff, in press), soccer (Robinson & Howe, 1978), and squash players (Cox & Kerr, 1990), indicating that participants who were defeated in competition experienced a lowering of positive affect in relation to pre-competition levels.

The finding that winning competitors did not experience a decline in positive affect suggests that playing itself, regardless of outcome, does not produce a decrease in positive affect. Hence, the decrease in positive affect in the losing athletes is more likely due to losing than mere playing. The findings of the decline for losing adolescent competitors support Wehlage's (1980) comments that likened competition loss to a psychological grief reaction due to the occurrence of affective changes. The finding that males and females did not differ significantly in their positive-affect decline suggests that the effect is a broad one.

The second hypothesis was supported by results that indicated participants in the experimental group exposed to the self-efficacy intervention experienced less decline in positive affect than control group participants. This effect was shown to be similar for males and females. The size of the effect with regard to self-report data was moderate. The finding provides support for Bandura's (1997) theoretical view that high self-efficacy tends to lead to high positive affect.

The present study found, as did the study of Arathoon and Malouff (in press), that prompting athletes to think theoretically adaptive thoughts helped prevent a decline in positive affect after losing. The current finding extends the finding of Arathoon and Malouff (in press) to adolescents as well as adults, to males as well as females, and to soccer and netball players as well as field hockey players. The findings with regard to the observer rating of positive affect extend the self-report findings of Arathoon and Malouff to the realm of systematically observed signs of positive affect, which one might think less susceptible to experimenter-demand effects. The current findings also show that somewhat different thoughts from those suggested to the players in the study of Arathoon and Malouff can have a positive effect.

The present study found, as in the study of Arathoon and Malouff (in press), that the types of thoughts most commonly chosen by defeated athletes were those that dealt with performing well. In the study of Arathoon and Malouff, the thoughts selected most were "something [I] did well in the game" and "we didn't win but we really played well." In the present study the two thoughts most selected were "something you did really well during the game" and "winning your next game and how you will feel." Thinking along those lines of good and successful performance could be at the heart of self-efficacy and positive affect for athletes.

The results should be interpreted with consideration of several methodological characteristics of the study. First, the observer measure lacked demonstrated reliability and validity. However, the results of the observer ratings were consistent with the self-report results and also with casual observations in another study of losing woman field hockey players (Arathoon & Malouff, in press). Second, the study did not examine whether the intervention procedure based on self-efficacy theory produced changes in self-efficacy or was more effective than any other type of cognitive intervention. The effects might be due to competitors merely being distracted from their loss. Future research might shed light on this issue. At any rate, the intervention did produce a valuable effect in adolescent athletes. Third, to control for extraneous influences, the control group participants were asked to wait quietly for a minute or so while experimental participants completed the self-efficacy intervention. It is possible that during this period, control group participants actually dwelled on their loss and as a result experienced greater decline of positive affect than they might have under ordinary circumstances. However, it is quite common for athletes after a game to remain silent for a minute or so as they start to gather gear, change clothes, or go home, so the control condition created nothing unusual.

Fourth, it is possible that playing in a game we expected them to lose might have influenced the positive affect of the players at pre or post-game. Perhaps they also expected to lose and so had less of a decline in positive affect than if they had expected to win. However, for the main analysis between intervention and control group members, this expectation effect, if any, would have been equivalent for both groups and so not affected group differences.

Although the study had certain methodological limitations, it also had methodological strengths, for instance in the random assignment of participants to conditions and use of a well-validated self-report measure of positive affect as well as an observation measure. The safest conclusion is that the findings provide some support for the theory of self-efficacy and some support for a specific application of self-efficacy principles to helping adolescent athletes cope with losing by prompting them to think about some good aspects of their recent or other performance in the sport. The main implication of the findings is that the self-efficacy intervention is worthy of further examination. The high participation levels of adolescents in organized sport (see, e.g., Australian Bureau of Statistics, 1997) provide coaches and parents with many opportunities to test informally the ability of self-efficacy strategies to help individual athletes cope with losing. Large-scale experimental research might profitably clarify whether the specific self-efficacy intervention thoughts (1) produce a positive effect on self-efficacy and (2) are of more benefit than other thoughts.

## REFERENCES

Abadie, B. R. (1989). Effect of competitive outcome on state anxiety. *Perceptual and Motor Skills, 69*, 1057–1058.

Australian Bureau of Statistics (1997). Participation in sport and physical activities, 1995–96. (No.4177.0). Canberra: Author.

Arathoon, S. M., & Malouff, J. M. (in press). The effectiveness of a brief cognitive intervention to help athletes cope with competition loss. *Journal of Sport Behavior.*

Bandura, A. (1977). Self-efficacy: Toward a unifying theory of behavioral change. *Psychological Review, 84*, 191–215.

Bandura, A. (1997). Self-efficacy. *The exercise of control.* NY: W.H. Freeman and Company.

Brewer, D., Doughtie, E. B., & Lubin, B. (1980). Induction of mood and mood shift. *Journal of Clinical Psychology, 36*, 215–225.

Cobb, N. J. (1998). *Adolescence: continuity, change and diversity.* Mayfield, CA: Mayfield Publishing Company.

Cohen, J. (1988). *Statistical power analysis for the behavioral sciences* (2nd ed.). Hillsdale, NJ: Erlbaum.

Cox, T., & Kerr, J. H. (1990). Self-reported mood in competitive squash. *Personality and Individual Differences, 11*, 199–203.

Dagleish, T., & Power, M. J. (Eds.). (1999). *Handbook of cognition and emotion.* New York: Wiley.

Ekman, P. (1999). Basic Emotions. In T. Dagleish and M. J. Power (Eds.), *Handbook of cognition and emotion* (pp. 45–60). New York: Wiley.

Ellis, H. C., & Moore, B. A. (1999). Mood and memory. In T. Dagleish and M.J. Power (Eds.), *Handbook of cognition and emotion* (pp. 193–210). New York: Wiley.

Feltz, D. L., & Lirgg, C. D. (2001). Self-efficacy beliefs of athletes, teams and coaches. In R. N. Singer, H. A. Hausenblas, and C. M. Janelle (Eds.), *Handbook of sports psychology* (pp. 340–361). New York: Wiley.

Forgas, J. P., Bower, G. H., & Moylan, S. (1990). Praise or blame? Affective influences on attributions for achievement. *Journal of Personality and Social Psychology, 59*, 809–819.

Hanin, Y. L. (2000). *Emotions in sport.* Champaign, IL: Human Kinetics.

Heimpel, S. A., Wood, J. V., Marshall, M. A., & Brown, J.D. (2002). Do people with low self-esteem really want to feel better? Self-esteem differences in motivation to repair negative moods. *Journal of Personality and Social Psychology, 82*, 128–147.

Howell, D. C. (1997). *Statistical methods for psychology.* Belmont, CA: Wadsworth Publishing Company.

Huebner, E. S., & Dew, T. (1995). Preliminary validation of the Positive and Negative Affect Schedule with adolescents. *Journal of Psychoeducational Assessment, 13,* 286–293.

Isen, A. M. (1999). Positive affect. In T. Dagleish and M. J. Power (Eds.), *Handbook of cognition and emotion* (pp. 521–539). New York: Wiley.

Isberg, L. (2000). Anger, aggressive behavior and athletic performance. In U.L. Hanin (Ed.), *Emotions in sport* (pp. 113–133). Champaign, IL: Human Kinetics.

Kazdin, A. E. (1998). *Research designs in clinical psychology.* (3rd ed.). Needham Heights, MA: Allyn and Bacon.

Lane, A. M., & Terry, P. C. (2000). The nature of mood: development of a conceptual model with focus on depression. *Journal of Applied Sport Psychology, 12,* 16–33.

McAuley, E., & Gross, J. B. (1983). Perceptions of causality in sport: an application of the causal dimension scale. *Journal of Sport Psychology, 5,* 72–76.

Morris, W. N. (1989). *Mood: the frame of mind.* New York: Springer-Verlag.

Parrott, W. G, & Hertel, P. (1999). Research methods in cognition and emotion. In T. Dagleish and M. J. Power (Eds.), *Handbook of cognition and emotion* (pp. 61–82). New York: Wiley.

Robinson, D. W., & Howe, B. L. (1978). Causal attributions and mood state relationships of soccer players in a sport achievement setting. *Journal of Sport Behavior, 1,* 137–146.

Sanderson, F. H., & Ashton, M. K. (1981). Analysis of anxiety levels before and after badminton competition. *International Journal of Sport Psychology, 12,* 23–28.

Tabachnick, B. G, & Fidell, L. S. (2001). *Using multivariate statistics.* Boston: Allyn and Bacon.

Thayer, R. E., Newman, J. R., & McClain, T. M. (1994). Self-regulation of mood: strategies for changing a bad mood, raising energy, and reducing tension. *Journal of Personality and Social Psychology, 67,* 910–925.

Velten, E. (1968). A laboratory task for induction of mood states. *Behavior Research and Therapy, 6,* 473–482.

Watson, D., & Clark, L. A. (1997). Measurement and mismeasurement of mood: recurrent and emergent issues. *Journal of Personality Assessment, 68,* 267–296.

Watson, D., Clark, L. A., & Tellegen, A. (1988). Development and validation of brief measures of positive and negative affect: The PANAS scales. *Journal of Personality and Social Psychology, 54,* 1063–1070.

Wehlage, D. F. (1980). Managing the emotional reaction to loss in athletics. *Athletic Training, 15,* 144–146.

## AUTHORS' NOTES

We thank the competitors, parents, caregivers, coaches and committee members of the Wellington Netball Association and the Wellington Junior Soccer Association, for cooperation with this study.

This paper is based on the 4th year thesis of Lisa J. Brown, who was supervised by John M. Malouff in consultation with Nicola S. Schutte.

## AUTHOR AFFILIATION

Lisa J. Brown, John M. Malouff, and Nicola S. Schutte
University of New England, Australia

## AUTHOR AFFILIATION

Address Correspondence to: John M. Malouff, School of Psychology, University of New England, Armidale, NSW, 2351, Australia. Email: jmalouff@une.edu.au.

## CHAPTER ACTIVITY QUESTIONS

1. What was the problem or behavior the authors were trying to address in this article?
2. Which constructs did they use?
3. What was the intervention they developed based on the constructs?
4. How was this intervention similar or different from the ones you identified in your brainstorming session?
5. Using the results of your brainstorming session, what else could have been done?

## CHAPTER REFERENCES

Bandura, A. (1977). Self-Efficacy: Toward a unifying theory of behavioral change. *Psychological Review, 84*(2), 191–215.

Bandura, A., & Adams, N. (1977). Analysis of Self-Efficacy Theory of behavior change. *Cognitive Therapy and Research, 1*(4), 287–310.

Bandura, A. (1994). Self-Efficacy. In V.S. Ramachaudran (Ed.), *Encyclopedia of Human Behavior* (Vol. 4, pp. 71–81). New York: Academic Press. (Reprinted in H. Friedman [Ed.], *Encyclopedia of Mental Health*. San Diego: Academic Press, 1998.)

Bandura, A. (1997). *Self-Efficacy: The Exercise of Control*. New York: Freeman.

Bandura, A. (2004). Swimming against the mainstream: The early years from chilly tributary to transformative mainstream. *Behavior Research and Therapy, 42*, 613–630.

Brown, L.J., Malouff, J.M., & Schutte, N.S. (2005). The effectiveness of a self-efficacy intervention for helping adolescents cope with sport-competition loss. *Journal of Sport Behavior, 28*(2), 136–150.

Centers for Disease Control. (2012). Cost of falls among older adults. Retrieved March 15, 2013, from http://www.cdc.gov/HomeandRecreationalSafety/Falls/fallcost.html.

Cheal, B., & Clemson, L. (2001). Older people enhancing self-efficacy in fall-risk situations. *Australian Occupational Therapy Journal, 48,* 80–91.

Froman, R.D., & Owen, S.V. (1989). Infant care self-efficacy. *Scholarly Inquiry for Nursing Practice: An International Journal, 3*(3), 199–210.

Froman, R.D., & Owen, S.V. (1990). Mothers' and nurses' perceptions of infant care skills. *Research in Nursing and Health, 13,* 247–253.

Gross, D., Rocissano, L., & Roncoli, M. (1989). Maternal confidence during toddlerhood: Comparing preterm and full-term groups. *Research in Nursing and Health, 18*(6), 489–499.

Jackson, D. (2010). How personal trainers can use Self-Efficacy Theory to enhance exercise behavior in beginning exercisers. *Strength and Conditioning Journal, 32*(3), 67–71.

Maliski, S.L., Clerkin, B., & Litwin, M.S. (2004). Describing a nurse case manager intervention to empower low-income men with prostate cancer. *Oncology Nursing Forum, 31*(1), 57–63.

Pajares, F. (2002). Overview of Social Cognitive Theory and of self-efficacy. Retrieved March 15, 2013, from http://www.uky.edu/~eushe2/Pajares/eff.html.

Rowe, M.M., & Moore, T.A. (1998). Self-report measures of dental fear: Gender difference. *American Journal of Health Behavior, 22*(4), 243–247.

Strauser, D. (1995). Applications of Self-Efficacy Theory in rehabilitation counseling. *Journal of Rehabilitation, 61*(1), 7–11.

Tripp, M.K., Herrmann, N.B, Parcel, G.S., Chamberlain, R.M., & Gritz, E.R. (2000). Sun protection is fun! A skin cancer prevention program for pre-schools. *Journal of School Health, 70* (10), 395–401.

# The Theory of Reasoned Action and the Theory of Planned Behavior

## STUDENT LEARNING OUTCOMES

After reading this chapter the student will be able to:

- Explain the concept of the Theory of Reasoned Action (TRA) and the Theory of Planned Behavior (TPB).
- Explain how the constructs of attitude, subjective norm, volitional control, and behavioral control influence intention.
- Differentiate between the TRA and the TPB.
- Use the theory to explain at least one behavior.

## THEORY ESSENCE SENTENCE

Health behavior results from intention influenced by attitude, norms, and control.

---

**Self-Efficacy Constructs Chart**

**Attitude:**
A series of beliefs about something that affects the way we think and behave

**Subjective norms:**
The behaviors we perceive important people expect of us and our desire to comply with these expectations

**Volitional control:**
The extent to which we can decide to do something, at will

**Behavioral control:**
The extent of ease or difficulty we believe the performance of a behavior to be

---

# IN THE BEGINNING

In the 1960s and 70s attitudes were seen as comprising a person's beliefs, feelings, and actions toward an object (behavior). Given this, the assumption was that attitude was strongly related to behavior; that is, human behavior is determined by attitudes toward the behavior. Although research repeatedly failed to show a strong relationship between the two, there was, nonetheless, widespread acceptance of this assumption—that behavior was largely determined by attitude (Fishbein & Ajzen, 1975). In 1975, Fishbein and Ajzen (1975) conducted a review of previous studies of attitude and behavior. Once again, they found little evidence that supported a relationship between the two, again confirming the assumption was false. They argued that although attitude *should* be related to behavior, it is not necessarily so and that behavior is rather driven by intention to perform a behavior rather than the attitude toward the behavior.

# THEORETICAL CONCEPT

The Theory of Reasoned Action (TRA) and the Theory of Planned Behavior (TBP) propose that behavior is based on the concept of intention. *Intention* is the extent to which someone is ready to engage in a certain behavior, or the likelihood that someone will engage in a particular behavior (Fishbein, 1967; Ajzen & Fishbein, 1980). People are more likely to do something if they plan or aim to do it than if they do not.

# THEORETICAL CONSTRUCTS

Intention in the TRA/TBP is influenced by the following factors: attitudes, subjective norms, volitional control, and behavioral control.

## ATTITUDES

Attitudes are formed by a series of beliefs and result in a value being placed on the outcome of the behavior (Ajzen, 2002a). If the outcome or result of a behavior is seen as being positive, valuable, beneficial, desirable, advantageous, or a good thing, then a person's attitude will be favorable and his or her likelihood of engaging in that behavior would be greater. For example, if someone believes eating soy is healthier than eating animal protein, is better for the environment, and carries less of a chance of foodborne illness, the individual's attitude toward eating soy products would be favorable. Conversely, an unfavorable attitude toward soy consumption may result from the beliefs that soy products have an unpleasant taste and texture and are too expensive (Rah, Hasler, Painter, & Chapman, 2004). These attitudes would either positively or negatively influence the intention to eat soy products.

Another example of how intention to engage in a behavior is impacted by attitude and beliefs is seen in infant feeding choice. If a woman believes breastfeeding will protect her baby against infection (Swanson & Power, 2004), is healthier for her, and is more convenient, these beliefs are consistent with a positive attitude and she is more likely to breastfeed. If she believes breastfeeding is embarrassing (Swanson & Power, 2004), hurts, and restricts her activity (negative attitude), she is more likely to bottle feed.

Among college students, attitudes toward tobacco were found to play a role in those who began smoking at age 18 or older. Among the attitudinal differences found in one study were a more positive attitude toward having a relationship with a smoker, and less positive attitudes toward smoking restrictions on campus and other anti-smoking policies (Stockdale, Dawson-Owens, & Sagrestano, 2005). When the contribution of attitude toward smoking was compared in African American and Caucasian college students, attitudes emerged as having some predictive value for both, although was not found to be a strong predictor (Nehl et al., 2009)

## SUBJECTIVE NORMS

In addition to attitude, intention is influenced by subjective norms. A *subjective norm* is the perceived social pressure to engage or not to engage in a certain behavior.

It is determined by normative beliefs. These are the behaviors that *we perceive* important people in our lives expect from us (Ajzen, 2002a). These important people are often family members, friends or peers, religious figures, health care providers, or others we hold in high esteem—people we like to please. Subjective norms, then, result from the behaviors we perceive these important people expect from us, and our desire to comply with their perceived expectations (**Figure 3–1**). Note that these expectations may or may not be based in reality, as they are our *perceptions*.

Continuing with the soy consumption example used previously, if a health care provider and family member suggest that an individual eat soy products, and if the person wants to make these others happy, there is a greater willingness to comply and a greater likelihood of soy consumption (Rah et al., 2004). On the other hand, if the health care provider does not make the suggestion to consume soy and there is limited family support to try this food source, then the likelihood of soy being eaten is greatly diminished.

Just as we have seen earlier how attitude and beliefs influence infant feeding choice, so too do subjective norms. The decision women make about feeding method for their first baby is influenced by their own mothers, friends, partners, and medical professionals (Swanson & Power, 2004). These new moms will choose the method they perceive to be the preference of these important people. The same is true when we look at condom use among adolescent

© ZouZou/Shutterstock, Inc.

**FIGURE 3–1** We want to please the important people in our lives

mothers. The extent of importance given to the parents', peers', and sexual partner's approval or disapproval of condom use influences intention to use (Koniak-Griffin & Stein, 2006).

Although one would presume peer group expectations to be strong motivators for other behaviors among college students, surprisingly, parental subjective norms are the strong motivators for college students to wear bike helmets. That is—the desire to comply with parental expectations of helmet use is a strong predictor of use. Given this, one approach to ultimately increasing helmet use on campuses is to work with parents of young children to insist that they wear helmets (Ross, Ross, Farber, Davidson, Trevino et al., 2011).

## VOLITIONAL CONTROL

Although the Theory of Reasoned Action tells us behavior is the result of a person's intention to do something, in order for this to happen, the behavior has to be under volitional control. A behavior under volitional control is one in which the person is able to decide, at will, to engage in or not (Ajzen, 1991). Whether you eat breakfast in the morning is under volitional control. The type of exercise you do (if any) is under volitional control. Having your blood pressure checked is under volitional control.

In some situations a person may not have complete control over a behavior even though the intention to engage in the behavior is great. For example, a woman may intend to practice safer sex. However, the actual use of the (male) condom is not in her control. Thus, she has limited volitional control over this behavior even though her intention is great. Condom use is significantly more likely if, in addition to her intention to use a condom, her male partner also intends to use a condom (DeVisser & Smith, 2004). On the other hand, she can say no to sex without a condom. She does have volitional control over engaging in intercourse (except in the case of rape).

If we look at participating in a team sport, making the team is a good example of a behavior that is not under volitional control. A person may have great intention to join the university lacrosse team, have a really positive attitude toward team sports and exercise, and want to make his parents happy by engaging in a sport in college, but alas, does not make the team. Making the team is not completely under his control because there is no way to affect the skill level of the other people he is competing against (**Figure 3–2**).

**FIGURE 3-2**  Making the team is not under volitional control

## BEHAVIORAL CONTROL

In situations where there is less volitional control, even when intention is great, the TRA is not very useful in predicting or explaining behavior. To address this, the construct of behavioral control was added to the theory, and with this, the *Theory of Planned Behavior* was born (Ajzen, 1991; Ajzen, 2002b). Therefore, the Theory of Planned Behavior is nothing more than the Theory of Reasoned Action with another construct added.

The construct of behavioral control is similar to the construct of self-efficacy in Social Cognitive Theory (Ajzen, 2002b) and the concept of Self-Efficacy Theory. However, behavioral control differs from self-efficacy in that self-efficacy is concerned with one's perception of *ability* to perform a behavior, whereas behavioral control is concerned with "perceived *control* over performance of a behavior" (Ajzen, 2002b, p. 4), or how easy or difficult it is to perform the behavior (Ajzen, 1991).

Behavioral control is impacted by a set of control beliefs. These are beliefs the person has that help or hinder performance of the behavior (Ajzen, 2002b); that is, they affect the perception of how easy or difficult it is to carry out the behavior (Ajzen, 1991). For the lacrosse player who didn't make the team, behavioral control influenced his intention to try out. He believed it would be easy for him to make the team. In the condom example, although the woman has limited volitional control, she may believe it is easy to get her partner to use a condom.

In trying to understand nonsmoking behavior in African American and Caucasian college students, of all the constructs of the Theory of Planned

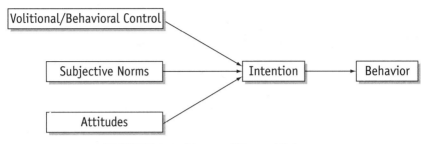

**FIGURE 3–3** Theory of Planned Behavior

*Source:* Adapted from: Rah, J.H., Hasler, C.M., Painter, J.E., & Chapman-Novakoski, K.M. (2004). Applying the Theory of Planned Behavior to Women's Behavioral Attitudes on and Consumption of Soy Products. *Journal of Nutrition Education, 36*(5), 238-244.

Behavior, perceived behavioral control (PBC) emerges as the strongest predictor of nonsmoking intention for both groups of students. PBC in the case of non-smoking is the perception of how easy or difficult it is to not smoke (Nehl et al., 2009). If the perception is that refraining from smoking is easy, then the intention to not smoke is greater, and the likelihood of smoking lessened. On the other hand, if the perception is that refraining from smoking is very difficult, then smoking is more likely. The importance of this is its application in practice. Given the importance of perceived behavioral control in the initiation of smoking among college students, interventions that enhance the sense of control are needed (Wang, 2001).

This was also found to be true with bike helmet use among college students (Ross et al., 2011). To increase the positive contribution behavioral control makes to helmet use, hands-on interventions were suggested to change the perception of choosing a correct helmet and using it from something that was difficult to something that was easy to do.

In summary, according to the Theory of Reasoned Action and the Theory of Planned Behavior, attitudes, subjective norms, volitional control, and behavioral control affect intention and, therefore, our behavior. (See **Figure 3–3**.)

# THEORY IN ACTION—CLASS ACTIVITY

The makers of HPV vaccine target mothers of girls ages 9 to 14 in their ads. Brainstorm the attitudes/beliefs, and subjective norms you think might influence mothers' decisions about vaccinating their daughters against this STI. Now, read the following article and answer the questions at the end.

# Chapter 3 Article: Using the Theory of Planned Behavior to Predict Mothers' Intentions to Vaccinate Their Daughters Against HPV[1]

*Askelson, Natoshia M; Campo, Shelly; Lowe, John B; Smith, Sandi; Dennis, Leslie K et al.*

## Abstract (summary)

This study assessed mothers' intentions to vaccinate their daughters against human papillomavirus (HPV) using the theory of planned behavior (TPB). Experience with sexually transmitted infections (STIs), beliefs about the vaccine encouraging sexual activity, and perception of daughters' risk for HPV were also examined for a relationship with intention. A random sample of mothers in a rural, Midwestern state were mailed a survey with questions pertaining to the intention to vaccinate. Attitudes were the strongest predictor of mothers' intentions to vaccinate, but intentions were not high. Subjective norms also influence intention. Mothers' risk perceptions, experience with STIs, and beliefs about the vaccine encouraging sexual activity were not related to intention. Mothers' perceptions of the daughters' risks for HPV were surprisingly low. This research provides a foundation for designing interventions to increase HPV vaccination rates. Further research should explore ways to influence mothers' attitudes and to uncover the referent groups mothers refer to for vaccination behavior.

**Keywords:** communicable diseases; family life/sexuality; health education; immunizations; quantitative research

The Food and Drug Administration approved the first vaccine against human papillomavirus (HPV), Merck's Gardasil1, for preventing HPV infection types 6, 11, 16, and 18. The Advisory Committee on Immunization Practices (ACIP) recommended that this vaccine be given to females as early as

---

[1] Reproduced from Askelson, N.M., Campo, S., Lowe, J.B., Smith, S., Dennis, L.K., Andsager, J. (2010). Using the Theory of Planned Behavior to Predict Mothers' Intentions to Vaccinate Their Daughters Against HPV. *The Journal of School Nursing, 26*(3), 194–202.

9–10 years of age, be routinely given to 11- to 12-year-olds, and females up to age 26 should be vaccinated if they had previously not been vaccinated (Advisory Committee on Immunization Practices, 2006). Although recommendations exist, a recommendation alone does not mean that girls and adolescents will be immunized, as seen in the case of the hepatitis B vaccine (Rosenthal, Kottenhahn, Biro, & Succup, 1995). It is important to assess influences of mothers' intentions to vaccinate, so that interventions and messages can be designed to encourage vaccination. Much of the previous research on vaccine acceptability was conducted before the vaccine was actually approved and available in health care settings. Factors influencing vaccination adoption beyond vaccine recommendations are reported below. Influencing factors can include risk perceptions, attitudes, subjective norms, perceived behavioral control, mothers' perceptions of the vaccine encouraging sexually activity, and experience with sexually transmitted infections (STIs).

The theory of planned behavior (TPB) posits that attitudes, subjective norms, and perceived behavioral control drive people's intention to perform a behavior, which in turn influences whether they engage in a behavior (Ajzen, 1984). Subjective norms are what important referent groups want an individual to do and an individual's willingness to comply with these groups. Perceived behavioral control is the amount of control a person believes to have over performing a behavior. Additionally, intentions are directly related to behavior. Specifically related to the HPV vaccine, there has been little preliminary research using the constructs of the TPB (Ogilvie et al., 2007). Research on decision making about other immunizations points to mothers' desires to want to do what their doctors want, to maintain the norm of vaccination, and to support the social contract implicit in the vaccination of children (Benin, Wisler-Scher, Colson, Shapiro, & Holmboe, 2006).

Risk perception is another possible influencer of the intent to vaccinate. Previous research indicates that parents who perceived their children at risk for HPV were more likely to be in favor of vaccination (Brabin, Roberts, Farzaneh, & Kitchener, 2006; Dempsey, Zimet, Davis, & Koutsky, 2006; Olshen, Woods, Austin, Luskin, Bauchner, 2005; Zimet et al., 2005). However, many parents do not think that their children are at risk for STIs including HPV (Olshen et al., 2005). Parents underestimate their children's risk behaviors, especially among younger adolescents and children (O'Donnell et al., 2008; Young & Zimmerman, 1998).

Mothers' experiences with STIs and the experiences of women they know have the potential to influence whether mothers would intend to vaccinate their daughters. A qualitative study conducted before the vaccine was released suggested that mother's experience with STIs positively influenced their support of a vaccine to protect their children against STIs (Mays, Sturm, & Zimet, 2004). Other research found that parents who had experience with STIs were more likely to accept the vaccine (Dempsey et al., 2006; Zimet et al., 2005). Knowing someone with an abnormal Papanicolaou test was also related to parents wanting a child to receive the HPV vaccine (Davis, Dickman, Ferris, & Dias, 2004). Women who had experience with HPV or abnormal Papanicolaou test were also more likely to know more about HPV (Tiro, Meissner, Kobrin, & Chollette, 2007).

Early research on the acceptability of the HPV vaccine indicated that parents and others were concerned that the vaccine might encourage sexual activity among adolescents (Brabin et al., 2006; Dailard, 2006). People have argued that adolescents will decide to become sexually active or engage in risky sexual behavior (i.e., not using condoms) because they will believe that the vaccine decreases their risk for the negative consequences of sexual activity.

The purpose of this research was to investigate the influences of mothers' intentions to vaccinate their 9- to 15-year-old daughters against HPV. Specifically, this study examined how attitudes, subjective norms, and perceived behavioral control might influence intention to vaccinate against HPV. Additionally, the study was designed to investigate how mothers' personal experiences with STIs as well as the experiences of women they know might influence their intention to vaccinate their daughters with HPV. Finally, mothers' perceptions about their daughters' risk for HPV and their opinions about the vaccine encouraging sexual activity were explored. Mothers were the focus of this study because the vaccine manufacturer's media information campaign had targeted mothers (Merck, 2007).

## METHOD

The survey was pretested with 10 mothers. Based on the pretest, the survey length was shortened and questions that were confusing were either changed with input from the mother or eliminated. The survey was given to a random sample of 1,207 mothers who had daughters aged 9–15 in a rural, Midwest state. A power analysis was done to determine the sample size. Sample size was based on the number of girls in this age group (144,260 girls) in this state according to the 2000 US Census (US Census Bureau, 2007). The sample was drawn from all women who were registered to vote in 2007 and who gave birth in the state to daughters born in 1993–1999, in an effort to obtain a true sample of mothers from this state. Voter registration rates in this state are high, with approximately 96% of adults registered to vote (Iowa State, Secretary of State, 2008). Birth certificate data from all female children born in the state, who were currently 9–15 years old, were matched with voter registration data to provide the most current addresses of mothers.

The survey was mailed to potential participants, followed by a reminder postcard 10 days later. Ten days after the postcard, a second copy of the survey was mailed. There were 306 completed or partially complete surveys returned. The response rate was 25.43% (American Association for Public Opinion Research, 2008). For this analysis, mothers who had reported already vaccinating their daughter, mothers whose daughters did not live with them at least half the time, and mothers who reported on daughters outside of the 9- to 15-year-old age were not included in the analysis. The remaining 217 were used for the analysis. The research project was reviewed and approved of by the institutional review board and the survey was accompanied with a letter that contained the elements of consent.

## THEORY OF PLANNED BEHAVIOR

The questions measuring attitudes, subjective norms, and perceived behavioral control were based on the questions from the theory's creator (Ajzen, 2004). The mothers were asked to respond to statements using a Likert-type, 7-point scale with the higher score (7) representing a more favorable response. To assess mothers' intentions, they were asked about how likely they were to have their 9- to 15-year-old daughter vaccinated. They were also asked at what age they would vaccinate their daughter.

To measure subjective norms, mothers were asked to rate how much they agreed with each statement: "Most people who are important to me think that I should vaccinate my daughter," "It is expected of me that I will vaccinate my daughter against HPV," and "The people in my life whose opinions I value would want me to vaccinate my daughter." These measures were combined to form a total measure of subjective norms.

There were three measures of attitude toward vaccinating daughters who were 9–15 years old. Mothers were asked whether vaccinating "is necessary," "is a good idea," and "is beneficial." Again, the mean of the sum of these three responses provided the entire measure of attitude toward vaccinating daughters age 9–15.

Mothers were asked to respond to five different statements pertaining to perceived behavioral control: "For me, vaccinating my daughter against HPV is possible," "If I wanted to get my daughter vaccinated in the next 6 months it would be easy," "How much control do you have over your daughter getting vaccinated?" and "It is mostly up to me whether or not my daughter gets vaccinated against HPV." For the final perceived behavioral control measure, mothers were asked how much they disagreed with the statement: "The cost of the vaccine (about $360) is a barrier to my daughter getting vaccinated."

## OTHER MEASURES

Other questions pertaining to mothers' perception of risk for their daughters, perception of the vaccine as promoting sexual activity, and STI experience were asked. The measure of STI experience for mothers and other women they know was based on a similar, previously published measure used to assess life experience with HPV (Dempsey et al., 2006). Mothers responded whether they had been told that they had an abnormal Papanicolaou test, HPV/genital warts, cervical cancer, or other STIs. The answers to each of these four questions were coded zero for no experience and one for experience. The answers to the four questions were summed to provide a total experience score. They were also asked whether they knew of someone who had been told that they had an abnormal Papanicolaou test, HPV/genital warts, cervical cancer, or other STIs. These answers were also summed to provide a cumulative measure of experience for women the mothers knew. Mothers were also asked how much they agreed with the statement "My daughter is or will be at risk for HPV" on a 7-point Likert-type scale. Mothers responded to the statement, "Vaccinating my daughter against HPV will encourage her to be sexually active . . . will have NO effect on her decision to be sexually active" with a 7-point scale (having no effect was 7). Mothers were also asked if they had discussed whether to vaccinate their daughter with the child's other parent. The age of the daughters, mothers' age, health insurance status of the daughters, household income, educational attainment of the mothers, and mothers' race and ethnicity were also obtained.

## ANALYSIS

The analysis was conducted using SPSS version 15.0. Descriptive statistics were calculated. Confirmatory factor analysis was used to establish the validity of the constructs of the TPB. Factor analysis was done using a varimax rotation. Linear regression was used to estimate the influence of the constructs of the TPB and the measures of risk perception, disinhibiting impact of the vaccine, and STI experience on mothers' intention to vaccinate.

# RESULTS

There were 217 respondents who were used in the analyses in this research. The majority of the respondents had at least graduated from college (63.3%, n = 134) and household income levels for most were $50,000 or above. The sample was predominantly White and there was almost no racial or ethnic diversity among the mothers. The mean age of the mothers was 40.30 (SD = 5.50) with a range of 27 to 56 years old. Daughters were between 9 and 15 years old, with a mean age of 11.21 (SD = 1.82). All of the mothers reported that their daughters had health insurance. Ninety percent (n = 190) had private health insurance and just 10% (n = 21) had public health insurance.

Results for the survey questions are presented in **Table 1**. The table shows the means and standard deviations for all the variables. For the measures of attitudes and subjective norms, which had high Cronbach's αs, the factor loadings and the αs are presented. Because of poor internal consistency (Cronbach's α .38), the perceived behavioral control variables could not be simply summed. Other combinations of these measures did not prove to have acceptable reliability; therefore, the variables were used individually. The confirmatory factor analysis confirmed that these variables did not load together or in other combinations; thus, the constructs of the TPB (attitudes, subjective norms, and perceived behavioral control) were entered into a linear regression model.

Linear regression was used to estimate the influence of the constructs of the TPB on mothers' intentions to vaccinate their daughters and the influence of

**Table 1** Variables for Mothers' Intentions to Vaccinate 9- to 15-Year-Old Daughters Against HPV ($N = 217$)

| Variables (all Variables on a Scale of 1–7) | Mean (SD) | Factor Loading | Cronbach's α |
|---|---|---|---|
| Intention to vaccinate | 4.71 (2.21) | | |
| How likely are you to vaccinate? | | | |
|   Attitudes | 5.21 (1.81) | | .96 |
|     Vaccinating is necessary | 4.81 (1.99) | 0.94 | |
|     Vaccinating is a good idea | 5.39 (1.86) | 0.98 | |
|     Vaccinating is beneficial | 5.39 (1.80) | 0.97 | |
|   Perceived behavioral control (PBC) | | | |
|     PBC vaccinating is possible | 5.83 (1.56) | | |
|     PBC vaccinating is easy | 5.85 (1.63) | | |
|     PBC vaccinating is in my control | 6.68 (0.68) | | |
|     PBC vaccinating is up to me | 6.42 (1.12) | | |
|     PBC cost is barrier | 4.41 (2.29) | | |
|   Subjective norms | 4.56 (1.63) | | .88 |
|     Most people think I should vaccinate my daughter | 4.69 (2.05) | 0.94 | |
|     It is expected of me that I will vaccinate | 4.01 (1.89) | 0.83 | |
|     The people in my life would want me to vaccinate | 4.89 (1.83) | 0.92 | |
| Mothers' STI experience[a] | 0.55 (0.83) | | |
| Others STI experience[a] | 1.35 (1.37) | | |
| Risk for HPV | 3.43 (1.74) | | |
| Vaccine encourages sexual activity | 6.15 (1.35) | | |

*Notes:* HPV = human papillomavirus; STI = sexually transmitted infection.

[a] Mean of total experiences.

risk perceptions, experience, and mothers' assessment of the vaccine's impact on sexual activity; F (11, 173) = 31.17, p < .001. The regression analysis results are shown in **Table 2**. The adjusted $R^2$ for this model is .66, which indicates that the model accounts for 66% of the variance and is a good fit for the data.

Intent to vaccinate was influenced by mothers' positive attitudes about the vaccine in such a way that more positive attitudes increased the likelihood of vaccinating (β = .61, p < .001). The results of the linear regression also indicated

**Table 2** Linear Regression of Factors That Predict Mothers' Intentions to Vaccinate Daughters Against HPV ($N = 217$)

|  | B | SE | β |
|---|---|---|---|
| Attitude | 0.74 | 0.11 | .61** |
| Subjective norms | 0.22 | 0.11 | .16* |
| PBC vaccinating is possible | 0.15 | 0.10 | .12 |
| PBC vaccinating is easy | −0.02 | 0.07 | −.02 |
| PBC vaccinating is in my control | −0.06 | 0.18 | −.02 |
| PBC vaccinating is up to me | 0.07 | 0.10 | .03 |
| PBC cost is barrier | 0.08 | 0.05 | .08 |
| Mothers' STI experience | −0.02 | 0.12 | −.01 |
| Others STI experience | 0.09 | 0.08 | .05 |
| Risk for HPV | −0.08 | 0.06 | −.06 |
| Vaccine encourages sexual activity | −0.01 | 0.08 | −0.01 |
| Adjusted $R^2 = .66$ | | | |

*$p < .05$.
**$p < .001$.
Notes: HPV = human papillomavirus; PBC = perceived behavioral control; STI = sexually transmitted infection.

that those with subjective norms that were in support of the vaccine were more likely to intend to vaccinate ($\beta = .16$, $p < .05$). Perceived behavioral control did not influence intentions. There was no evidence that mothers' perceptions of risk of HPV for their daughters influenced intention to vaccinate. Furthermore, there was no support for the influence of maternal STI experience and STI experience of women the mothers knew on the intention to vaccinate. Mothers' concerns about the vaccine encouraging sexual activity also did not predict mothers' intentions to vaccinate. Mothers believed that the vaccine would have little effect on their daughter's decision to be sexually active, contrary to what we hypothesized.

# DISCUSSION

This study had several strengths. Very few previous studies on HPV vaccine acceptability have used any theory or theoretical construct (Zimet, Liddon, Rosenthal, Lazcano-Ponce, & Allen, 2006), as this study had. The value of a random sample from a rural state was another unique feature of this study. This research points to the importance of mothers' attitudes and subjective norms in predicting intention to vaccinate and indicates that mothers' intentions to vaccinate are not overwhelming. The model presented also had a high $R^2$ value, indicating that much of the variance in intention to vaccinate was explained by the constructs of the TPB. Because of the importance of mothers' attitudes and the influence of subjective norms, further research should explore ways to influence their attitudes, heighten the importance of subjective norms that support vaccination, and help mothers understand their daughters' risks.

Attitudes were the strongest predictor of mothers' intentions to vaccinate. The importance of attitudes has been cited in previous HPV vaccine acceptability research (Dempsey et al., 2006; Ogilvie et al., 2007). Mothers from this rural, Midwestern state had fairly positive attitudes toward the vaccine. They believed it was a good idea and beneficial, while they were slightly less in agreement about whether the vaccine was necessary. Their view that the vaccine was not necessary might be related to their assessment that their daughters were not at risk for HPV. Other studies have indicated that risk perception and acceptability are related (Brabin et al., 2006; Dempsey et al., 2006; Mays et al., 2004; Zimet et al., 2005).

Subjective norms were the only other predictor of intention in this model. Mothers' responses to the subjective norms questions were more neutral, leaning slightly positive. Subjective norms in the form of health care providers' opinions have been shown in previous research to be influential (Dempsey et al., 2006). The current study did not look at specific people or groups of people, so it is not clear who the important persons or referent group would be for these mothers. Future research should explore this issue.

Perceived behavioral control was a problematic construct, as the measures for this construct did not hold together in the factor analysis. Mothers in this study indicated that their perceived behavioral control was very high when it came to vaccinating their daughters. That is, it appears that vaccinating against HPV was a behavior that mothers perceive as in their control, indicating that vaccinating their daughters was "possible" and "easy." Cost was not perceived as a barrier, most likely because all of the daughters in this sample had health insurance and the vaccine is covered by health insurance in this state. Only 3% of the children in this state are without health insurance, so cost would have minimal impact (Damiano et al., 2007). The construct of perceived behavioral control requires further investigation across a diverse sample.

Only about 48% of mothers who responded indicated that they agreed or strongly agreed with the statement that they were intending to vaccinate their daughters. The average age mothers reported for intending to vaccinate their daughters (13.20 years) was higher than the recommendations of 11–12 years. Other research before the Food and Drug Administration approval of the vaccine has indicated more support from mothers for vaccination than this current research study (Brabin et al., 2006). Other past research has also shown that mothers are more willing to vaccinate at older ages (Dempsey et al., 2006).

## Experience With STIs

Mothers' experience with STIs and the experience of women whom mothers know were not related to intention in this study, which is in contrast with past research conducted before the vaccine was available (Davis et al., 2004; Dempsey et al., 2006; Mays et al., 2004; Tiro et al., 2007; Zimet et al., 2005). Mothers' experience should be substantial, as yearly some 3.5 million women in the United States have an abnormal Papanicolaou test result (Dailard, 2006), but women might not be sharing this information with each other. For women in the age group of the mothers, national HPV prevalence ranges from 19.6% to 27.5% (Dunne et al., 2007), and about 11,070 women were diagnosed with cervical cancer in 2007 (Jemal et al., 2008).

## Risk Perceptions

Despite almost one third of mothers reporting knowing someone with genital warts/HPV, most did not think it was likely that their daughters were at risk for acquiring these infections and this perception had no impact on their intentions to vaccinate. Previous research has suggested that there is a relationship between risk perception and acceptability of the vaccine (Brabin et al., 2006; Dempsey et al., 2006; Mays et al., 2004; Olshen et al., 2005; Zimet et al., 2005). Mothers in this study perceived very low risk for their daughters. In accordance with the previous literature on parents' inability to estimate risk behaviors in their children (Bylund, Imes, & Baxter, 2005; O'Donnell et al., 2008; Young & Zimmerman, 1998), these mothers are likely underestimating their daughters' risk. Prevalence of HPV is 24.5% in females 14–19 years old (Dunne et al., 2007). Daughters are also likely to become sexually active before the age of 18, with one study reporting 36% of high school females being sexually active (Melhado, 2008). By the 12th grade, 61% of students report being sexually active (Brener, Kann, Lowry, Wechsler, & Romero, 2006). Even if they do not have sex as a teenager, the vaccine would protect them later in life. A woman's lifetime risk for HPV infection is 50% (Centers for Disease Control and Prevention, 2004).

Furthermore, because risk is a concept poorly understood by the general public and influenced by culture and society (Wilkinson, 2001), it is possible that mothers were not able to estimate risk of a disease, even if they recognized the disease to be very prevalent. Mothers' risk perceptions, which were low, were also not associated with mothers' intentions to vaccinate; therefore, mothers were choosing to vaccinate based on their attitude toward the vaccine and subjective norms, not how much danger their daughters were in without the vaccine. This is an interesting paradox that needs to be further explored.

Interestingly, mothers from this study strongly agreed that the vaccine would have no effect on their daughters' decisions to be sexually active. Not only does this finding go against early arguments made that the vaccine would encourage sexual activity among adolescents (Brabin et al., 2006; Dailard, 2006), but this might also indicate that mothers see decisions to be sexually active as being complicated and not easily influenced by one thing, such as a vaccination. This finding has practical significance, as the popular press has highlighted this concern of encouraging sexual activity (Senator: HPV vaccine more deserved debate, 2007).

The low response rate might contribute to a response bias in this study. Although the response rate was low in this survey, additional items from the survey measured parenting style (Baumrind, 1991) and family communication patterns (Ritchie, 1991). The distribution of mothers for both of these scales mirrored those seen in other research with mothers and parents (Huebner & Howell, 2003; Ritchie & Fitzpatrick, 1990). This provides some evidence that the mothers who responded to the survey are not unlike other mothers in regard to important characteristics like parenting style and family communication patterns.

## IMPLICATIONS FOR SCHOOL NURSES

Because mothers in this study were not overwhelmingly indicating that they intended to vaccinate their daughters and were not intending to vaccine at the recommended ages, it will be up to health care providers and public health practitioners to encourage mothers to vaccinate their daughters. Efforts will need to be focused on strengthening mothers' positive attitudes about the vaccine as it pertains to their daughters to change mothers' intentions. It is possible to increase mothers' positive attitudes toward the vaccine. Mothers did not universally believe that the vaccine is necessary. More work needs to be done to show mothers that HPV is common and a threat to their daughters. These messages may also have to be coupled with messages about daughters being at risk, if not immediately, then later in life when they are sexually active and have partners who could expose them to the virus. More emphasis could also be placed on the concepts of the vaccine being "a good idea" and "beneficial." Furthermore, more information and messages directed at the effectiveness of this highly effective vaccine might move attitudes in a more positive direction. School nurses are in a pivotal position to coordinate efforts in the health care community to raise awareness of the need for HPV vaccine and the subsequent recommendations for administration.

Future research needs to establish how school nurses can most effectively communicate with parents about vaccinations. The research should focus on what messages need to be communicated and how they should be communicated to inform and motivate parents to vaccinate their children. Messages about how these groups of people support the vaccination of girls at the recommended ages could motivate mothers to have their daughters vaccinated.

Furthermore, interventions also need to give mothers an accurate perception of risk. Although perceptions of risk did not influence intentions, it is still important for mothers to understand the real risks their daughters face. Parents with inaccurate risk perceptions are less likely to parent in ways that protect their children, such as talking to them about the issue (Eisenberg, Sieving, Bearinger, Swain, & Resnick, 2006; Swain, Ackerman, & Ackerman, 2006). Information about an average adolescent's risk for sexual activity and HPV need to be addressed, not only to impress upon mothers the risks their daughters face but also to encourage mothers to address their daughters' sexual development.

*"Mothers' experiences with STIs and the experiences of women they know have the potential to influence whether mothers would intend to vaccinate their daughters."*

*"Despite almost one third of mothers reporting knowing someone with genital warts/HPV, most did not think it was likely that their daughters were at risk for acquiring these infections and this perception had no impact on their intentions to vaccinate."*

*"Information about an average adolescent's risk for sexual activity and HPV need to be addressed, not only to impress upon mothers the risks their daughters face but also to encourage mothers to address their daughters' sexual development."*

# REFERENCES

Advisory Committee on Immunization Practices. (2006). ACIP Recommendations. Retrieved December 16, 2006, from www.cdc.gov/nip/publications/acip-list.html.

Ajzen, I. (1984). From intentions to actions: A theory of planned behavior. In J. Kuhl & J. Beckman (Eds.), *Action control: From cognition to behavior*. New York, NY: Springer-Verlag.

Ajzen, I. (2004). Theory of planned behavior. Retrieved November 20, 2006, from http://www.people.umass.edu/aizen/tpb.html.

American Association for Public Opinion Research. (2008). Standard definitions: Final dispositions of case codes and outcome rates for surveys. Retrieved March 20, 2008, from http://www.aapor.org/uploads/Standard_Definitions_07_08_Final.pdf.

Baumrind, D. (1991). The influence of parenting style on adolescent competence and substance use. *Journal of Early Adolescence, 11*, 56–95.

Benin, A. L., Wisler-Scher, D. J., Colson, E., Shapiro, E. D., & Holmboe, E. S. (2006). Qualitative analysis of mothers' decision-making about vaccines for infants: The importance of trust. *Pediatrics, 117*, 1532–1541.

Brabin, L., Roberts, S. A., Farzaneh, F., & Kitchener, H. C. (2006). Future acceptance of adolescent human papillomavirus vaccination: A survey of parental attitudes. *Vaccine, 24*, 3087–3094.

Brener, N., Kann, L., Lowry, R., Wechsler, H., & Romero, L. (2006). Trends in HIV-related risk behaviors among high school students—United States, 1991–2005. *Morbidity and Mortality Weekly Report, 55*, 851–854.

Bylund, C. L., Imes, R. S., & Baxter, L. A. (2005). Accuracy of parents' perceptions of their college student children's health and health risk behaviors. *Journal of American College Health, 54*, 31–37.

Centers for Disease Control and Prevention. (2004). Genital HPV Infection Fact Sheet. Rockville, MD: CDC National Prevention Information Network.

Dailard, C. (2006). Achieving universal vaccination against cervical cancer in the United States: The need and the means. *Guttmacher Policy Review, 9*, 12–19.

Damiano, P., Willard, J., Borst, J., Dhooge, L., Hageman, G., Kane, D., & Penziner, A. (2007). Health insurance coverage of children in Iowa: Results from the Iowa Child and Family Household Health Survey. Retrieved September 19, 2008, from http://ppc.uiowa.edu/health/ICHHS/ECR/pdf/ insuranceFinal12_19_07.pdf.

Davis, K., Dickman, E. D., Ferris, D., & Dias, J. K. (2004). Human papillomavirus vaccine acceptability among parents of 10- to 15-year-old adolescents. *Obstetrical & Gynecological Survey, 59*, 820–822.

Dempsey, A. F., Zimet, G. D., Davis, R. L., & Koutsky, L. (2006). Factors that are associated with parental acceptance of human papillomavirus vaccines: A randomized intervention study of written information about HPV. *Pediatrics, 117*, 1486–1493.

Dunne, E. F., Unger, E. R., Sternberg, M., McQuillan, G., Swan, D. C., Patel, S. S., & Markowitz, L. E. (2007). Prevalence of HPV infection among adolescent females in the United States. *Journal of the American Medical Association, 297*, 813–819.

Eisenberg, M. E., Sieving, R. E., Bearinger, L. H., Swain, C., & Resnick, M. D. (2006). Parents' communication with adolescents about sexual behavior: A missed opportunity for prevention? *Journal of Youth and Adolescence, 35*, 893–902.

Huebner, A. J., & Howell, L. W. (2003). Examining the relationship between adolescent sexual risk-taking and perceptions of monitoring, communication, and parenting styles. *Journal of Adolescent Health, 33*, 71–78.

Iowa State, Secretary of State. (2008). Voter/elections. Retrieved September 19, 2008, from http://www.sos.state.ia.us/elections/voterreg/reg_to_vote.html.

Jemal, A., Siegel, R., Ward, E., Hao, Y., Xu, J., Murray, T., & Thun, M. J. (2008). Cancer Statistics, 2006. CA: *A Cancer Journal for Clinicians, 58*, 71–96.

Mays, R. M., Sturm, L. A., & Zimet, G. D. (2004). Parental perspectives on vaccinating children against sexually transmitted infections. *Social Science and Medicine, 58*, 1405–1431.

Melhado, L. (2008). Prevalence of sexual risk behaviors among U.S. high school students declined between 1991–2007. *Perspectives on Sexual and Reproductive Health, 40*, 180–181.

Merck & Company, Inc. (2007). Questions to ask your doctor or health care professional. Retrieved March 30, 2007, from http://www.gardasil.com/ask-your-doctor-about-hpv.html

O'Donnell, L., Stueve, A., Duran, R., Myint-U, A., Agronick, G., San Doval, A., & Wilson-Simmons, R. (2008). Parenting practices, parents' underestimation of daughters' risks, and alcohol and sexual behaviors of urban girls. *Journal of Adolescent Health, 31*, 496–502.

Ogilvie, G. S., Remple, V. P., Marra, F., McNeil, S. A., Naus, M., Pielak, K. L., & . . . Patrick, D. M. (2007). Parental intention to have daughters receive the human papillomavirus vaccine. *Canadian Medical Association Journal, 177*, 1506–1512.

Olshen, E., Woods, E. R., Austin, S. B., Luskin, M., & Bauchner, H. (2005). Parental acceptance of the human papillomavirus vaccine. *Journal of Adolescent Health, 37*, 248–251.

Ritchie, L. D. (1991). Family communication patterns: An epistemic analysis and conceptual reinterpretation. *Communication Research, 18*, 548–565.

Ritchie, L. D., & Fitzpatrick, M. A. (1990). Family communication patterns: Measuring intrapersonal perceptions of interpersonal relationships. *Communication Research, 17*, 523–544.

Rosenthal, S. L., Kottenhahn, R. K., Biro, F. M., & Succup, P. A. (1995). Hepatitis B vaccine acceptance among adolescents and their parents. *Journal of Adolescent Health, 17*, 248–254.

Senator: HPV vaccine more deserved debate. (2007, February 5). *The Dallas News*, Retrieved September 26, 2007, from http://www.dallasnews.com/sharedcontent/dws/news/texassouthwest/ stories/020607dntexvaccine.5378d899.html.

Swain, C., Ackerman, L. K., & Ackerman, M. A. (2006). The influence of individual characteristics and contraceptive beliefs on parent-teen sexual communications: A structural model. *Journal of Adolescent Health, 38*, 753–759.

Tiro, J. A., Meissner, H. I., Kobrin, S., & Chollette, V. (2007).What do women in the U.S. know about human papillomavirus and cervical cancer. *Cancer Epidemiology Biomakers & Prevention, 16*, 288–294.

US Census Bureau. (2007). American Fact Finder. Retrieved March 27, 2007, from http://factfinder.census.gov.

Wilkinson, I. (2001). Social theories of risk perception: At once indispensable and insufficient. *Current Sociology, 49*, 1–22.

Young, T. L., & Zimmerman, R. (1998). Clueless: Parental knowledge of risk behaviors of middle school students. *Archives of Pediatric Adolescent Medicine, 152*, 1137–1139.

Zimet, G. D., Liddon, N., Rosenthal, S. L., Lazcano-Ponce, E., & Allen, B. (2006). Psychosocial aspects of vaccine acceptability. *Vaccine, 24*, 201–209.

Zimet, G. D., Mays, R. M., Sturm, L. A., Ravert, A. A., Perkins, S. M., & Juliar, B. E. (2005). Parental attitudes about sexually transmitted infection vaccination for their adolescent children. *Archives of Pediatric and Adolescent Medicine, 159*, 132–137.

## AUTHOR AFFILIATION

Natoshia M. Askelson, MPH, PhD, Shelly Campo, PhD, John B. Lowe, PhD, Sandi Smith, PhD, Leslie K. Dennis, PhD, and Julie Andsager, PhD

## AUTHOR AFFILIATION

Natoshia M. Askelson, MPH, PhD, is an assistant research scientist at the Department of Community and Behavioral Health, University of Iowa.

Shelly Campo, PhD, is an associate professor at the Department of Community and Behavioral Health and Department of Communication Studies, University of Iowa.

John B. Lowe, PhD, is the Head of the School of Health and Sport Sciences at the University of the Sunshine Coast, Australia.

Sandi Smith, PhD, is a professor at the Department of Communication, Michigan State University.

Leslie K. Dennis, PhD, is an associate professor at the Department of Epidemiology, University of Iowa.

Julie Andsager, PhD, is a professor, Department of Journalism & Mass Communication, University of Iowa.

## CHAPTER ACTIVITY QUESTIONS

1. Which constructs had the greatest impact on the mothers' intention to vaccinate their daughters?
2. How did this compare to the outcome of your brainstorming session?

# CHAPTER REFERENCES

Ajzen, I. (1991). The Theory of Planned Behavior. *Organizational Behavior and Human Decision Process, 50*, 179–211

Ajzen, I. (2002a). Theory of Planned Behavior. Retrieved October 24, 2004, from http://www-unix.oit.umass.edu/~aizen/index.html.

Ajzen, I. (2002b). Perceived behavioral control, self-efficacy, locus of control and the Theory of Planned Behavior. *Journal of Applied Social Psychology, 32*, 1–20.

Ajzen, I., & Fishbein, M. (1980). *Understanding Attitudes and Predicting Social Behavior.* Englewood Cliffs, NJ: Prentice-Hall.

DeVisser, R.O., & Smith, A.M.A. (2004). Which intention? Whose intention? Condom use and theories of individual decision making. *Psychology, Health & Medicine, 9*(2), 193–204.

Fishbein, M. (1967). *Readings in Attitude Theory and Measurement.* New York: Wiley.

Fishbein, M., & Ajzen, I. (1975). Belief, attitude, intention and behavior: An introduction to theory and research. Reading, MA: Addison-Wesley. Retrieved March 15, 2013, from http://people.umass.edu/aizen/f&a1975.html.

Koniak-Griffin, D., & Stein, J.A. (2006). Predictors of sexual risk behaviors among adolescent mothers in a human immunodeficiency virus prevention program. *Journal of Adolescent Health, 38*, 297e1–297e11.

Nehl, E.J., Blanchard, C.M., Peng, C.J., Rhodes, R.E., Kupperman, J., Sparling, P.B., Courneya, K., Baker, F. (2009). Understanding nonsmoking in African American and Caucasian college students: An application of the Theory of Planned Behavior. *Behavioral Medicine, 35,* 23–28.

Rah, J.H., Hasler, C.M., Painter, J.E., & Chapman-Novakofski, K.M. (2004). Applying the Theory of Planned Behavior to women's behavioral attitudes on and consumption of soy products. *Journal of Nutrition Education and Behavior, 36*(5), 238–244.

Stockdale, M.S., Dawson-Owens, H.I., & Sagrestano, L.M. (2005). Social, attitudinal, and demographic correlates of adolescents vs college age tobacco initiation. *American Journal of Health Behavior, 29,* 311–323.

Swanson, V., & Power, K.G. (2004). Initiation and continuation of breastfeeding: Theory of Planned Behavior. *Journal of Advanced Nursing, 50*(3), 272–282.

Wang, M.Q. (2001). Social, environmental influences on adolescents smoking progression. *American Journal of Health Behavior, 25*, 418–425.

# Health Belief Model

## STUDENT LEARNING OUTCOMES

After reading this chapter the student will be able to:

- Explain the original concept of the Health Belief Model (HBM).
- Discuss how the constructs of perceived seriousness, susceptibility, benefits, and barriers might predict health behavior.
- Analyze the impact of the modifying variables on health behavior.
- Identify cues to action and how they motivate behavior.
- Use the model to explain at least one behavior.

## THEORY ESSENCE SENTENCE

Personal beliefs influence health behavior.

---

**Health Belief Model Constructs Chart**

**Perceived susceptibility:**
An individual's assessment of his or her chances of getting the disease

**Perceived benefits:**
An individual's conclusion as to whether the new behavior is better than what he or she is already doing

**Perceived barriers:**
An individual's opinion as to what will stop him or her from adopting the new behavior

**Perceived seriousness:**
An individual's judgment as to the severity of the disease

**Modifying variables:**
An individual's personal factors that affect whether the new behavior is adopted

**Cues to action:**
Those factors that will start a person on the way to changing behavior

**Self-efficacy:**
Personal belief in one's own ability to do something

---

# IN THE BEGINNING

The Health Belief Model was developed by researchers at the U.S. Public Health Service in the late 1950s. At the time, a great emphasis was being placed on screening programs for disease prevention and early detection. Although public health practitioners were in favor of screenings, the public was not very receptive to being tested for diseases of which they didn't have symptoms. This was particularly true for tuberculosis (TB) (Hochbaum, 1958; Rosenstock, 1960).

Although TB screening programs were attracting some people, they were not attracting the large numbers who were known to be at risk for the disease. Consequently, there was a need to understand why some people went for the screening, but why so many others did not (Hochbaum, 1958; Rosenstock, 1960). To find out, researchers at the U.S. Public Health Service conducted a study to identify the combination of psychological, social, and physical factors (observations) that determined whether a person wanted to be screened for TB, when, and at what type of facility (Hochbaum, 1958).

Because the researchers were all social psychologists, their approach was based on the idea that behavior is the result of how people perceive their environment. That is, individual beliefs or perceptions are what determine behavior. Using this as the foundation, it was reasoned that in order for people to take action to prevent a disease they didn't have, or to be screened/tested for a disease they didn't have symptoms of, certain beliefs or perceptions about the disease needed to exist.

The outcome of the study identified three sets of factors that determined participation in a voluntary screening program: psychological readiness, situational influences, and environmental conditions (Rosenstock, 1958). Factors identified as being indicative of people's psychological readiness to be screened for TB included the belief that they had TB, were at risk of getting TB, or that they would benefit from being tested for TB. Situational influences included having bodily changes thought to be symptoms of TB and other people's opinions of whether they should or shouldn't be screened. And lastly, if the environmental conditions were provided an opportunity to be screened and if it was convenient (Rosenstock, 1958). The conclusions drawn from this study formed the basis of the Health Belief Model.

# THEORETICAL CONCEPT

The Health Belief Model (HBM) is by far the most commonly used theory in health education and health promotion (Glanz, Rimer, & Viswanath, 2008; National Cancer Institute [NCI], 2005). The underlying concept of the HBM is that health behavior is determined by personal beliefs or perceptions about a disease and the strategies available to decrease its occurrence (Hochbaum, 1958). Personal perception is influenced by the whole range of intrapersonal factors affecting health behavior, including, but not limited to: knowledge, attitudes, beliefs, experiences, skills, culture, and religion.

# THEORETICAL CONSTRUCTS

The following four perceptions serve as the main constructs of the model: perceived seriousness, perceived susceptibility, perceived benefits, and perceived barriers. Each of these perceptions, individually or in combination, can be used to explain health behavior. More recently, other constructs have been added to the HBM; thus, the model has been expanded to include cues to action, motivating factors, and self-efficacy.

## PERCEIVED SERIOUSNESS

The construct of perceived seriousness speaks to an individual's belief about the seriousness or severity of a disease. While the perception of seriousness is often based on medical information or knowledge, it may also come from beliefs a person has about the consequences an illness might have on him or her personally. For example, most of us perceive seasonal flu as a relatively minor ailment. We get it, stay home a few days, and get better. However, if you have asthma, contracting the flu could land you in the hospital. In this case, your perception of the flu might be that it is a serious disease. Or, if you are self-employed, having the flu might mean a week or more of lost wages. Again, this would influence your perception of the seriousness of this illness.

Perception of seriousness can also be colored by past experience with the illness. No doubt, most people would consider skin cancer a serious disease. However, the perception of serious might be diminished in someone who had a cancerous lesion removed and recovered without much more than a sore area and a Band-Aid for a few days.

## PERCEIVED SUSCEPTIBILITY

Personal risk or susceptibility is one of the more powerful perceptions in prompting people to adopt healthier behaviors. The greater the perceived risk, the greater the likelihood of engaging in behaviors to decrease the risk. This is what prompts men who have sex with men to be vaccinated against hepatitis B (de Wit, Vet, Schutten, & van Steenbergen, 2005) and to use condoms in an effort to decrease susceptibility to HIV infection (Belcher, Sternberg, Wolotski, Halkitis, & Hoff, 2005). Perceived susceptibility motivates people to be vaccinated for influenza (Chen, Fox, Cantrell, Stockdale, & Kagawa-Singer, 2007) to use sunscreen to prevent skin cancer, and to floss their teeth to prevent gum disease and tooth loss (**Figure 4–1**).

It is only logical that when people believe they are at risk for a disease, they will be more likely to do something to prevent it from happening. Unfortunately, the opposite also occurs. When people believe they are not at risk or have a low risk of susceptibility, unhealthy behaviors tend to result. This is exactly what has been found with older adults and HIV prevention behavior. Because older adults generally do not perceive themselves to be at risk for HIV infection, many do not practice safer sex (Rose, 1995; Maes & Louis, 2003). This same scenario was found with Asian American college students earlier in the HIV/AIDS epidemic. They tended to view epidemic as a non-Asian problem; thus, their perception of susceptibility to HIV infection was low and not associated with practicing safer sex behaviors (Yep, 1993).

Unfortunately, this lack of perceived susceptibility to sexually transmitted infections (STIs) is still alive and well on campuses, albeit not necessarily because of ethnicity as seen in the previous example. Rather, students under estimate *their* risk of contracting infections from their partners, because they underestimate their partners susceptibility. (They ignore the old adage that you are sleeping with everyone your partner has ever slept with.) Consequently, they do not protect themselves against STIs, especially when sexual activity is restricted to oral sex. This is particularly evident if they attend schools in a geographic area that has a low incidence of HIV/AIDS (Downing-Matibag & Geisinger, 2009).

**FIGURE 4–1**  Risk avoidance is a powerful motivator for change

What we have seen so far is that a perception of increased susceptibility or risk is linked to healthier behaviors, and perception of decreased susceptibility to unhealthy behaviors. However, this is not always the case. In college students, perception of susceptibility is rarely linked to the adoption of healthier behaviors (Courtenay, 1998), even when the perception of risk is high. For example, even if college students consider themselves at risk for HIV because of their unsafe sex behaviors, they still do not practice safer sex (Lewis & Malow, 1997), nor do they stop tanning even though they perceive themselves to be at increased risk for skin cancer (Lamanna, 2004). Perception of susceptibility explains behavior in some situations, but not all.

When the perception of susceptibility is combined with seriousness, it results in perceived threat (Stretcher & Rosenstock, 1997). If the perception of threat is to a serious disease for which there is a real risk, behavior is likely to change. This is what happened in Germany in 2001 after an outbreak of bovine spongiform encephalitis (BSE), better known as mad cow disease. Although mad cow disease does not occur in people, research suggests that eating cattle with the disease can result in variant Creutzfeldt-Jakob disease (CJD). Variant CJD, like BSE, affects the brain, causing tiny holes that make it appear spongelike. Both diseases are untreatable and fatal

(National Institute of Neurological Disorders and Stroke, 2007). The perception of threat of contracting this disease through eating beef was one factor related to declining meat consumption in Germany (Weitkunat et al., 2003). People changed their behavior based on the perception of threat of a fatal disease.

Another example in which perception of threat is linked to behavior change is found in colon cancer survivors. Colorectal cancer is a very serious disease with a high risk of recurrence. It is the perception of the threat of recurrence that increases the likelihood of behavior change in people previously treated for this disease. In particular, changes occur in their diets, exercise, and weight (Mullens, McCaul, Erickson, & Sandgren, 2003).

We see the same thing when people perceive a threat of developing non-insulin-dependent diabetes mellitus (NIDDM). Among people whose parents had or have the disease, the perception of threat of developing it themselves is predictive of more health-enhancing, risk-reducing behaviors. Most important, they are more likely than others to engage in behaviors to control their weight (Forsyth, 1997), given that obesity is a known risk factor for NIDDM.

Just as perception of increased susceptibility does not always lead to behavior change, as we saw earlier in the chapter with college students, neither does a perception of increased threat. This is the scenario with older adults and safe food-handling behaviors. Older adults are among the groups most vulnerable to foodborne illness (Gerba, Row, & Haas, 1996) and are among those for whom it can be particularly serious. Even though they perceive a threat of illness from foodborne sources, they still do not use safe food-handling practices (Hanson & Benedict, 2002) all of the time.

## PERCEIVED BENEFITS

The construct of perceived benefits is a person's opinion of the value or usefulness of a new behavior in decreasing the risk of developing a disease. People tend to adopt healthier behaviors when they believe the new behavior will decrease their chances of developing a disease. Would people strive to exercise if they didn't believe it was beneficial? Would people quit smoking if they didn't believe it was better for their health? Would people use sunscreen if they didn't believe it worked? Probably not.

A prime example of this is seen among parents who either do not have their children vaccinated for vaccine preventable diseases (VPD), or delay having them vaccinated. Children whose parents do not see a benefit in vaccination—that is, are more likely to agree vaccines may have serious side effects and that too many vaccines overwhelm the immune system, tend to not to have their children vaccinated. Conversely, parents who see a benefit to vaccination—that is, agree vaccines are effective in preventing diseases and are safe and necessary to protect the health of the child, are more likely to have their children vaccinated. (Smith, et al., 2011).

Perceived benefits play an important role in the adoption of secondary prevention behaviors, as well. A good example of this is screening for colon cancer. One of the screening tests for colon cancer is a colonoscopy. It requires a few days of preparation prior to the procedure to completely cleanse the colon: a diet restricted to clear liquids followed by cathartics. The procedure involves the insertion of a very long, flexible tube instrument with a camera on the end into the rectum to view the length of the colon. The procedure itself is done under anesthesia, so it is not uncomfortable, but it does take time afterward to recover, and the preparation is time consuming. Regardless of the inconvenience, this is presently the best method for early detection of colon cancer, the third leading cause of cancer deaths in the United States. When colon cancer is found early, it has a 90% cure rate. However, only 36% of people over age 50 (who are most at risk) have this screening done (New York-Presbyterian Hospital, 2006). What makes some people undergo screening and others not? Among women, those who perceive a benefit from colonoscopy (early detection) are more likely to undergo screening than those who do not see the screening as having a benefit (Frank & Swedmark, 2004).

## PERCEIVED BARRIERS

Since change is not something that comes easily to most people, the last construct of the HBM addresses the issue of perceived barriers to change. This is an individual's own evaluation of the obstacles in the way of him or her adopting a new behavior. Of all the constructs, perceived barriers are the most significant in determining behavior change (Janz & Becker, 1984).

In order for a new behavior to be adopted, a person needs to believe the benefits of the new behavior outweigh the consequences of continuing the old behavior (Centers for Disease Control and Prevention, 2004). This enables barriers to be overcome and the new behavior to be adopted (**Figure 4–2**).

Even though there is much education on college campuses about HIV/AIDS risk reduction, and even though students demonstrate they are knowledgeable about HIV/AIDS, condom use among African American college students remains inconsistent (Winfield & Whaley, 2002) leaving them exposed to a greater risk of infection. There is obviously something else at play here. Using the HBM to explain what that something else might be reveals that perceived barriers may be a contributing factor. Barriers such as perceived difficulty in doing the things that need to be done to protect oneself, for example. Further, research has suggested that African American men use condoms more frequently when they perceive there are fewer barriers

**FIGURE 4-2**  Barriers can be overcome

to their use. This is important to recognize as HIV/AIDS prevention often focuses on empowering women to negotiate safer sex rather than addressing it as a shared responsibility (Winfield & Whaley, 2002) and addressing the perceived barriers of both men and women.

## MODIFYING VARIABLES

The four major constructs of perception are modified by other variables, such as culture, education level, past experiences, skill, and motivation, to name a few. These are individual characteristics that influence personal perceptions. For example, if someone is diagnosed with basal cell skin cancer and successfully treated, he or she may have a heightened perception of susceptibility because of this past experience and be more conscious of sun exposure because of past experience. Conversely, this past experience could diminish the person's perception of seriousness because the cancer was easily treated and cured.

In personal health classes on many campuses, students are required to complete a behavior change project. They choose an unhealthy behavior and develop a plan to change it and adopt a more healthy behavior. The modifying variable behind this is motivation. The motivation is a grade.

**FIGURE 4-3** Cue to action—don't drink and drive

## CUES TO ACTION

In addition to the four beliefs or perceptions and modifying variables, the HBM suggests that behavior is also influenced by cues to action. Cues to action are events, people, or things that move people to change their behavior. Examples include illness of a family member, media reports (Graham, 2002), mass media campaigns, advice from others, reminder postcards from a health care provider (Ali, 2002), or health warning labels on a product (**Figure 4-3**).

Knowing a fellow church member with prostate cancer is a significant cue to action for African American men to attend prostate cancer education programs (Weinrich et al., 1998). Hearing TV or radio news stories about foodborne illness and reading the safe handling instructions on packages of raw meat and poultry are cues to action associated with safer food-handling behaviors (Hanson & Benedict, 2002). Having displays on college campuses of cars involved in fatal crashes from drunk driving is an example of a cue to action—don't drink and drive.

## SELF-EFFICACY

In 1988, self-efficacy was added to the original four beliefs of the HBM (Rosenstock, Strecher, & Becker, 1988). Self-efficacy is the belief in one's own ability to do something (Bandura, 1977). People generally do not try to do something new unless they think they can do it. If someone believes a new behavior is useful (perceived benefit), but does not think he or she is capable of doing it (perceived barrier), chances are that it will not be tried.

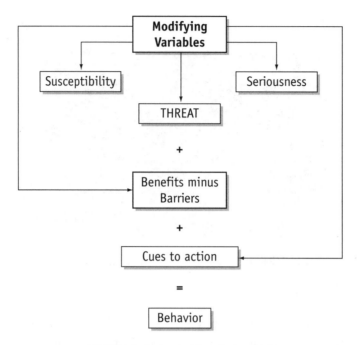

**FIGURE 4–4**  Health Belief Model

Adapted from Stretcher, V. & Rosenstock, I.M. (1997). The Health Belief Model. In Glanz, K., Lewis, F.M., & Rimer, B.K. (Eds). *Health Behavior and Health Education Theory, Research and Practice*. San Francisco: Jossey-Bass.

When we look at osteoporosis, exercise self-efficacy and exercise barriers are the strongest predictors of whether one practices behaviors known to prevent this disease. Women who do not engage in the recommended levels of weight-bearing exercise tend to have low exercise self-efficacy, meaning they do not believe they can exercise, and perceive there to be significant barriers to exercise (Wallace, 2002). As a result, these women do not exercise.

In summary, according to the Health Belief Model, modifying variables, cues to action, and self-efficacy affect our perception of susceptibility, seriousness, benefits, and barriers and, therefore, our behavior (**Figure 4–4**).

# THEORY IN ACTION—CLASS ACTIVITY

Use the constructs of the HBM to explain your own daily physical activity. Then, think about how those same constructs might help you to increase your physical activity. Share this insight with others in your class. Now, read the following article and answer the questions at the end.

# Chapter 4 Article: A Community-wide Media Campaign to Promote Walking in a Missouri Town[1]

*Wray, Ricardo J; Jupka, Keri; Ludwig-Bell, Cathy*

## Introduction

Engaging in moderate physical activity for 30 minutes five or more times per week substantially reduces the risk of coronary heart disease, stroke, colon cancer, diabetes, high blood pressure, and obesity, and walking is an easy and accessible way to achieve this goal. A theory-based mass media campaign promoted walking and local community-sponsored wellness initiatives through four types of media (billboard, newspaper, radio, and poster advertisements) in St Joseph, Mo, over 5 months during the summer of 2003.

## Methods

The *Walk Missouri* campaign was conducted in four phases: 1) formative research, 2) program design and pretesting, 3) implementation, and 4) impact assessment. Using a postcampaign-only, cross-sectional design, a telephone survey (N = 297) was conducted in St Joseph to assess campaign impact. Study outcomes were pro-walking beliefs and behaviors.

## Results

One in three survey respondents reported seeing or hearing campaign messages on one or more types of media. Reported exposure to the campaign was significantly associated with two of four pro-walking belief scales (social and pleasure benefits) and with one of three community-sponsored activities (participation in a community-sponsored walk) controlling for demographic, health status, and environmental factors. Exposure was also significantly associated with one

---

[1] Reproduced from Wray, R.J., Jupka, K., Ludwig-Bell, C. (2005). A community-wide media campaign to promote walking in a Missouri town. *Preventing Chronic Disease, 2*(4). Available from: http://www.cdc.gov/pcd/issues/2005/oct/05_0010.htm.

of three general walking behaviors (number of days per week walking) when controlling for age and health status but not when beliefs were introduced into the model, consistent with an a priori theoretical mechanism: the mediating effect of pro-walking beliefs on the exposure–walking association.

## Conclusion

These results suggest that a media campaign can enhance the success of community-based efforts to promote pro-walking beliefs and behaviors.

# INTRODUCTION

Sedentary lifestyles contribute to chronic diseases, such as cardiovascular disease, cancer, and diabetes, and to risk factors including obesity (1). In 2003, the majority of U.S. adults (52.8%) were not physically active at levels that promote health (2). In Missouri, 54.9% of the adult population in 2003 failed to get enough physical activity to provide any health benefits (2). *Healthy People 2010* includes several goals that seek to increase physical activity levels in the United States (3).

Walking is an easy and accessible way to achieve the recommended amount of daily activity (4,5). Thirty minutes of brisk walking five or more times per week substantially reduces the risk of developing or dying of coronary heart disease, stroke, colon cancer, diabetes, high blood pressure, and obesity (6).

Known determinants of physical activity participation fall into multiple categories, including demographics (7), psychosocial factors (8–10), social support (7), and neighborhood and other environmental factors (11–13). Media-based interventions have been implemented to promote physical activity in recent years, but three recent reviews of media-based programs have disagreed on their potential to change behavior (14–16). Our review of studies on eight media campaigns in five countries offers moderate evidence of impact on behavior change. The data suggest success in reaching audiences, with exposure rates (percentage of a population that reports seeing or hearing campaign messages) ranging from 38% to 90% (17–22) and campaign-message recall rates (the percentage of the population that is able to recall a specific campaign message) ranging from 23% (19) to 30% (17). These studies also report shifts in cognition related to moderate physical activity. For example, in a study in Australia, 62% of individuals exposed to media campaigns reported awareness of the benefits of moderate physical exercise (compared with 29% of control populations) (21). In a national study in

NewZealand, the percentage of adults intending to be more active increased from 2% in 1999 to 9% in 2002, following a media campaign (22).

The data on behavior change, however, are mixed. Campaigns in the United Kingdom (18) and Scotland (23) resulted in no increase or a negligible increase in physical activity despite moderate levels of exposure to media campaigns. In Brazil, a citywide campaign achieved a campaign-message recall rate of 56% and was associated with a reduction in sedentary lifestyles (19). Two national campaigns in Australia in 1990 and 1991 were shown to increase intention to engage in physical activity and physical activity behavior in older adults in the first year, but physical activity levels reached a plateau in the second year (24). A national campaign in New Zealand was associated with a 5% increase in the proportion of walkers in a national survey, but the gain declined to baseline in the second year (22). A campaign in New South Wales, Australia, was shown to increase knowledge about the benefits of physical activity and lead to increases in self-efficacy for physical activity; residents were twice as likely to engage in physical activity as residents in other states (20). A 6% national decline in physical activity improved in New South Wales to 4.4% during the period of the campaign (21). Finally, in Wheeling, WVa, a campaign reaching 90% of the population affected stages of change as well as perceived behavioral control and intention. In this quasi-experimental study, the proportion of walkers in the intervention community increased after the campaign more than it increased in a comparison community where no campaign was implemented (25).

Some consensus for an integrated approach to increase physical activity—including environmental and policy changes, community-based programs, and media campaigns—has emerged (14–16, 26). For example, in its recent evaluation of interventions promoting physical activity, the Centers for Disease Control and Prevention's (CDC's) *Guide to Community Preventive Services (Community Guide)* strongly recommends community-wide initiatives that include informational components, but it finds insufficient evidence to recommend media-only approaches (16). It is not clear which, if any, informational elements should be included in an integrated campaign to promote physical activity. This gap in knowledge has led to research designed to address two important questions. Can mass media-based interventions support community-based activities? If so, how do media campaigns contribute to community-based interventions designed to promote physical activity? To answer these questions, we describe the design, development, implementation, and impact assessment of *Walk Missouri,* a mass media campaign designed to promote walking in a Missouri town.

# METHODS

## CAMPAIGN DESIGN AND DEVELOPMENT

The *Walk Missouri* campaign was conducted in four phases: 1) formative research, 2) program design and pretesting, 3) implementation, and 4) impact assessment. Elements of the health belief model (HBM) (27) provided a framework for the effort from formative research through assessment. Perceived susceptibility and perceived severity, two elements of the HBM, were not included in this study because their predictive ability has been questioned in other research (28,29); perceived barriers and perceived benefits were included in the framework because they have been shown to be strongly correlated with physical activity behavior (7).

## PHASE 1: FORMATIVE RESEARCH

We conducted 24 focus groups in 2001 in both midsize and large metropolitan areas across Missouri. The demographic characteristics of the focus group members participating in the formative research are shown in **Table 1**. Focus group questions were designed to identify perceived benefits of and barriers to

**Table 1** Demographic Characteristics of Focus Group Participants, *Walk Missouri* Campaign, 2001–2002

| Characteristics | Formative Research Focus Groups (N = 24) | Pretest Focus Groups (N = 16) |
|---|---|---|
| No. participants | 174 | 118 |
| Female, % | Not collected | 80 |
| Age, median, y (range) | 44 (18–83) | 46 (18–83) |
| Education, mean, y (range) | 14.3 (8–16+) | 14.5 (9–16+) |
| Household income, mean, $ | 30,000–39,999 | 30,000–39,999 |
| **Race and ethnicity, %** | | |
| White | 83 | 83 |
| African American | 15 | 14 |
| Native American | 1 | 1 |
| Hispanic | 1 | 1 |
| Other | 0 | 1 |

walking as well as possible cues to action. Focus group findings indicated that participants responded more readily to messages emphasizing ways to overcome barriers and the short-term benefits of walking rather than long-term health benefits. These findings informed messages that emphasized the short-term positive outcomes of walking and identified strategies to overcome obstacles.

## PHASE 2: MESSAGE DEVELOPMENT AND PRETESTING

Behavioral messages for the media campaign were developed as cues to action, reminding Missourians of the short-term health benefits of walking (e.g., losing weight), the social benefits (e.g., spending time with loved ones), and the pleasure benefits (e.g., having fun). Messages also communicated ways to overcome barriers (e.g., providing ideas on how to incorporate walking into a busy schedule). Messages included phrases and themes drawn from the formative research focus groups. Messages used a question-and-answer format, with a message answering one of four questions: when, where, why, or with whom do you walk? Answers were emphasized more than questions (i.e., were spoken first in radio advertisements or were set in larger typeface on billboards and posters and in newspaper advertisements). Messages also used the phrase "do it" to pique curiosity.

Print, radio, and television messages were developed and tested with 16 focus groups representing a range of audience segments across Missouri. **Table 1** shows the characteristics of this second group of participants. The campaign strategy was received positively by the focus groups, and message materials were selected for the campaign.

## PHASE 3: IMPLEMENTATION

The multimedia campaign took place during a 5-month period from May through September 2003. The media plan consisted of billboard, newspaper, radio, and poster advertisements. (Television spots were not used because of the expense of buying airtime.) The strategy for media placement was to achieve the greatest visibility at the outset, in May and June, followed by reduced numbers of advertisements from July through September. In a press conference to kick off the campaign, local political leaders and coalition partners announced the *Walk Missouri* campaign to local radio, television, and newspaper outlets. **Table 2** shows the amount and cost of media space and time purchased.

**Table 2** Media Purchases for *Walk Missouri* Campaign, St Joseph, Mo, 2003

| Type | Amount Spent, $ | No. Advertisements |
|------|-----------------|--------------------|
| Billboards | 2760 | 8 |
| Newspapers | 5862 | 16 |
| Radio | 9876 | 1296 |
| Posters | 800 | 200 |
| **Total** | **19,298** | **1520** |

**Table 3** Messages Promoted in *Walk Missouri* Campaign, St Joseph, Mo, 2003

| Type | Messages Used |
|------|---------------|
| Billboards | · I like to do it with my best friend. *Who do you walk with?* |
| | · Sunday afternoons are a family affair. *When do you walk?* |
| | · We like to do it in nature's backyard. *Where do you walk?* |
| | · We do it because it's better than television. *Why do you walk?* |
| | · It's like recess for grown-ups. *Why do you walk?* |
| Radio | · We do it as a church group. I do it with my coworkers on my lunch hour. We do it together. I do it with friends at the gym. *Who do you walk with?* |
| | · I do it first thing in the morning to start the day off right. I do it on my lunch hour; it feels great. I do it on my way to work and on my way home. I do it after dinner to help me wind down. *When do you walk?* |
| | · I do it around my neighborhood every morning. I do it at the mall. I do it at the gym. I do it at the park. I do it around the softball field while my daughter practices. *Where do you walk?* |
| | · We do it because a family who plays together, stays together. I do it because it's easy to fit into my busy schedule. I do it to feel better and have more energy. I do it to lose weight. I do it because it's fun. *Why do you walk?* |
| Newspaper | · My co-worker and I keep each other on track. *Who do you walk with?* |
| | · Sunday afternoons are a family affair. *When do you walk?* |
| | · We like to do it in nature's backyard. *Where do you walk?* |
| | · I do it to set a good example. *Why do you walk?* |
| Posters | · It's great for catching up with my buddy. *Who do you walk with?* |
| | · We like to do it on cool, cloudy days. *When do you walk?* |
| | · We like to do it in nature. *Where do you walk?* |
| | · I do it for my health. *Why do you walk?* |

**Table 3** presents a complete list of messages included in all types of media in the St Joseph, Mo, campaign.

The campaign was designed to reach adult residents of St Joseph, Mo. A midsize town with a population of 84,909 in 2003 (30), St Joseph is located about 45 miles north of Kansas City, Mo. The community was chosen because of its cooperation during the first two stages of the study and its commitment to physical activity initiatives. St Joseph had already developed local initiatives to increase physical activity, including an extensive network of walking trails and an active worksite wellness coalition *(Get Movin' St. Joe)* led by the Buchanan County Health Department, the YMCA, and Heartland Health, the owner of a local hospital. The *Get Movin' St. Joe* coalition was active in the community, working with worksites, schools, and athletic organizations for at least 1 year before the *Walk Missouri* campaign. Although the worksite wellness coalition advertised its events through its affiliated groups, it had not engaged in mass media advertising. Consistent with the *Community Guide* recommendation for community-wide campaigns (16), the *Walk Missouri* campaign tapped into these local initiatives, augmenting available resources and increasing campaign reach.

The *Get Movin' St. Joe* coalition organizers participated in implementing the *Walk Missouri* campaign. Local walking resources and activities organized by *Get Movin' St. Joe* were incorporated into *Walk Missouri* newspaper and radio advertisements. For example, the *Get Movin' St. Joe* logo was incorporated into the *Walk Missouri* campaign advertisements. Local collaborators increased visibility of the *Walk Missouri* campaign by distributing and displaying *Walk Missouri* campaign posters in community centers, businesses associated with the worksite wellness program, and other locations across the town. In this way, the *Walk Missouri* media effort helped to advertise community-sponsored walking activities and resources while capitalizing on local efforts to expand *Walk Missouri* campaign reach.

## PHASE 4: IMPACT ASSESSMENT

The objectives of the *Walk Missouri* campaign were as follows:

- To increase knowledge and positive beliefs about the social and short-term health benefits as well as pleasures of walking;
- To increase knowledge and positive beliefs about ways to overcome barriers to walking;
- To increase participation in community walking and wellness activities; and
- To increase amount and frequency of walking.

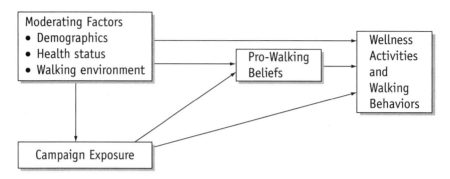

A community-wide campaign to promote walking in a Missouri town

*Source:* Reproduced from Wray, R.J., Jupka, K., Ludwig-Bell, C. (2005). A community-wide media campaign to promote walking in a Missouri town. *Preventing Chronic Disease, 2*(4). Available from: http://www.cdc.gov/pcd/issues/2005/oct/05_0010.htm.

The figure shows the conceptual framework of the evaluation, including the hypothesis that exposure to the *Walk Missouri* campaign could achieve a direct effect on walking behaviors, indicated by the arrow linking exposure to behaviors. Alternately, there might be an indirect effect of exposure on behaviors, mediated by pro-walking beliefs, indicated by the arrows linking exposure with beliefs and beliefs with behaviors. In testing for either of these effects, we controlled for likely moderating factors.

# EVALUATION METHODS

## SURVEY DESIGN AND SAMPLE

The Saint Louis University Institutional Review Board approved this study. A postcampaign-only design was used: phone numbers for residents living within the city of St Joseph were purchased from a market research firm, and a random-digit–dial telephone survey was conducted. Individuals were eligible to participate if they identified themselves as adult (aged 18 years or older) residents of St Joseph. Trained callers conducted the interviews between July 31 and October 31, 2003. The survey required an average of 15 minutes to complete. Individual numbers were dialed numerous times before being eliminated from the survey. A total of 297 interviews were completed with the funds available for evaluation.

## MEASURES

*Exposure.* As in the evaluation of other media campaigns (31), various campaign exposure measures were used to evaluate the *Walk Missouri* campaign, including campaign-exposure questions, media-type–exposure questions, and dose-exposure questions. Both prompted and unprompted questions were asked. (The Appendix provides all survey items used in the analysis.) To discern media-type dose exposure, individuals were first asked if they had been exposed to any campaign advertisements through billboards, radio, or newspapers or if they had seen any campaign posters or news stories about the campaign. (News stories were initiated by local newspapers in response to the press conference and the campaign.) Individuals who answered in the affirmative for a media type were then asked how many times they had been exposed to that type. For example, respondents who answered *yes* for billboards were asked in how many locations they had noticed billboards sponsored by the campaign (with answers ranging from one to six billboards). Respondents who answered *yes* for radio were asked how many times they had heard radio advertisements sponsored by the campaign (with survey items offering ranges of 1 to 5, 6 to 10, 11 to 20, 21 to 50, 51 to 100, or more than 100 times).

Two variables were developed for analysis of exposure: a four-level dose-exposure scale and a dichotomous variable (exposed and unexposed). The four-level dose-exposure scale summed the five media-type dose-exposure items in the survey. A higher value on this scale signifies either more types of media through which the campaign was seen or heard or a greater number of messages seen or heard through fewer types of media. Because the scale was highly skewed toward no exposure, the scale was recoded as a four-category variable (none, low, medium, and high exposure) to make coefficients more stable. A value of 1 (low) signifies that the respondent reported seeing one billboard, newspaper advertisement, or newspaper story; heard only five or fewer radio advertisements; or saw only five or fewer posters. A value of 2 (medium) signifies that the respondent reported exposure to the campaign through two or three types of media or exposure to more advertisements through one or two types of media. A value of 3 (high) signifies that the respondent reported exposure on four or more types of media or exposure to more advertisements on fewer types of media. Because of varying ranges within survey items and different kinds of exposure to messages on different types of media, it was not practicable to convert the scale into levels of frequency of exposure. The four-level scale was used to assess associations of amount of exposure with study outcomes; it was also recoded into a new dichotomous variable (exposed and unexposed) to test for group differences.

*Beliefs.* The survey asked participants 12 questions about their opinions of exercise using a 5-point Likert scale. Four subscales were computed from nine survey items to measure theoretical belief constructs. Despite a small number of items in each subscale (only two or three), the Cronbach $\alpha$ calculated for each subscale was near or higher than minimum desired level of $\alpha = .70$ for social benefits ($\alpha = .66$), pleasure benefits ($\alpha = .58$), health benefits ($\alpha = .73$), and social support ($\alpha = .60$). (A fifth subscale for overcoming barriers was dropped from the analysis because of an unacceptably low Cronbach $\alpha$ of .46.) Subscales were computed using belief items that were recoded to three levels because the individual items and the resulting scales had normal distributions and would provide more stable results in statistical analyses. Strongly disagree, disagree, and neutral were consolidated as one value coded as 1; agree was coded as 2; and strongly agree was coded as 3. To make them comparable, each subscale was computed to three value scales by dividing the summed scale by the original number of items. To test for a mediating effect of beliefs on the association between exposure and behaviors, a single all-beliefs scale was computed from all 12 belief items in the survey (Cronbach $\alpha = .75$).

*Behavior measures.* The survey asked six walking-behavior questions. Three dichotomous (yes or no) measures inquired about walking and wellness activities sponsored by *Get Movin' St. Joe*. One dichotomous (yes or no) and two continuous measures of walking behavior were adapted from physical activity measures in the 2000 Behavioral Risk Factor Surveillance System (BRFSS).

*Moderators.* Various measures were included to control for possible alternative explanations for evaluation results. Demographic measures included sex, age, race, and level of education. Health-related measures included health status, medical diagnosis of chronic disease or overweight, medical advice to walk more, and recent injury. Perceived safety of the participant's walking environment was assessed using six Likert items. Cronbach $\alpha$ for the scale was .63.

*Analysis.* Our conceptual framework (Figure) offers the hypothesis that exposed individuals are more likely to hold beliefs consistent with campaign themes and more likely to engage in walking activities than individuals not exposed to the campaign and controlling for likely alternative explanations. In the multivariate analyses, we controlled for moderators that were significantly associated with outcomes. In addition, we hypothesized that beliefs had a mediating effect on the association between exposure and behaviors.

Group differences for the exposed and unexposed portions of the sample were assessed using two-tailed $t$ tests for ordinal and continuous outcomes and chi-square tests for dichotomous outcomes. Associations between amount of exposure and outcomes were assessed using the Spearman rank correlation ($\rho$). For multivariate analyses, linear regression was used for ordinal and continuous outcomes, and logistic regression was used for dichotomous outcomes. When beliefs were significantly associated with behaviors, stepwise regression was used to test a mediating effect of beliefs on any associations between exposure and behaviors.

# RESULTS

## RESPONSE RATE

During data collection, 4668 phone numbers were used, 2866 of which were out of scope (e.g., businesses, out-of-service numbers, numbers failing to be answered after multiple calls). Of the remaining 1802 numbers, 1461 refused participation before we were able to determine eligibility. Of the remaining 341, five respondents were aged younger than 18 years, bringing our total number of eligible respondents to 336. The total number of completed interviews was 297, resulting in a cooperation rate of 88% (297/336). Compared with the Council of American Survey Research Organization (CASRO) response rates of 54.6% found for the BRFSS Missouri, which include estimates of eligible households among households for which eligibility was not determined, our response rate was low at 17% (32). However, our response rate proved to be better than the rate of 9.1% provided for random-digit–dial surveys tracked by the Market Research Association (33). Low response rates for random-digit–dial surveys are increasingly a problem for evaluators of health promotion interventions (34).

# SURVEY FINDINGS

## SAMPLE CHARACTERISTICS AND EXPOSURE LEVELS

The sample had more women and was older, better educated, and more diverse than the U.S. census indicates for this area (**Table 4**). Thirty-two percent of the sample reported exposure to the campaign through news and advertising media. Exposure levels by type of media ranged from 7% (newspaper

**Table 4** Demographic Characteristics of Respondents and Results of Telephone Survey to Assess *Walk Missouri* Media Campaign Impact on Community, St Joseph, Mo, 2003

| Characteristic (No. respondents) | Measure | Exposure to *Walk Missouri* Campaign | Measure |
|---|---|---|---|
| Female (295) | 62% | Exposed through media (297) | 32% |
| Age, mean, y (290) | 47±17.43 | **Posters** | |
| **Education (290)** | | Respondents exposed | 11% |
| Some or completed high school | 41% | Median no. seen | 1–5 |
| Some college or received college degree | 47% | **Newspaper ads** | |
| Some graduate school or completed graduate degree | 11% | Respondents exposed | 7% |
| Not sure | 1% | Median no. seen | 2 |
| **Race and ethnicity (296)** | | **Newspaper stories** | |
| African American | 4% | Respondents exposed | 13% |
| White | 84% | Median no. seen | 2 |
| Hispanic | 3% | Radio ads | |
| Native American | 3% | Respondents exposed | 8% |
| Asian or other | 6% | Median no. heard | 6–10 |
| **Levels of exposure to media in general** | | **Billboards** | |
| No. hours per week listening to radio, median (296) | 2 | Respondents exposed | 13% |
| No. days per week reading newspaper, median (296) | 7 | Median no. seen | 1 |
| **Frequency of observing types of media[a]** | | **Dose-exposure scale (297)[b]** | |
| Posters (296), median | Sometimes | 0 (none) | 68% |
| Newspaper ads (293), median | Often | 1 (low) | 11% |
| Billboards (296), median | Sometimes | 2 (medium) | 10% |
| | | 3 (high) | 11% |

[a]1–4 scale where 1 = never, 2 = rarely, 3 = sometimes, 4 = often.

[b]Dose-exposure scale is the recoded sum of the items measuring number of advertisements to which respondents reported exposure; a higher value signifies either a greater number of types of media through which the campaign was seen or heard or a greater number of messages seen or heard through fewer types of media.

advertisements) to 13% (newspaper articles and billboards). Among respondents reporting exposure to the campaign through different types of media, the median number of advertisements reported for each type of media was one to five posters, two newspaper advertisements, two newspaper stories, one billboard, and six to 10 radio advertisements. The exposed respondents (32%) were distributed evenly to low (11%), medium (10%), and high (11%) levels within the dose-exposure scale. A separate analysis found no demographic differences between exposed and unexposed groups, nor was any association found between dose exposure and demographic characteristics.

## BELIEFS

On a scale of 1 to 3, with 2 indicating agree, survey participants rated all beliefs as approximately 2 (**Table 5**). The mean for the all-beliefs scale was 4, also equivalent to agree, on the 5-point scale. The exposed group reported greater agreement with two of the four belief subscales (social benefits and pleasure benefits) than the unexposed group at a statistically significant level. Amount of exposure was associated with three of four subscales (social, pleasure, and health benefits) and the all-beliefs scale at a statistically significant level.

## BEHAVIORS

The exposed group reported a greater level of participation in three of six wellness or walking behaviors than the unexposed group at a statistically significant level. Amount of exposure was associated with the same three behaviors at a statistically significant level. Two of the outcomes were wellness behaviors: participation in a community-sponsored walk or participation in a health fair. The third outcome was a general walking behavior: the number of days per week the respondent walked at least 10 minutes.

### ASSOCIATION OF EXPOSURES, BELIEFS, AND BEHAVIORS

Beliefs and behaviors associated with campaign exposure at the bivariate level were selected for multivariate analysis, controlling for variables associated with the dependent variable in bivariate analyses. Campaign-dose exposure remained associated with two of the four belief subscales (social benefits and pleasure benefits) when controlling for likely confounding factors (**Table 6**). The association of campaign-dose exposure with the health benefits subscale

**Table 5** Telephone Survey Results by Level of Exposure to *Walk Missouri* Media Campaign, St Joseph, Mo, 2003

| | Grand Mean Score (SD) | Unexposed Respondents (Mean Score) | Exposed Respondents (Mean Score) | Test of Difference[a] (P value) | Low Exposure (Mean Score) | Medium Exposure (Mean Score) | High Exposure (Mean Score) | Test of Association (P value) |
|---|---|---|---|---|---|---|---|---|
| **Belief subscale[b] (no. respondents)** | | | | | | | | |
| Social benefits (293) | 1.95(0.55) | 1.90 | 2.05 | $t_{291} = -2.24$ (.03) | 1.83 | 2.16 | 2.18 | $\rho = 0.15$ (.01) |
| Pleasure benefits (295) | 2.25(0.46) | 2.20 | 2.36 | $t_{293} = -2.84$ (.005) | 2.31 | 2.28 | 2.48 | $\rho = 0.18$ (.002) |
| Health benefits (290) | 2.22(0.51) | 2.18 | 2.30 | $t_{288} = -1.81$ (.07) | 2.28 | 2.25 | 2.35 | $\rho = 0.12$ (.04) |
| Social support (290) | 1.67(0.58) | 1.64 | 1.72 | $t_{288} = -1.04$ (.30) | 1.72 | 1.71 | 1.73 | $\rho = 0.03$ (.56) |
| All beliefs (279) | 3.82(0.49) | 3.78 | 3.89 | $t_{277} = -1.76$ (.08) | 3.86 | 3.89 | 3.92 | $\rho = 0.13$ (.04) |
| **Behaviors (no. respondents)** | | | | | | | | |
| Participated in sponsored walk (*Walk Missouri* or *Get Movin' St. Joe*) (295) | 2% | 0.5% | 4.3% | $X^2_1 = 5.4$ (.02) | 3% | 3% | 6% | $\rho = 0.14$ (.01) |
| Participated in worksite wellness activities (295) | 11% | 10% | 13% | $X^2_1 = 0.6$ (.44) | 13% | 0% | 24% | $\rho = 0.06$ (.21) |

| | | | | | | | |
|---|---|---|---|---|---|---|---|
| Participated in health fair sponsored by a local health care provider (295) | 13% | 10% | 20% | $X^2_1 = 5.9$ (.02) | 28% | 7% | 24% | $\rho = 0.13$ (.02) |
| Walked for at least 10 min at a time during usual week (296) | 89% | 89% | 88% | $X^2_1 = 0.01$ (.94) | 84% | 90% | 90% | $\rho = 0.01$ (.93) |
| No. days per week walked at least 10 min at a time (260) | 4.73 | 4.52 | 5.2 | $t_7 = -2.34$ (.02) | 5.19 | 5.12 | 5.27 | $\rho = 0.16$ (.01) |
| On days walked at least 10 min, total minutes walked on a scale of 1-6[c] (248) | 3 | 3.54 | 3.63 | $t_5 = -0.38$ (.71) | 3.48 | 3.96 | 3.48 | $\rho = 0.02$ (.74) |

[a]All $t$ tests are unpaired, two-tailed tests.

[b]Belief subscales were computed by summing belief items that were recoded to three levels (with strongly disagree, disagree, and neutral consolidated as 1, agree as 2, and strongly agree as 3). The subscales were then computed to three value scales by dividing the summed scale by the original number of items. The all-beliefs scale was computed by summing 12 original 5-point Likert items, then dividing by 12.

[c]Survey provided six categories (Appendix) with three representing 30-39 minutes.

**Table 6** Linear Regression Analysis for Belief Subscales, *Walk Missouri* Campaign, St Joseph, Mo, 2003

| Independent Variables | Social Benefits[a] | | | Pleasure Benefits[b] | | | Health Benefits[c] | | | All Beliefs[d] | | |
|---|---|---|---|---|---|---|---|---|---|---|---|---|
| | B (95% CI)[e] | SE | P | B (95% CI) | SE | P | B (95% CI) | SE | P | B (95% CI) | SE | P |
| Age | −0.005 (−0.01 to 0.003) | .004 | .20 | Excluded[f] | | | Excluded | | | Excluded | | |
| School | Excluded | | | 0.06 (0.003 to 0.12) | .03 | .04 | 0.08 (−0.02 to 0.18) | .05 | .11 | Excluded | | |
| Sex | Excluded | | | Excluded | | | 0.51 (0.16 to 0.87) | .18 | .01 | 1.46 (0.15 to 2.77) | .67 | .03 |
| Health status | 0.11 (−0.02 to 0.25) | .07 | .10 | 0.14 (0.04 to 0.25) | .05 | .01 | 0.22 (0.04 to 0.40) | .09 | .02 | 1.26 (0.61 to 1.92) | .33 | <.001 |
| Told overweight | −0.28 (−0.59 to 0.03) | .16 | .08 | Excluded | | | Excluded | | | Excluded | | |
| Advised by doctor to walk | 0.02 (−0.29 to 0.32) | .15 | .90 | Excluded | | | Excluded | | | Excluded | | |
| Injury | Excluded | | | Excluded | | | Excluded | | | −2.58 (−4.68 to −0.49) | 1.07 | .02 |

| Variable | Model a[^a] B (95% CI) | | | Model b[^b] B (95% CI) | | | Model c[^c] B (95% CI) | | | Model d[^d] B (95% CI) | | |
|---|---|---|---|---|---|---|---|---|---|---|---|---|
| Walking environment | 0.05 (0.01 to 0.08) | .02 | .01 | 0.05 (0.02 to 0.08) | .01 | .001 | 0.08 (0.03 to 0.12) | .02 | .001 | 0.44 (0.27 to 0.61) | .09 | <.001 |
| Campaign dose exposure | 0.16 (0.05 to 0.28) | .06 | .01 | 0.14 (0.04 to 0.24) | .05 | .006 | 0.11 (−0.05 to 0.28) | .08 | .17 | 0.44 (−0.16 to 1.05) | .31 | .15 |

[^a]: Belief in social benefits = 2.73 − (.005 × Age) + (.11 × Health status) − (.28 × Told overweight) + (.02 × Advised by doctor) + (.05 × Walking environment) + (.16 × Campaign dose exposure). Adjusted $R^2$ = 0.09.
[^b]: Belief in pleasure benefits = 2.67 + (.06 × School) + (.14 × Health status) + (.05 × Walking environment) + (.14 × Campaign dose exposure). Adjusted $R^2$ = 0.11.
[^c]: Belief in health benefits = 3.59 + (.08 × School) + (.51 × Sex) + (.22 × Health status) + (.08 × Walking environment) + (.11 × Campaign dose exposure). Adjusted $R^2$ = 0.09.
[^d]: All walking beliefs = 30.88 + (1.46 × Sex) + (1.26 × Health status) − (2.58 × Injury) + (.44 × Walking environment) + (.44 × Campaign dose exposure). Adjusted $R^2$ = 0.18.
[^e]: B indicates unstandardized regression coefficient; CI, confidence interval.
[^f]: Variables were included in analyses only when they were associated with the dependent variable at the bivariate level.

and all-beliefs subscale was not statistically significant when controlling for other factors.

Campaign-dose exposure remained associated with participation in a community-sponsored walk at a statistically significant level when controlling for educational level. In this analysis, the odds ratio of dose exposure was 2.14 (confidence interval, 1.04–4.41; $P$ = .04); exposed respondents were more than twice as likely to participate in the community-sponsored walks than unexposed respondents. In another multivariate analysis (not shown), dose exposure was not associated with participation in community-sponsored health fairs when controlling for other factors.

Campaign-dose exposure was associated with the number of days per week walking at a statistically significant level when controlling for age and health status (**Table 7**). However, when the all-beliefs scale was introduced in the second step of the linear regression, the coefficient for campaign exposure lost statistical significance.

# DISCUSSION

Impact assessment of media campaigns seeks to answer the question "Did exposure to the campaign lead to changes in beliefs and behavioral outcomes?" The evidence presented here shows that exposure to the *Walk Missouri* campaign

Table 7  Stepwise Linear Regression for Number of Days Walked per Week, *Walk Missouri* Campaign, St Joseph, Mo, 2003[a]

| Independent Variables | First Step | | | Second Step | | |
|---|---|---|---|---|---|---|
| | B (95% CI)[b] | SE | P | B (95% CI) | SE | P |
| Age | −0.02 (−0.04 to −0.003) | 0.01 | .02 | −0.02 (−0.04 to −0.006) | 0.01 | .01 |
| Health status | 0.62 (0.35 to 0.89) | 0.14 | <.001 | 0.51 (0.24 to 0.79) | 0.14 | <.001 |
| Campaign dose exposure | 0.29 (0.04 to 0.53) | 0.12 | .02 | 0.24 (−0.01 to 0.48) | 0.12 | .054 |
| All beliefs scale | Excluded in first step | | | 0.08 (0.04 to 0.3) | | <.001 |

[a]Number of days walked per week = −.133 − (.02 × Age) − (.52 × Health status) + (.24 × Campaign dose exposure) + (.08 × All-beliefs scale). Adjusted explained variance ($R^2$) = 0.15.
[b]B indicates unstandardized regression coefficient; CI, confidence interval.

had limited effects, producing small increases in positive walking beliefs and behaviors among residents of St Joseph. Effect sizes were small, with Spearman ρs of between 0.13 and 0.18 for statistically significant associations of beliefs and behaviors with campaign-dose exposure. Among exposed respondents, 4.3% reported participation in community-sponsored walks, compared with 0.5% of unexposed respondents. Exposed respondents reported walking for at least 10 minutes per day 5.2 days of the week, compared with 4.5 days per week for unexposed respondents.

When an external control community and baseline measures are not possible for assessing the impact of media campaigns, alternative approaches can offer evidence of effects when they show 1) moderate levels of campaign reach; 2) associations of exposure with behaviors, controlling for alternative explanations; 3) and confirmation of an a priori hypothesis positing mediation of exposure–behavior associations by beliefs promoted by the campaign (35). The *Walk Missouri* evaluation set out to provide such evidence. First, survey respondents reported a moderate level of exposure to the campaign, with about one in three respondents reporting some exposure. This level of exposure was near the 36% average for health-behavior media campaigns found in a recent meta-analysis (36). Second, exposure was significantly associated with three of six walking-behavior measures, and one association remained when controlling for several known predictors: demographic characteristics, health status, perceptions of the walking environment, and health beliefs.

Third, in addition to differences between exposed and unexposed groups, there was a dose-response relationship between exposure and outcomes, with higher levels of agreement on beliefs and positive walking behavior corresponding to higher levels of exposure.

Fourth, the association of exposure and number of days walking was mediated by health beliefs, providing evidence of a theoretically informed causal mechanism. For one wellness behavior—participation in community-sponsored walking activities—beliefs did not mediate the association with exposure. We conclude that campaign information on walking opportunities increased knowledge about these activities, leading to a slight increase in walking.

The single-site, postcampaign-only design limited the power of the study in several ways. Lack of an external control community and baseline measures may have weakened the study's internal validity. We cannot rule out the possibility of reverse causal direction—that walking adherents were more likely to pay attention to and recall the campaign. Nor can we conclude that the associations we found were not the result of other unmeasured third factors. The low response rate for our random-digit–dial survey may have introduced selectivity bias into the sample and limited our ability to generalize even to the medium-size midwestern town of St Joseph. Self-report measures are vulnerable to socially desirable responses, although there is no evidence that this necessarily contributed to differences between groups.

Acknowledging these limitations and caveats, our study provides information for public health communication researchers and practitioners about the potential for media interventions to promote physical activity. The study elucidates how a media campaign can contribute to a community-sponsored effort to promote walking behavior.

## EVIDENCE DESPITE A SIMPLE DESIGN

Elements of this single-site, postcampaign-only, cross-sectional design support our claim of limited effect. Careful and multiple measurements of exposure allowed for the creation of an unexposed comparison group. Two measures of exposure confirmed both group differences and dose-response associations of exposure and outcomes. A dose-response relationship suggested a possible causal relationship between exposure to the media campaign and increased likelihood of undertaking walking behaviors (37). We account for likely alternative explanations for associations of exposure with outcomes by including moderating factors in multivariate analysis. Empirical support for a theoretical mechanism is established in a test of the mediating effect of pro-walking beliefs on the association of campaign exposure and walking behavior. Combined, these results strengthen our claim of limited effect by ruling out alternative explanations and supporting an a priori theoretical approach that underlies the campaign strategy and study design (35).

## SUPPORT FOR THE MESSAGE STRATEGY

The association of exposure with social and pleasure benefits suggests that the campaign was most successful in communicating these ideas. Although health benefits, social support, and overcoming barriers were also included in the messages, they did not appear to have as much of an impact on the intended audience.

## SUCCESSFUL INTEGRATION INTO LOCAL ACTIVITIES

Originally envisioned and designed as a stand-alone media campaign, *Walk Missouri* was successfully integrated into local community-sponsored activities, consistent with recommendations from the literature (14–16,26), including the *Community Guide,* which strongly recommends programs that include informational promotional components. The local community coalition welcomed the opportunity to serve as the pilot community for the campaign, indicating that campaign themes and messages complemented their activities. It was not difficult to integrate information about local community activities and the coalition into *Walk Missouri* message materials, including scheduled walks and other wellness activities, lists of participating sponsors, and the *Get Movin' St. Joe* logo. Adaptation of the *Walk Missouri* campaign materials provided practical, useful information grounded in local events and organizations and proved pertinent for residents of St Joseph.

The scale of the initiative was closer to the community-based initiative of Wheeling, WVa (25), than the national and statewide campaigns implemented in New Zealand and Australia (20,22), all of which included investments in community-based programs. The *Walk Missouri* campaign incorporated information about community-sponsored activities, but *Walk Missouri* did not otherwise fund or support local activities. Nonetheless, it can be argued that in actively linking with community-based initiatives, the campaign fit more closely within the category of community-wide activities than in the media-alone category suggested by the *Community Guide* (16).

## MEDIA CONTRIBUTIONS TO BEHAVIOR CHANGE

The limited effect achieved by the *Walk Missouri* campaign is similar to the results of other media campaigns promoting general health behaviors as well as the few media campaigns that have promoted walking. The difference in wellness behaviors between exposed and unexposed groups was small (between 3 and 10 percentage points), consistent with research on the effects of health campaigns on behavior (36), and with previous efforts to promote physical activity through media interventions (20,22).

The study provides tentative evidence of independent and complementary effects of media campaigns on community-based interventions. We argue that the *Walk Missouri* media campaign expanded the reach of the local initiative, *Get Movin' St. Joe.* Originating as a worksite-wellness effort and a community coalition, *Get Movin' St. Joe* benefited from the visibility provided by the many posters, newspaper advertisements, billboards, and radio spots of *Walk Missouri,* and as a result, *Get Movin' St. Joe* reached a wider audience.

The study design does not allow us to differentiate between effects of media exposure and exposure to other community-sponsored activities; however, the evidence does permit us to discern how the campaign affected walking behavior. The evidence suggests that the campaign achieved behavioral results in two ways. First, campaign exposure was associated with participation in community-sponsored walks, consistent with a direct effect of exposure on behavior. Integration of information about community-sponsored walking activities and resources into media messages rendered them practical and useful. In this way, the media campaign was *complementary* to the community-sponsored events and may well have boosted attendance.

Second, the association of exposure with number of days of walking was mediated by pro-walking beliefs, consistent with an indirect effect of exposure on behavior. This finding suggests an independent effect of the campaign on walking behavior. General walking behavior did not rely on coalition activities. More importantly, the pro-walking beliefs that mediated the exposure–behavior association were consistent with campaign themes highlighted in *Walk Missouri*. These results begin to distinguish the mechanisms by which communication elements of a community-wide campaign contribute to increases in physical activity directly by advertising events and indirectly through changed beliefs and attitudes about walking.

### IMPORTANT IMPACT ON THE MARGIN

For a limited time, residents of St Joseph who were exposed to the campaign may have walked almost 1 day more per week than residents who were not exposed. More people may have attended coalition events because they heard about them through radio spots. Incremental increases in levels of physical activity at the population level contribute to major gains in public health (38).

By accounting for alternative explanations and substantiating a theory-based mechanism for impact, a simple study design with a small sample can provide persuasive evidence of campaign effects. The results of this small study with limited resources provide encouraging evidence that a media campaign can enhance the success of community-based efforts to promote positive walking beliefs and behaviors.

# ACKNOWLEDGMENTS

This publication was supported by award number U50/CCU721332-01 from the Centers for Disease Control and Prevention (CDC). The Walk Missouri project was a collaborative effort of the Health Communication Research

Laboratory in the Saint Louis University School of Public Health (SLU–SPH) and the Heart Disease and Stroke Program of the Missouri Department of Health and Senior Services (MDHSS), with the support of the Preventive Health & Human Services (PHHS) Catalog of Federal Domestic Assistance 93.99, and the Division of Nutrition and Physical Activity, CDC. We acknowledge our state and county health departments and community collaborators for making the project and this assessment possible: the MDHSS, Buchanan County and Marion County health departments, the St Joseph chapter of the YMCA, and Heartland Health. Atlanta-based CDC colleagues at the Division of Nutrition and Physical Activity offered invaluable guidance for the analysis, and the paper benefited from the review of our SLU–SPH colleagues. The authors are responsible for any errors in analysis or interpretation. The contents of the paper are the sole responsibility of the authors and do not necessarily represent the views of the CDC.

# Appendix

## Survey Questions for the Walk Missouri Media Campaign

### EXPOSURE QUESTIONS

1a. In the past 30 days, do you remember seeing any posters sponsored by the *Walk Missouri* campaign displayed in the St Joe area?
1. Yes
2. No (skip to next question)
3. Not sure (skip to next question)
4. Refuse (skip to next question)

1b. In the last 30 days, in how many different locations have you noticed a poster sponsored by the *Walk Missouri* campaign in your community? (*Read the ranges if respondent has trouble answering.*)
1. 1 to 5
2. 6 to 10
3. 11 to 20
4. 21 to 50
5. 51 to 100
6. Over 100

2a. In the last 30 days, do you remember seeing any newspaper advertisements sponsored by the *Walk Missouri* campaign?
1. Yes
2. No (skip to next question)
3. Not sure (skip to next question)
4. Refuse (skip to next question)

2b. In the last 30 days, how many times have you seen *Walk Missouri* advertisements in your local newspapers?
   1. 1 time
   2. 2 times
   3. 3 times
   4. 4 times
   5. 5 or more times (specify)
   6. Not sure

3a. In the last 30 days, do you remember seeing any local news stories about *Walk Missouri* or *Get Movin' St. Joe*?
   1. Yes
   2. No (skip to next question)
   3. Not sure (skip to next question)
   4. Refuse (skip to next question)

3b. How many news articles have your seen or read in the last 30 days that mention *Walk Missouri* or *Get Movin' St. Joe*?
   1. 1 time
   2. 2 times
   3. 3 times
   4. 4 times
   5. 5 or more times (specify)

4a. In the last 30 days, do you remember hearing radio ads sponsored by *Walk Missouri*?
   1. Yes
   2. No (skip to next question)
   3. Not sure (skip to next question)
   4. Refuse (skip to next question)

4b. In the last 30 days, how many times have you heard radio ads sponsored by *Walk Missouri*?
   1. 1 to 5 times
   2. 6 to 10 times
   3. 11 to 20 times
   4. 21 to 50 times
   5. 51 to 100 times
   6. Over 100 times

5a.  In the last 30 days, do you remember seeing any billboard advertisements sponsored by *Walk Missouri*?

1. Yes
2. No (skip to next question)
3. Not sure (skip to next question)
4. Refuse (skip to next question)

5b.  In the last 30 days, in how many different locations have you noticed a billboard sponsored by the *Walk Missouri* campaign in your community?

1. 1
2. 2
3. 3
4. 4
5. 5
6. 6 or more times (specify)

## BELIEF QUESTIONS

I would now like to ask you a few questions about your opinions of exercise. Please indicate whether you

- 1 = Strongly agree
- 2 = Agree
- 3 = Neither agree nor disagree
- 4 = Disagree
- 5 = Strongly disagree
- 6 = Not sure
- 7 = Refuse

1.  Exercise is a good way to spend time with people who are important to me.
2.  Exercise is a good time for me to catch up with my friends.
3.  People who are important to me encourage me to walk regularly.
4.  Walking is good way to ensure I have good health.
5.  Walking is good way to control my weight.
6.  I can walk almost anywhere at any time.
7.  In order to get the benefits of walking, it has to be hard work.
8.  Walking helps me deal with stress.
9.  Walking is a good way to enjoy the outdoors.
10. It is important to me that my family and friends know I walk for exercise.

11. I can find time to walk.
12. Walking can be fun.

## BEHAVIOR QUESTIONS

1. In the past 30 days, have you participated in a walk sponsored by *Walk Missouri* or *Get Movin' St. Joe*?
   1. Yes
   2. No

2. In the past 30 days, have you participated in any wellness activities at your worksite?
   1. Yes
   2. No

3. In the past 30 days, have you attended a health fair sponsored by a local health care provider such as the hospital or health department?
   1. Yes
   2. No

4. In a usual week, do you walk for at least 10 minutes at a time while at work, for recreation, for exercise, to get to and from places, or for any other reason?
   1. Yes
   2. No

5. In the past week, how many days per week did you walk for at least 10 minutes at a time?
   - 0 = 0 days
   - 1 = 1 day
   - 2 = 2 days
   - 3 = 3 days
   - 4 = 4 days
   - 5 = 5 days
   - 6 = 6 days
   - 7 = 7 days

6. In the past week, how many days per week did you walk for at least 10 minutes at a time?
   - 1 = 10–19 minutes
   - 2 = 20–29 minutes

- 3 = 30–39 minutes
- 4 = 40–49 minutes
- 5 = 50–59 minutes
- 6 = 60 minutes or more

## MODERATOR QUESTIONS: DEMOGRAPHICS, HEALTH STATUS, AND WALKING ENVIRONMENT

1. What year were you born? 19__

2. What is the highest year of school completed?
   1. Some high school
   2. High school diploma or equivalent
   3. Some college
   4. Associate's degree
   5. Bachelors degree
   6. Some graduate work
   7. Graduate or advanced degree
   8. Not sure/silent code

3. Would you characterize yourself as . . . ?
   1. African American
   2. Asian
   3. Caucasian
   4. Hispanic
   5. Native American
   6. Other (specify)
   7. Not sure/silent code

4. I am sorry, but I have to ask all of the questions. Are you . . .
   1. Male
   2. Female

5. Would you say that in general your health is . . .
   1. Excellent
   2. Very good
   3. Good
   4. Fair

5. Poor

6. Don't know

6. Have your ever been told by your doctor that you are overweight or have a chronic disease such as heart disease, high blood pressure, high cholesterol, diabetes, arthritis, osteoporosis, or another chronic disease?
   - 1 = Yes
   - 0 = No
   - 2 = Not sure/don't know

7. Have you ever been told by your doctor that you should walk or exercise more?
   - 1 = Yes
   - 0 = No
   - 2 = Not sure/don't know

8. There are many types of injuries, such as a broken bone, a cut, a bruise, a pulled muscle, or a sprained ankle. In the last 30 days, have you been injured badly enough that you needed to change your daily activities for at least 1 week?
   - 1 = Yes
   - 0 = No
   - 2 = Not sure/don't know

9. Please indicate whether you . . .
   - 1 = Strongly agree
   - 2 = Agree
   - 3 = Neither agree nor disagree
   - 4 = Disagree
   - 5 = Strongly disagree
   - 6 = Not sure/silent code

   a. There are many places to walk (for example, a store, a workplace, etc.) within easy walking distance from my home.
   b. I often walk to places near my home.
   c. There are good sidewalks on most of the streets in my community.
   d. There are interesting things to look at while walking in my neighborhood.
   e. I feel safe walking around my neighborhood.

10. Do you find your neighborhood . . .
    - 1 = Very pleasant
    - 2 = Somewhat pleasant
    - 3 = Not very pleasant
    - 4 = Not at all pleasant
    - 5 = Not sure/silent code

## FOOTNOTES

The opinions expressed by authors contributing to this journal do not necessarily reflect the opinions of the U.S. Department of Health and Human Services, the Public Health Service, Centers for Disease Control and Prevention, or the authors' affiliated institutions. Use of trade names is for identification only and does not imply endorsement by any of the groups named above.

*Suggested citation for this article*: Wray RJ, Jupka K, Ludwig-Bell C. A community-wide media campaign to promote walking in a Missouri town. Prev Chronic Dis [serial online] 2005 Oct [date cited]. Available from: http://www.cdc.gov/pcd/issues/2005/oct/05_0010.htm

## CONTRIBUTOR INFORMATION

Ricardo J Wray, Saint Louis University School of Public Health. 3545 Lafayette Ave, St Louis, MO 63104, Phone: 314-977-4075, Email: wray@slu.edu .

Keri Jupka, Health Communication Research Laboratory, Saint Louis University School of Public Health, St Louis, Mo.

Cathy Ludwig-Bell, Southern Illinois University Edwardsville, Edwardsville, Ill.

## REFERENCES

1. Centers for Disease Control and Prevention Chronic disease overview. Atlanta (GA): Centers for Disease Control and Prevention; 2004. May, Available from: http://www.cdc.gov/nccdphp/overview.htm.
2. Centers for Disease Control and Prevention Behavioral Risk Factor Surveillance System prevalence data. Atlanta (GA): Centers for Disease Control and Prevention; 2004. Oct, C1995–2003. Available from: http://apps.nccd.cdc.gov/brfss/.
3. U.S. Department of Health and Human Services Healthy People 2010. Conference ed. Washington (DC): U.S. Government Printing Office; 2000.
4. Siegel PZ, Brackbill RM, Heath GW. The epidemiology of walking for exercise: implications for promoting activity among sedentary group. *Am J Public Health*. 1995 May;*85*(5): 706–710.
5. Eyler A, Brownson R, Bacak S, Housemann R. The epidemiology of walking for physical activity in the United States. *Med Sci Sports Exerc.* 2003;*35*(9):1529–1536.

6. Centers for Disease Control and Prevention. A report of the surgeon general: physical activity and health. At-a-glance 1996. Atlanta (GA): Centers for Disease Control and Prevention; 1996.

7. King AC, Blair SN, Bild DE, Dishman RK, Dubbert PM, Marcus BH, et al. Determinants of physical activity and interventions in adults. *Med Sci Sports Exerc.* 1992;*24*(6 Suppl):S221–S236.

8. Ainsworth BE, Wilcox S, Thompson WW, Richter DL, Henderson KA. Personal, social, and physical environmental correlates of physical activity in African-American women in South Carolina. *Am J Prev Med.* 2003;*25*(3 Suppl 1):23–29.

9. Courneya KS, Friedenreich CM, Sela RA, Quinney HA, Rhodes RE. Correlates of adherence and contamination in a randomized controlled trial of exercise in cancer survivors: an application of the theory of planned behavior and the five factor model of personality. *Ann Behav Med.* 2002;*24*(4):257–268.

10. Wankel LM. The importance of enjoyment to adherence and psychological benefits from physical activity. *Int J Sport Psychol* 1993;*24*:151–169.

11. Boslaugh SE, Luke DA, Brownson RC, Naleid KS, Kreuter MW. Perceptions of neighborhood environment for physical activity: is it "who you are" or "where you live?". *J Urban Health.* 2004;*81*(4):671–681.

12. Saelens BE, Sallis JF, Black JB, Chen D. Neighborhood-based differences in physical activity: an environment scale evaluation. *Am J Public Health.* 2003;*93*(9):1552–1558.

13. Wilcox S, Castro C, King AC, Housemann R, Brownson RC. Determinants of leisure time physical activity in rural compared with urban older and ethnically diverse women in the United States. *J Epidemiol Community Health.* 2000;*54*(9):667–672.

14. Marcus BH, Owen N, Forsyth LH, Cavill NA, Fridinger F. Physical activity interventions using mass media, print media, and information technology. *Am J Prev Med.* 1998;*15*(4):362–378.

15. Marshall A, Owen N, Bauman A. Mediated approaches for influencing physical activity: update of the evidence on mass media, print, telephone and website delivery interventions. *J Sci Med Sport.* 2004;*7*(1 Suppl):74–80.

16. Kahn EB, Ramsey LT, Brownson RC, Heath GW, Howze EH, Powell KE, et al. The effectiveness of interventions to increase physical activity. A systematic review. *Am J Prev Med.* 2002;*22*(4 Suppl):73–107.

17. Wardle J, Rapoport L, Miles A, Afuape T, Duman M. Mass education for obesity prevention: the penetration of the BBC's 'Fighting Fat, Fighting Fit' campaign. *Health Educ Res.* 2001;*16*(3):343–355.

18. Hillsdon M, Cavill N, Nanchahal K, Diamond A, White IR. National level promotion of physical activity: results from England's ACTIVE for LIFE campaign. *J Epidemiol Community Health.* 2001;*55*(10):755–761.

19. Matsudo V, Matsudo S, Andrade D, Araujo T, Andrade E, de Oliveira LC, et al. Promotion of physical activity in a developing country: the Agita Sao Paulo experience. *Public Health Nutr.* 2002;*5*(1A):253–261.

20. Bauman AE, Bellew B, Owen N, Vita P. Impact of an Australian mass media campaign targeting physical activity in 1998. *Am J Prev Med.* 2001;*21*(1):41–47.

21. Bauman A, Armstrong T, Davies J, Owen N, Brown W, Bellew B, et al. Trends in physical activity participation and the impact of integrated campaigns among Australian adults, 1997–99. *Aust N Z J Public Health.* 2003;*27*(1):76–79.

22. Bauman A, McLean G, Hurdle D, Walker S, Boyd J, van Aalst I, et al. Evaluation of the national 'Push Play' campaign in New Zealand—creating population awareness of physical activity. *N Z Med J.* 2003;*116*(1179):U535.

23. Wimbush E. A moderate approach to promoting physical activity: the evidence and implication. *Health Educ J.* 1994;*53*(3):322–336.

24. Owen N, Bauman A, Booth M, Oldenburg B, Magnus P. Serial mass-media campaigns to promote physical activity: reinforcing or redundant? *Am J Public Health.* 1995;*85*(2):244–248.

25. Reger B, Cooper L, Booth-Butterfield S, Smith H, Bauman A, Wootan M, et al. Wheeling Walks: A community campaign using paid media to encourage walking among sedentary older adults. *Prev Med.* 2002;*35*:285–292.

26. Cavill N. National campaigns to promote physical activity: can they make a difference. *Int J Obes Relat Metab Disord.* 1998;*22*(Suppl 2):S48–S51.

27. Rosenstock I. The health belief model: explaining health behavior through expectancies. In: Glanz K, Lewis F, Rimer B, editors. *Health behavior and health education: theory, research, and practice.* 1st ed. Jossey-Bass; San Francisco (CA): 1991.

28. Strecher V, Rosenstock I. The health belief model. In: Glanz K, Lewis F, Rimer B, editors. *Health behavior and health education: theory, research, and practice.* 2nd ed. Jossey-Bass; San Francisco (CA): 1997. pp. 41–59.

29. Manne S, Markowitz A, Winawer S, Guillem J, Meropol N, Haller D, et al. Understanding intention to undergo colonoscopy among intermediate-risk siblings of colorectal cancer patients: a test of a mediational model. *Prev Med.* 2003;*36*(1): 71–84.

30. United States Census Bureau. United States Census Bureau; Washington (DC): Oct, 2004. Available from: http://quickfacts.census.gov/qfd/states/29/29021.html.

31. Valente T. *Evaluating health promotion programs.* Oxford University Press; New York (NY): 2002.

32. Centers for Disease Control and Prevention Summ data quality rep. Atlanta (GA): Centers for Disease Control and Prevention; 2004.

33. Tracking system: cooperation, refusal and response rates. The Council for Marketing and Opinion Research; Wethersfield (CT): 2005.

34. Mokdad A, Stroup D, Giles W. Public health surveillance for behavioral risk factors in a changing environment. Recommendations from the Behavioral Risk Factor Surveillance Team. Centers for Disease Control and Prevention. *MMWR Recomm Rep.* 2003;*52*(RR-9):1–12.

35. Hornik R. Evaluation design for public health communication. In: Hornik R, editor. *Public health communication: evidence for behavior change.* Lawrence Erlbaum; Mahwah (NJ): 2002. pp. 385–385.

36. Snyder L, Hamilton M. A meta-analysis of U.S. health campaign effects on behavior: emphasize enforcement, exposure, and new information, and beware the secular trend. In: Hornik R, editor. *Public health communication: evidence for behavior change.* Lawrence Erlbaum; Mahwah (NJ): 2002. pp. 357–383.

37. Hennekens C, Buring J, Mayrent S. *Epidemiology in medicine.* Little, Brown and Company; Boston (MA): 1987.

38. Sorensen G, Emmons K, Hunt MK, Jonston D. Implications of the results of community intervention trials. *Annu Rev Public Health.* 1998;*19*:379–416.

## CHAPTER ACTIVITY QUESTIONS

1. What constructs were used as the framework for the program and why?
2. How did results from the focus group influence the constructs used?
3. Give examples of the how the constructs were used in the development of the program.
4. What modifying factors were identified? Brainstorm how they might have influenced the outcome of this program.

## CHAPTER REFERENCES

Belcher, L., Sternberg, M.R., Wolotski, R.J., Halkitis, P., & Hoff, C. (2005). Condom use and perceived risk of HIV transmission among sexually active HIV positive men who have sex with men. *AIDS Education and Prevention, 17*(1), 79–89.

Chen, J.K., Fox, S.A., Cantrell, C.H., Stockdale, S.E., & Kagawa-Singer, M. (2007). Health disparities and prevention: Racial/ethnic barriers to flu vaccinations. *Journal of Community Health, 32*(1), 5–20.

Courtenay, W.H. (1998). College men's health: An overview and call to action. *Journal of American College Health, 46*(6), 279–287.

de Wit, J.B.F., Vet, R., Schutten, M., & van Steenbergen, J. (2005). Social-cognitive determinants of vaccination behavior against hepatitis B: An assessment among men who have sex with men. *Preventive Medicine, 40*(6), 795–802.

Downing-Matibag, T.M., & Geisinger, B. (2009). Hooking up and sexual risk taking among college students: A Health Belief Model perspective. *Qualitative Health Research, 19*(9), 1196–1209.

Forsyth, L.H., & Goetsch, V.L. (1997). Perceived threat of illness and health protective behaviors in offspring of adults with non-insulin dependent diabetes mellitus. *Behavioral Medicine, 23*(3), 112–120.

Frank, D., Swedmark, J., & Grubbs, L. (2004). Colon cancer screening in African American women. *ABNF Journal, 15*(4), 67–70.

Gerba, C.P., Rose, J.B., & Haas, C.N. (1996). Sensitive populations: Who is at the greatest risk? *International Journal of Food Microbiology, 30*, 113–123.

Glanz, K., Rimer, B.K., & Viswanath, K. (Eds.). (2008) *Health Behavior and Health Education* (4th ed.). San Francisco: Jossey-Bass.

Graham, M.E. (2002). Health beliefs and self breast examination in black women. *Journal of Cultural Diversity, 9*(2), 49–54.

Hanson, J.A., & Benedict, J.A. (2002). Use of Health Belief Model to examine older adults' food-handling behaviors. *Journal of Nutrition Education, 34*, S25–S30.

Hochbaum, G.M. (1958). *Public Participation in Medical Screening Programs: A Sociopsychological Study* (Public Health Service Publication No. 572). Washington, DC: Government Printing Office.

Janz, N.K., & Becker, M.H. (1984). The Health Belief Model: A decade later. *Health Education Quarterly, 11*(1), 1–47.

Lamanna, L.M. (2004). College students' knowledge and attitudes about cancer and perceived risks of developing skin cancer. *Dermatology Nursing, 16*(2), 161–176.

Lewis, J.E., & Malow, R.M. (1997). HIV/AIDS risks in heterosexual college students. *Journal of American College Health, 45*(4), 147–155.

Maes, C.A., & Louis, M. (2003). Knowledge of AIDS, perceived risk of AIDS, and at-risk sexual behaviors of older adults. *The Journal of the American Academy of Nurse Practitioners, 15*(11), 509–516.

Mullens, A.B., McCaul, K.D., Erickson, S.C., & Sandgren, A.K. (2003). Coping after cancer: Risk perceptions, worry, and health behaviors among colorectal cancer survivors. *Psycho-oncology, 13*, 367–376.

National Cancer Institute. (2005). *Theory at a Glance: A Guide for Health Promotion Practice.* (2nd ed.) Washington, DC: U.S. Department of Health and Human Services. Retrieved July 29, 2012, from http://www.cancer.gov/cancertopics/cancerlibrary/theory.pdf.

National Institute of Neurological Disorders and Stroke. (2007). Transmissible spongiform encephalopathies information page. Retrieved March 29, 2007, from http://www.ninds.nih.gov/disorders/tse/tse.htm.

New York-Presbyterian Hospital. (2006). Colonoscopy promoted during colorectal cancer awareness month. Retrieved April 22, 2007, from http://www.nyp.org/news/health/060322.html.

Rose, M.A. (1995). Knowledge of human immunodeficiency virus and acquired immunodeficiency syndrome, perception of risk, and behaviors among older adults. *Holistic Nursing Practice, 10*(1), 10–17.

Rosenstock, I.M. (1960). What research in motivation suggests for public health. *American Journal of Public Health, 50*(3), 295–302.

Rosenstock, I.M, Strecher, V.J., & Becker, M.H. (1988). Social learning theory and the Health Belief Model. *Health Education Quarterly, 15*(2), 175–183.

Smith, P.J., Humiston, S.G., Marguse, E.K., Zhao, Z., Dorell, C.G., Howes, C., & Hibbs, B. (2011). Parental delay or refusal of vaccine doses, childhood vaccination coverage at 24 months of age, and the Health Belief Model. *Public Health Reports, 126* (supp 2), 135–146.

Stretcher, V., & Rosenstock, I.M. (1997). The Health Belief Model. In K. Glanz, F.M. Lewis, & B.K. Rimer (Eds.), *Health Behavior and Health Education: Theory, Research and Practice* (2nd ed.). San Francisco: Jossey-Bass.

Weinrich, S., Hodlford, D., Boyd, M., Creanga, D., Cover, K., Johnson, A., Frank-Stromborg, M., & Weinrich, M. (1998). Prostate cancer education in African American churches. *Public Health Nursing, 15*(3), 188–195.

Weitkunat, R., Pottgieber, C., Meyer, N., Crispin, A., Fischer, R., Schotten, K., Kerr, J., & Uberia, K. (2003). Perceived risk of bovine spongiform encephalopathy and dietary behavior. *Journal of Health Psychology, 8*(3), 373–382.

Wallace, S.L. (2002). Osteoporosis prevention in college women: Application of the Expanded Health Belief Model. *American Journal of Health Behavior, 26*(3), 163–172.

Winfield, E.B., & Whaley, A.I. (2002). A comprehensive test of the Health Belief Model in predicting condom use among African American college students. *Journal of Black Psychology, 28*(4), 330–346.

Yep, G.A. (1993). HIV prevention among Asian American college students: Does the Health Belief Model work? *Journal of American College Health, 41*(5), 199–205.

# Attribution Theory

## THEORY ESSENCE SENTENCE

There is a cause or explanation for things that happen.

### Attribution Theory Constructs Chart

**Locus of control:**
The extent to which a person has control over life events

**Stability:**
The extent to which a cause is permanent or temporary

**Controllability:**
The extent to which a person can willfully change the cause

# IN THE BEGINNING

Attribution Theory grew out of a desire to identify an overarching theory to explain what motivates people (Weiner, 2010). Much of the research that lead to this theory focused on perceived attributional causes of achievement – that is, success or failure relative to a specific behavior and the internal factors or external situations that influence the outcome (Weiner, 1985; Kearsely, 2006). Originally conceived by Heider in the 1950s, he proposed that success and failure could be explained by the following formula "Can × Try." "Can" is the relation between ability and the difficulty of the task, multiplied by "try," which is the effort put forth by the person (Weiner, 2010). A psychologist by training, Heider believed that people strived to understand why others behave the way they did and to determine whether their behavior was caused by internal factors (personality or disposition) or external situations (Strickland, 2006).

Attribution Theory also has roots in two other theories used to explain motivation, Drive Theory and Expectancy/value Theory. Drive Theory explains behavior as being determined by drive × habit. That is, behavior depends on the degree of need (drive) multiplied by the strength of behavior patterns (habit) strengthened by rewards. Expectancy/value Theory explains behavior as being determined by expectancy × value and motives. That is, behavior depends on what one is going to get (expects) multiplied by the incentive (value) and the subjective likelihood of getting it, and the need for achievement (primary motive) (Weiner, 2010).

Additionally, the concept of locus of control was added to this mix (Rotter, 1966). It seemed logical that people who had high needs for achievement would view the world as being in their control—(outcomes are controlled by their skills—internal controls) in contrast to people with low achievement needs (outcomes are the result of luck—external controls), and that locus of control might be a significant determinant of success or failure (Weiner, 2010). In 1971, Weiner combined the four characteristics related to success and failure—ability, effort, difficulty of task, and locus of control—and added causal stability and control to develop the framework of Attribution Theory (Weiner, 2010).

# THEORETICAL CONCEPT

In 1982, there was a football team in Los Angeles—the Los Angeles Rams—that had a really bad season. "Here it is Thanksgiving week, and the Los Angeles Rams are looking like the biggest turkeys in town. Coach Ray Malavasi has eliminated bad luck, biorhythms, and sunspots" as the reason for his team's poor performance (Robert, 1982). Clearly, poor Coach Malavasi was trying to attribute his team's lousy game (failure) to some external cause in order to explain why they played (behaved) so poorly.

Why is it so important that we attribute a cause to an outcome? Sometimes we need to assign causation to certain behaviors, events, or outcomes to avoid them (if undesirable) or repeat them (if desirable) in the future. Sometimes we want to assign causation just for the sake of having an explanation. Other times, we need to attribute a cause because it helps us psychologically deal with a specific event (Weiner, 1985). Sometimes, it is important for us to understand why certain events happen so we can either repeat the causes (behaviors/actions) to repeat the outcome if it is positive (successful), or change the causes if the outcome is negative (failure) (Weiner, 1985). As the saying goes, "If you keep doing the same thing, you'll keep getting the same thing." Now, this is fine if the results are what you want. But if they aren't what you want, then knowing the cause will enable you to change what you are doing so you won't keep getting the same undesirable outcome.

# THEORETICAL CONSTRUCTS

Since causality is the basis for this theory, understanding more about the causes helps us better understand why people behave in certain ways. To this end, three aspects of a cause, or causal dimensions, have been identified: locus, stability, and controllability (Weiner, 1985).

## LOCUS OF CONTROL

The causal dimension of locus is really referring to the idea of locus of control (Rotter, 1966). Locus of control has to do with the extent to which people believe they have control over events in their lives. Locus of control comes in two flavors, internal and external. A person with an internal locus of control believes events happen as a result of something within himself or herself (e.g., skill, intelligence, desire, commitment, work ethic, values, beliefs), attributes over which the person has control. A person with an external locus of control believes events happen because of things outside the realm of personal control or because of things in the environment. External causes are divided into those attributed to fate, luck, or chance and those attributed to powerful others. These powerful others can be significant in health because they are often physicians, dentists, therapists, and other health or medical personnel (Levenson, 1974; Wiegmann & Berven, 1998).

Whether someone attributes internal or external causes to a given situation varies from situation to situation (Rotter, 1993). This is typically seen in students.

If a student fails a course, the cause for the poor grade is inevitably external and often a powerful other—the professor (she is a tough grader; he didn't like me; his tests are too hard; she didn't teach us anything). However, if a student does really well in a course, then the cause for the good grade is attributed to attending class, taking notes, and studying—internal conditions over which the student has control. It is a rare student who will assign the cause of failure to internal conditions over which he or she had control. How many students do you know fail a course and say, "She was a great professor, but I just didn't care if I learned the information," or "I should have bought the book and read it, taken notes in class, handed in all of the assignments, and not partied as much" (**Figure 5–1**).

For a person diagnosed with HIV infection, among the many potential causes for this diagnosis is personal behavior (McDonell, 1993)—something the person did or didn't do. The infection may be attributed to internal causes, for example, not using condoms, or sharing unclean needles. On the other hand, the HIV infection may have been the result of external causes not under the person's control, such as luck or fate or the actions of others, as is the case with perinatal transmission, the rare transfusion transmission, or condom breakage.

When a poor outcome is attributed to internal causes, as is often the case with HIV infection, it leads to self-blame on the part of the infected individuals and is also seen as their "fault" by others. When people who need the help of others are held responsible for the circumstances that lead to need in the first place, help from others is often not forthcoming (McDonell, 1993). Thus, Attribution

© Sergey Dubrov/Shutterstock, Inc.

**Figure 5–1**  Internal cause for failing a course—sleeping on your notes

Theory helps to explain not only the behavior of the individual affected, but also that of those around him or her.

## STABILITY

There is more to an attributional cause than it simply being internal or external. Causes are also categorized by their stability, that is, how consistent or permanent they are (Wang, 2001).

Although it would be logical to assume that all internal causes of behavior are stable, consistent, and permanent, with no fluctuation in their capacity to cause a particular outcome, this is not necessarily true. For example, let's look at athletic ability as the internal cause of behavior. Athletic ability is pretty stable—it doesn't vary from day to day. Either you have it or you don't. However, other internal causes, such as mood, desire, drive, and effort, do vary. So although these are internal causes, they are not stable, permanent, or consistent (Weiner, 1985). They can fluctuate from day to day, from situation to situation.

The same is true of external causes. The external cause of luck, for instance, is unstable. Luck is inconsistent and certainly not permanent. Sometimes you have it, and unfortunately, sometimes you don't (**Figure 5–2**). On the other hand, task difficulty is an external cause, but one that is stable: if a task is difficult, it is difficult (Weiner, 1985). For example, maintaining a vegan lifestyle, even once you get the hang of it, is still difficult in our society.

© iQoncept/Shutterstock, Inc.

**Figure 5–2** Luck—sometimes you have it and sometimes you don't

The idea of cause stability has implications when we are trying to explain health behavior using the Attribution Theory. For instance, when an alcoholic relapses, he or she is more likely to attribute this negative behavior to an external, unstable cause (Seneviratne & Saunders, 2000): "When I wasn't looking, someone switched my soda with champagne, and since everyone was expected to join in the toast, I drank it. I won't ever take my eye off my soda again." The external cause was "someone," and the unstable aspect was that this was a temporary situation that won't happen again. Ah, the devil made me do it!

It is the rare individual who attributes his or her undesirable behavior (relapse) to internal, stable causes (Seneviratne & Saunders, 2000). If the alcoholic from the previous example were to do so, his or her explanation would be something along the lines of "I drank the champagne instead of soda because I wanted to get drunk, and the next time I have an opportunity to get drunk on Dom Perignon, I will do it again."

## CONTROLLABILITY

In addition to causes being stable or unstable, some causes can be controlled or changed and others cannot. Let's look at the controllability of the internal, *unstable* causes of behavior, effort, and mood (think depression). Effort can be willfully changed at any moment by the person, whereas mood cannot. Although both are internal and unstable, effort is controllable, whereas mood is uncontrollable (Rosenbaum, 1972; Weiner, 1985). When you are in a funk, you can't just change and immediately come out of it. You can, however, decide to put more effort into something right away.

The same issue of controllability is found among the internal, *stable* causes. For example, laziness is internal and stable. Although some people are lazy by nature, they do have control over it—they can change this if they choose to. This is not true of other internal, stable causes such as mathematic or artistic aptitude or physical coordination (Rosenbaum, 1972; Weiner, 1985). Some people have very little innate math ability, can't draw, and are clumsy. No matter how hard these folks try, they will never be math geniuses, famous painters, or Olympic gold medalists. These internal causes are just not changeable at will.

The construct of controllability has a real, practical application. It is the basis of stigmas or stereotypes. In general, people attribute negative outcomes, events, or conditions in other peoples' lives to internal but controllable causes. This is what happens with obesity. Obesity is seen as being the result of internal but controllable causes such as lack of willpower, overeating, laziness, and not exercising (Crandall & Schiffauer, 1998; Puhl & Brownwell, 2001, 2003), which may or may not be causing the increased weight at all. For the person who is genetically predisposed to obesity, this is an internal, uncontrollable cause. Keep in mind those somatotypes of ectoderm, mesoderm, and endoderm. There are internal and uncontrollable causes of body shape, height, and weight. Although these causes should not be used as an excuse for overeating or lack of exercise, not everyone has the genetic blueprint of the ectoderm.

With the stigma of obesity so strong, and blame for it placed within the obese person's control, it is no wonder that people will go to great lengths to avoid this outcome. Couple this with a culture that associates thinness with being "good" and fatness with being "bad" (Puhl & Brownell, 2003), we end up with an increased likelihood of depression and suicidal attempts in the obese (Carpenter, Hasin, Allison, & Faith, 2000) at one extreme and eating disorders and their health consequences at the other.

Dental caries are another example of a health problem that can be attributed to internal, controllable causes of laziness and poor motivation. If the same outcome of dental caries were attributed to dental phobia, the cause would still be internal, but uncontrollable. Another cause could be that the dentist did not remove old fillings. In this case, the cause would be external and uncontrollable (Kneckt & Knuuttila, 2000). This example shows us that in some situations, it is important to identify causality. After all, little would be gained by educating the lazy person if the culprit were the dentist!

If we look at peer victimization or bullying from an Attribution Theory perspective, we find that children use self-blame to explain why they are being bullied, that is they believe they deserve to be picked on. Attributing being bullied to self-blame reflects how the child sees him/herself. It is an internal, stable, and uncontrollable cause, which suggests that it cannot be changed and that the harassment will continue (Graham, 2006). A sad explanation indeed for a situation that is neither internal, stable, or uncontrollable.

Attribution Theory tells us that the explanations people give for certain events or situations that occur in their lives affect their emotions, expectations, and their behavior. In loneliness, a situation commonly seen among older adults, if the cause is believed to be controllable, then there is hope that the situation can be changed by changing one's behavior (Newall, Chipperfield, Clifton, Perry, & Swift, 2009). For example, perhaps by joining a community social group, planning a vacation with a tour group, volunteering at an agency or local food kitchen,

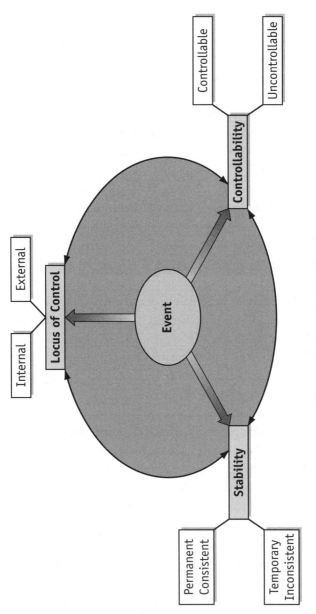

**Figure 5–3**  Attribution Flowchart

or taking a course at the local adult school. Older adults who have internal controllable beliefs about loneliness, are less lonely (Newall, et al., 2009).

Although not all health behaviors can be explained or changed on the basis of causal attribution, it can be a starting point. Assigning causation may not only help explain the behavior but also identify the type of intervention needed to achieve behavior change.

In summary, according to Attribution Theory, internal factors, external situations, locus of control, stability, and controllability explain behavior (**Figure 5–3**).

# THEORY IN ACTION—CLASS ACTIVITY

Brainstorm and list all the possible explanations as to why there is a rise in antibiotic-resistant bacteria. Then, read the following article and answer the questions at the end.

# Chapter 5 Article: Towards a Better Understanding of Patients' Perspectives of Antibiotic Resistance and MRSA: A Qualitative Study[1]

*Brooks, Lauren; Shaw, Alison; Sharp, Debbie; Hay, Alastair D.*

## Abstract

**Background.** Patients' expectations for antibiotics are known to influence prescribing, but little is known about patients' understanding of, and attitudes to, antibiotic resistance and whether these could modify treatment expectations.

**Objective.** To explore primary care patients' perspectives on antibiotic resistance and methicillin-resistant *Staphylococcus aureus* (MRSA) and understand how these could modify expectations for antibiotics.

**Methods.** A qualitative investigation using focus groups and semi-structured interviews with patients purposely sampled from low, intermediate and high antibiotic consumption groups from socio-economically contrasting general practices.

**Results.** There was uncertainty concerning the nature and implications of antibiotic resistance for both individuals and the wider community. While some patients viewed antibiotic resistance as a problem for society, most did not see it as something that would affect them personally. Many thought that science would provide the solution through the development of new drugs. Responsibility for antibiotic resistance was mostly attributed to 'other' patients and GPs who had respectively overused and overprescribed antibiotics in the past. As MRSA was mainly seen as a hospital-based problem, blame was largely directed at hospital management and, to a lesser degree, doctors, nurses and cleaners. Concerns about antibiotic resistance were not regarded as a reason to modify individual use of antibiotics.

---

[1] Reproduced from Brooks, L., Shaw, L., Sharp, D., & Hay, D.A. (2008). Towards a better understanding of patients' perspectives of antibiotic resistance and MRSA: a qualitative study. *Family Practice*, 25, 341–348.

**Conclusions.** Many primary care patients are unaware of what antibiotic resistance is and how it arises. The causes of, and responsibility for, antibiotic resistance are usually attributed to external rather than personal factors and patients perceive that its solutions are outside of their control.

**Keywords.** Antibacterial agents, drug resistance, patients' views, prescribing, qualitative research

# INTRODUCTION

Resistance to antibiotics is a major threat to public health.[1] In the UK, GPs are responsible for 80% of all antibiotics prescribed. They are mostly used for respiratory tract infections[2] despite evidence of marginal effectiveness for the most common respiratory presentations in primary care.[3-5] The decision to prescribe is made in partnership with patients and is determined by clinical as well as non-clinical factors.[6]

Previous research has examined patients' expectations regarding antibiotics and the impact on doctors' prescribing decisions. This indicates that GPs' perceptions that patients expect antibiotics can lead them at times to acquiesce to inappropriate treatment.[7-10] Qualitative research has highlighted the complexity of the GP–patient interaction and how patients may resist the doctor's recommendations not to prescribe.[11,12] The challenges that these interactions regarding antibiotic prescribing present for shared decision making have begun to be addressed.[12,13] Some research has examined how patients' attitudes to antibiotic prescribing can be changed, for example through use of the Internet.[14] Public education campaigns such as 'Not all bugs need drugs'[15] have sought to reduce patient expectations for antibiotics. Some have criticized such campaigns for the overly broad messages they convey, which fail to account for public knowledge and attitudes regarding antibiotic resistance.[16]

Methicillin-resistant *Staphylococcus aureus* (MRSA) is probably the best-known example of a resistant bacterium and has been the focus of intense scientific and political interest around the world.[17] Although there are high levels of awareness and concern about MRSA among hospital patients and visitors,[18,19] there has been little research focused on primary care patients' perspectives and understanding of antibiotic resistance more broadly. Such research is important as it may inform the future development of interventions to modify patients' expectations for antibiotics. A UK qualitative study of hospital patients with MRSA explored perceptions of MRSA infection and its treatment, but did not examine attitudes to antibiotic consumption or resistance.[20] A recent qualitative study explored public attitudes to antibiotic resistance,[16] but did not take account of individuals' prior antibiotic use. This paper builds on that research by exploring primary care patients' views of antibiotic resistance and MRSA among patients with differing levels of antibiotic use. It also examines their views of the relative benefits and threats of antibiotic use for individuals and the community and the impact this may have on their expectations for antibiotics.

# METHODS

## SAMPLING

We focused in depth on a purposeful sample of primary care patients selected in two stages. First, we recruited two general practices with contrasting levels of antibiotic use and practice populations: one a relatively low prescribing, affluent practice and the other a relatively high prescribing, deprived practice. Second, we wrote to adults identified from the practice records using a sampling frame that distinguished men and women, different age groups (16–49 and ≥50 years) and different levels of antibiotic use in the previous 12 months (0 versus 1 to 3 versus ≥4 courses). A total of 150 patients were invited to take part. Interested patients contacted the research team who then arranged the focus groups and interviews.

## DATA COLLECTION AND ANALYSIS

We collected and analysed data between April 2006 and March 2007, with preliminary analyses of early data informing the issues covered during later data collection in an iterative manner. LB conducted the focus groups (at the practices) and in-depth interviews (mostly at patients' homes) using a flexible topic guide. The topic guide covered issues relating to participants' knowledge, views and experiences of antibiotic use and prescribing, antibiotic resistance and MRSA. Focus groups were conducted first in order to identify the breadth of views held and tap into shared 'cultural' understandings. Group members were then invited to participate in a follow-up individual interview, for a more in-depth exploration of perspectives. Similar topics were covered within both the focus groups and interviews. However, during the interviews there was a greater focus on the

**Table 1**  Topics Covered in Focus Groups and Interviews

Introduction

Views of antibiotics and their use generally

Personal use of antibiotics

Views of situations when not acceptable/appropriate to use antibiotics

Understanding of antibiotic resistance and views of causes

Views of implications of antibiotics resistance for self and society

Understanding of MRSA and views of causes

Views of solutions and strategies for dealing with antibiotic resistance

Future use of antibiotics

Any other issues

individual's experiences of antibiotic use and how these related to their understandings of antibiotic resistance. An outline of the topics covered in groups and interviews is provided in **Table 1**. Focus groups and interviews ceased when no new themes or perspectives were emerging with additional data collection. All focus groups and interviews were audio recorded and transcribed verbatim.

We used a framework approach to analyse the data.[21] During the familiarization stage, LB read transcripts repeatedly and noted initial recurrent themes. We then constructed a thematic framework based on these emergent and a priori themes. The a priori themes reflected previous literature and the aims of the study, which were to explore patients' understanding of and attitudes to antibiotic resistance and MRSA, and their views regarding individual benefit versus societal harm that may play a part in decisions to consult for or consume antibiotics. A subset of the transcripts were read by AS and ADH (a social scientist and an academic GP) to check the credibility and trustworthiness of the developing analysis and incorporate the perspectives of researchers with different backgrounds. Additional emergent themes and subthemes were incorporated into the framework. LB then systematically coded transcripts using the modified thematic framework, aided by the software ATLAS.ti. Following this, LB created a data matrix that enabled mapping and interpretation of the themes, examining them for commonalities, differences and patterns across all participants/groups. LB led this stage but the interpretations were discussed and agreed with the other authors. **Table 2** shows the thematic framework as it developed during

**Table 2** Thematic Framework Used During Data Analysis

| Main themes | Subthemes |
| --- | --- |
| 1. Understanding of antibiotic resistance and MRSA[a] | Uncertainty about antibiotic resistance[b]<br>The body as resistant/immune[b]<br>Bacteria as resistant[b]<br>Uncertainty about MRSA[b]<br>Info sources[a] |
| 2. Responsibility and blame for AR and MRSA[b] | Irresponsible others (AR)[b]<br>Responsible selves (AR)[b]<br>GPs in the past (AR)[b]<br>Farming/veterinary (AR)[b]<br>Nature fighting back (AR)[b]<br>Poor hospital hygiene (MRSA)[b]<br>Contract cleaners (MRSA)[b]<br>Nurses (MRSA)[b]<br>Lack of discipline/authority (MRSA)[b]<br>Gov./mismanagement of NHS (MRSA)[b] |
| 3. Implications of AR for individual and societal risk[a] | Uncertainty of prevalence of AR[b]<br>Concerns about becoming immune[b]<br>Not concerned about resistance[b]<br>Fear of MRSA[b]<br>Scepticism about MRSA threat[b] |
| 4. Possible solutions: tackling the problem of resistance[a] | Lack of individual control[b]<br>Patient education[b]<br>Improving hospital hygiene[b]<br>Reducing GP antibiotic prescribing[b]<br>Faith in science[b] |

NHS, National Health Service; AR, antibiotic resistance

[a]Themes in the initial framework reflecting a priori themes derived from previous literature and topic guide.
[b]Emergent themes added to the final framework through the analysis of the data.

the process of analysis. It highlights both the emergent and a priori themes and subthemes included in the framework.

# RESULTS

Five focus groups comprising 23 patients and 20 follow-up interviews were conducted. **Table 3** shows that the participants were predominantly female with a

**Table 3** Characteristics of Participants

|  | No. of participants | |
|---|---|---|
|  | **Practice A (deprived)** | **Practice B (affluent)** |
| Men | 2 | 3 |
| Women | 8 | 10 |
| Age (years) | | |
| 16–49 | 1 | 5 |
| ≥50 | 9 | 8 |
| Employment (including retired) | | |
| Professional or higher managerial | 0 | 7 |
| Other non-manual | 6 | 3 |
| Skilled manual | 2 | 0 |
| Unskilled manual | 0 | 0 |
| Looking after home/family | 2 | 3 |
| Total household income | | |
| Less than £10k | 2 | 0 |
| £10–£20k | 5 | 2 |
| £20–£30k | 3 | 1 |
| £40–£50k | 0 | 3 |
| More than £50k | 0 | 7 |
| Highest educational qualification | | |
| No formal qualifications | 6 | 0 |
| O level/GCSE | 2 | 1 |
| A level | 1 | 2 |
| Degree | 0 | 8 |
| Professional qualification | 0 | 1 |
| NVQ | 1 | 1 |
| Antibiotic use (in past 12 months) | | |
| 0 courses | 1 | 3 |
| 1–3 courses | 3 | 8 |
| ≥4 courses | 6 | 2 |

GCSE, General Certificate of Secondary Education; NVQ, National Vocational Qualification.

broad range of income, qualifications and previous antibiotic use. Participants reported that they had used antibiotics for cellulitis, urinary tract infections, tooth abscesses, infected wounds, sinusitis, throat infections, tonsillitis and pneumonia. Several of the participants from the more than or equal to four courses category were advised to take antibiotics on a daily basis for conditions such as rosacea, bronchiectasis or following splenectomy. We refer to these individuals as long-term users of antibiotics.

We identified four key themes relating to patients' perspectives on antibiotic resistance. Each theme is illustrated with extracts from the focus groups and interviews, identified by pseudonym, age, gender, practice and level of antibiotic use. The data presented reflect the full range of expressed views.

### Theme 1. Uncertainty about antibiotic resistance and MRSA: 'bacteria becoming resistant' or 'bodies becoming immune'?

We identified a great deal of uncertainty among participants concerning antibiotic resistance, with over a quarter of the sample having never heard the term. Of the remaining participants, many found it difficult to explain what antibiotic resistance is, what causes it and its implications for patients. In contrast, all participants were familiar with the term MRSA and many had strong views about the incidence of MRSA in hospitals. However, when probed many were unsure about what MRSA was and how it affects people.

There was confusion for many participants about whether antibiotic resistance refers to the body or to bacteria becoming resistant to antibiotics (Box 1). Only a minority (six participants, five of whom were from the more affluent practice) described antibiotic resistance as bacteria developing resistance to a particular antibiotic or group of antibiotics over time. The more common understanding was that of bodily 'immunity', namely the body becoming immune or resistant to antibiotics through antibiotic use. Many believed that being personally resistant to antibiotics might lead one to need a different type of antibiotic or a stronger dose in the future. Furthermore, participants commonly perceived a relationship between their level of antibiotic use and their personal risk of developing immunity. Consequently, long-term users of antibiotics within the sample expressed more concern about developing immunity to antibiotics than those who used them less frequently.

MRSA was primarily seen as a hospital-based problem, with very few participants recognizing that it could also affect people in the community. A common understanding of MRSA was an infection that occurs in open wounds following

---

**Box 1** *Definitions of antibiotic resistance and MRSA*

### The body as resistant

'I suppose it's a point where your body is just sort of saying well look I've had enough, you know I've had all these different things and it's just saying you know, it's just becoming immune and not you know accepting them, that's the way I understand it' (53-year-old male, Practice A, more than or equal to four courses).

### Bacteria as resistant

'The bacteria mutate and develop resistance to the, the antibiotic, so that the antibiotics don't work as well, the penicillin and methicillin or whatever that we're using doesn't work to, to kill the infections, so the infections carry on' (38-year-old male, Practice B, one to three courses).

### MRSA: the hospital superbug

'It's [MRSA] just a superbug really in hospitals' (35-year-old male, Practice B, 0 courses).

---

surgery. Not all participants associated MRSA with antibiotic resistance. Participants' main sources of information on antibiotic resistance and MRSA were newspapers and television. Some had gained knowledge through personal experience of MRSA (three participants) or knowing somebody who had suffered from resistant infections while in hospital.

None of the participants had heard about antibiotic resistance through public information campaigns and only one participant had been informed about antibiotic resistance by a health professional (a dentist).

### Theme 2. Responsibility and Blame for Antibiotic Resistance and MRSA: 'Irresponsible Others' and 'Responsible Selves'

Ideas about responsibility and blame for antibiotic resistance were common in patients' accounts, although their perspectives on the appropriate targets of blame differed. There were also notable differences in terms of where participants attributed blame for MRSA and antibiotic resistance, respectively.

With regard to antibiotic resistance in general, the majority blamed either 'other' 'irresponsible' patients for misusing or overusing antibiotics, or overprescribing by GPs. The irresponsible patients were characterized as needlessly using antibiotics, failing to complete the course, disposing of unwanted antibiotics inappropriately or giving unused antibiotics to others. When blaming GPs, the majority attributed the problem to past prescribing practices (where antibiotics were 'handed out like sweets') and perceived a change towards more conservative prescribing.

> 'we used to go up and you used to be given antibiotics for that, but they're not giving it to you now. And I think well if, if they're not giving it to you then it's because you don't need it or it won't do any good so . . . they were giving it to you before . . . but not this generation, you know, the doctors before' (54-year-old woman, Practice A, more than or equal to four courses).

A smaller number of participants attributed blame to sources outside of medicine such as the farming industry and veterinary practice, for 'vast overuse of antibiotics'. In contrast, participants were keen to present themselves as responsible users of antibiotics. For example, the majority claimed they would never request antibiotics from their doctor, would not expect to be treated with antibiotics for 'minor complaints' (such as colds, coughs, sore throats and flu) and would be ready to 'listen to advice' from doctors about appropriate antibiotic use.

However, not all participants were willing to apportion blame. Some viewed antibiotic resistance as a process that occurs naturally and is therefore beyond human control. Three participants spoke about bacteria as naturally mutating and developing resistance to the drugs used to control them. Bacteria were anthropomorphized, being described as 'clever' and 'always one step ahead'. As one participant said: 'it's nature's way of beating us' (66-year-old woman, Practice A, one to three courses).

In contrast, as MRSA was mainly perceived to be a hospital-based problem, blame was largely directed at hospital management and, to a lesser degree, doctors, nurses and cleaners. Some individuals blamed nurses for specific behaviors that could spread infections and bacteria, for example, wearing their uniforms outside of the hospital or not ensuring that visitors adhere to hand-washing procedures. The government was also identified as indirectly to blame because of organizational changes within the National Health Service, such as the introduction of contract cleaners, resulting in inadequate cleaning. Within-participants accounts of the decline of hospital cleanliness were ideas about the erosion of authority and discipline within hospitals, which was seen to exacerbate such problems. There was much nostalgia, particularly among older participants, for a past when hospitals were portrayed as more hygienic and order was maintained by the authoritarian matron figure.

> Sylvia: Well, the staff in the hospitals, they're not as hygienic as they should be. When my husband was in a while back, this is in the heart ward, the person coming round with the tablets was coughing into her hand and then straight away putting . . .

> Steve: Well yeah

> Sylvia: . . . out the drugs for people

> Barbara: . . . for cleanliness

> Vera: These nurses aren't very clean are they?

> Sylvia: No

> Barbara: I mean years ago they were impeccable weren't they?

> Steve: Well that's because of the matron wasn't it? They used to check.

> (Focus Group 1, Practice A).

### Theme 3. Implications of antibiotic resistance: individual and societal risk

There was uncertainty among participants concerning the implications of antibiotic resistance both for individuals and the wider community. All were unclear about the potential impact of their personal antibiotic use on their own or their community's health. Some long-term users of antibiotics expressed concern about developing personal immunity:

> 'I'm scared that I'm going to get to a stage where antibiotics aren't . . . you know . . . I'm going to get immune to what I'm taking and need something stronger and more aggressive' (48-year-old woman, Practice A, more than or equal to four courses).

However, the majority did not perceive a relationship between their individual consumption of antibiotics and the development of antibiotic resistance in the community. They did not consider themselves to be at risk, because they either portrayed themselves as 'responsible' users of antibiotics or perceived that they had not consumed sufficient quantities of antibiotics for their bodies to build up resistance and become 'immune'. Thus, participants largely personalized the risk and reflected little on the extent to which antibiotic resistance is a community problem or one that should concern the general public.

Only a very small minority expressed concern about the consequences of resistant bacteria for society as a whole. Certain participants articulated concerns that antibiotic resistance could increasingly lead to particular infections becoming untreatable, with far reaching implications. While participants generally felt that resistance was being 'dealt with' sufficiently to avoid the occurrence of major problems, possible apocalyptic futures of a world where antibiotic resistance was rife were present in some accounts, with phrases like 'hell like', 'epidemic', 'could wipe out mankind' and 'genocide'.

In contrast, MRSA featured much more highly in participants' accounts as a possible threat to their personal health. The majority perceived MRSA as a very serious problem; several said it was something they worried about in general, with such feelings intensifying if they or a family member had to go into hospital. Such views were fuelled by media stories about the incidence of MRSA in hospitals. Nonetheless, others said that concerns about MRSA would not be prominent in their minds if, or when, they went into hospital and some described positive personal experiences of hospital care and hygiene that contradicted media accounts. A minority were skeptical about the threat posed by MRSA and felt that the television and news media exaggerated the danger.

### Theme 4. Possible solutions: tackling the problem of resistance

Participants had differing ideas concerning possible solutions to antibiotic resistance and MRSA. Most believed that individual patients could play only a minimal role in tackling the problem of resistance as it was largely outside of their control. They felt they did not have the knowledge to personally contribute to the solution: 'I think that's truly something that is a medical matter, that ordinary people . . . haven't got the knowledge' (66-year-old woman, Practice A, more than or equal to four courses). While suggesting that it was important that (other) patients limit their use of antibiotics, none of the participants felt that they needed to reduce their own antibiotic use.

As a result of their uncertainty about antibiotic resistance and the perception of irresponsible antibiotic use among other patients, participants commonly identified the need for further public education about resistance. A small number of participants felt that improving hospital hygiene (such as hand washing) could help prevent antibiotic resistance by limiting the spread of bacteria in the first instance. Reducing GP antibiotic prescribing was identified as another important area, though, as noted previously, many participants felt that this had largely been addressed. Participants placed strong faith in medicine and science, emphasizing the role of scientific research in providing the solution to antibiotic resistance, although there was ambiguity about the nature of those solutions:

> 'It's just all down to science I think . . . they just have to research and come up with answers don't they. They have to come up with the answers, I don't see any other possibility' (69-year-old woman, Practice A, one to three courses).

# DISCUSSION

## SUMMARY OF MAIN FINDINGS

This qualitative analysis suggests that there is uncertainty among patients concerning the nature and implications of antibiotic resistance. While some patients viewed it as a problem for wider society, most did not see it as something that would affect them personally or something they could control and therefore did not perceive a reason to modify their own individual antibiotic use. The characterization of antibiotic resistance as the 'body becoming immune' served to reinforce the view of antibiotic resistance as an individual problem (for patients who 'overuse' antibiotics) rather than one that can spread between individuals and so impact on the wider community. In seeking to explain the causes of antibiotic resistance, blame was primarily attributed to other patients who used antibiotics 'irresponsibly', GPs who had overprescribed antibiotics in the past and in the case of MRSA, poor hospital hygiene. There was strong faith in science and medicine to provide the solution to the problem of resistance.

## COMPARISON WITH THE LITERATURE

To our knowledge, perceptions of antibiotic resistance have only been explored in one other qualitative study using members of the public, in whom previous antibiotic use was not known.[16] That study reported a number of findings congruent with our data, most importantly, uncertainty about the causes of antibiotic resistance and the lack of individual responsibility for its control. Together, our data suggest that patients are either largely unaware of, or choosing to ignore, antibiotic resistance and its implications. This, combined with evidence that primary care clinicians regard the problem as clinically unimportant,[11,22] suggests that neither patients nor doctors are likely to raise this significant public health problem in the consultation.

Our findings are in line with survey data, which demonstrate relatively low levels of awareness and concern about the consequences of antibiotic resistance among the public. In a Scottish survey in 2000, 45% of respondents stated that they were not concerned about antibiotic resistance.[23] However, in a recent large British household survey, only 19% of respondents were not concerned about antibiotic resistance, suggesting an increased awareness through media publicity and public information campaigns.[24]

Our findings are also consistent with secondary care research that has reported uncertainty and confusion about MRSA among hospital patients and visitors.[19,20,25,26] Crucially, however, these studies have not explored patients' understandings of antibiotic resistance beyond hospital-acquired MRSA, their beliefs about responsibility and blame and the impact this may have on their expectations for antibiotics. These are gaps that our findings begin to address.

Previous research has demonstrated that information about antibiotics and antibiotic resistance supplied through community-wide campaigns, videos and the Internet can increase knowledge about antibiotic resistance and reduce patient expectations for antibiotics.[14,27–29] However, until recently, UK-based public education campaigns, such as 'Not all bugs need drugs', did not include information regarding antibiotic resistance, possibly explaining in part why our study patients knew so little about it. This is being addressed by the UK Department of Health, which launched a follow-up campaign in February 2008 called 'Getting better without antibiotics.'[30] This aims to maintain awareness about the role of antibiotics and has included some information regarding antibiotic resistance. In contrast, campaigns in the US ('Get Wise') and the European Union have long been including information about the dangers of antibiotic resistance.

## INTERPRETING OUR FINDINGS USING ATTRIBUTION THEORY

Many of our findings, notably those concerning patients' views of responsibility and blame for antibiotic resistance and MRSA, the implications of resistance and possible solutions, can largely be predicted by Attribution theory, a theoretical framework from Social Psychology.[31–33] It is useful to draw on this theory as it aids insightful explanation of the findings and permits the development of ideas about a theoretical framework for future interventions.

In simple terms, Attribution theory is concerned with how people explain events or behaviour (that of themselves or others) by attributing causes. It suggests that when people offer explanations about why things have happened, they offer one of two types: an external or an internal attribution. An external or 'situational' attribution assigns causality to an 'outside factor' (e.g. others, chance); by contrast, an internal or 'dispositional' attribution assigns causality to factors 'within the person' (the self).

Applying this theory to our findings, when seeking to explain why antibiotic resistance has developed, patients tended to make external attributions. They did not view themselves as potentially personally responsible; instead, they blamed others, attributing the cause of resistance to outside factors such as overprescribing of antibiotics by GPs in the past or irresponsible use of antibiotics by others. Similarly, in terms of MRSA, participants attributed causality to outside factors, such as poor hospital cleanliness and lack of attention to hygiene (e.g. hand washing) by others visiting hospitals, rather than seeing their own behaviour regarding antibiotics as a potential contributory factor to the societal problem of MRSA.

In addition, our finding that patients did not feel they could contribute to or control the development of antibiotic resistance or its solutions mirrors the concept of controllability suggested by Attribution theorists.[32,33] Controllability contrasts causes that one can control (such as one's own actions) from causes one cannot control (such as others' actions and 'chance'). In our study, patients tended to perceive the causes of antibiotic resistance as outside their control and put faith in external factors (science and medicine) to produce solutions to the problem.

Finally, the tendency of patients in our study to present themselves as responsible users of antibiotics reflects ideas within Attribution theory about motivations for attributions. Kelley and Michela[31] argue that there are motivations behind peoples' attributions, which largely derive from a concern to present the self in a positive light. In our study, participants tended to attribute positive behaviours to themselves (e.g. appropriate use of antibiotics), potentially motivated by the desire to present themselves favourably as responsible patients. Conversely, they tended to blame others for antibiotic resistance by attributing negative behaviour to them (e.g. irresponsible use of antibiotics by other patients or overprescribing of antibiotics by GPs), arguably motivated by self-protection.

## IMPLICATIONS FOR CLINICAL PRACTICE AND FUTURE INTERVENTION DEVELOPMENT

If antibiotic resistance is to be included among the issues that impact upon patient–clinician decisions about antibiotic use, then there is an urgent need for patient-based interventions, especially in the UK. Our data suggest that better information regarding what antibiotic resistance is and what it does could go some way to reduce public uncertainty. Drawing on Attribution theory to explain our findings, we suggest that a future intervention should also encourage patients first, to consider why antibiotic resistance develops (what is causing it?) and second, should include a dimension that assigns causality/responsibility to individuals (an internal attribution) rather than to others—that is, take into account the internal versus external attributions that patients may be making.

For example, such an intervention would encourage patients to think of antibiotic resistance as within their control and part of their personal responsibility. This is more likely to have an impact on patients' behaviour than an intervention that focuses on external factors that need to change. For example, '*You* are a person who uses antibiotics responsibly and you are helping to reduce resistance' rather than '*Your doctor* needs to be able to reduce prescribing of antibiotics'. Such an approach would also capitalize on the tendency of patients to present themselves as responsible users of antibiotics.

Future research should work with patients to develop such an intervention, for example guided by principles within the Medical Research Council's complex intervention framework.[34] Until such time, clinicians should probably not cite antibiotic resistance as a reason to withhold antibiotic treatment unless sufficient time is available to explore with the patient what it is, what causes it and how the patient's behaviour may contribute to the solution.

## STRENGTHS AND LIMITATIONS

The study strengths are that by using maximum variation sampling techniques, we were able to map the range of views of antibiotic resistance and MRSA held by primary care patients with differing characteristics, particularly previous levels of antibiotic use. The use of focus groups enabled us to examine patients' perspectives as generated through interaction with others, which mirrors (at least in part) how views are formed in everyday life. Combining focus groups with interviews allowed us to both explore the breadth of perspectives among patients and probe issues in depth. Both interviews and focus groups produce public accounts with patients presenting themselves as responsible users of antibiotics. A public information campaign and other future interventions would need to address this important barrier. Use of a theoretical framework (Attribution theory) helped to enhance our explanation of the findings and enabled us to consider the implications for developing theoretically informed interventions.

Limitations are that there were certain patient groups under-represented in our sample, notably younger men from lower socio-economic groups, and the views of these and the participants not responding to our study invitation may differ from those who did. However, with respect to our main findings, it seems unlikely that either young men or non-respondents would have higher levels of awareness of antibiotic resistance than our sample. The patients were drawn from two practices in one city in the south of England. However, our results mirror closely results from another country,[14] suggesting that our findings are relevant internationally.

## CONCLUSIONS

Many primary care patients are unaware of what antibiotic resistance is and how it arises. The causes of, and responsibility for, antibiotic resistance are usually attributed to external rather than personal factors and patients perceive that its solutions are outside of their control.

## DECLARATION

Funding: Royal College of General Practitioners (SFB/2005/16); South West General Practice Trust.

Ethical approval: We received ethical approval from the Southmead Research Ethics Committee (05/Q2002/105).

Conflicts of interest: None declared.

## ACKNOWLEDGMENTS

We thank all patients who took part in the research. We also thank staff at both practices for their support for the study, notably Ann Boote and Dr Michael Rossdale who assisted with the patient searches and mailing of information packs. This study was based in the Academic Unit of Primary Health Care, University of Bristol, which is a member of the National Institute for Health Research (NIHR) School for Primary Care Research. The NIHR School for Primary Care Research is a partnership between the Universities of Birmingham, Bristol, Cambridge, Manchester and Oxford. Contributors: ADH, AS and DS designed the study and secured the funding. LB conducted the focus groups and interviews, led the analysis (supported by AS and ADH) and drafted the manuscript. All authors contributed to and approved the final draft. ADH is the guarantor.

## FOOTNOTES

- Brooks L, Shaw A, Sharp D and Hay AD. Towards a better understanding of patients' perspectives of antibiotic resistance and MRSA: a qualitative study. *Family Practice* 2008; 25: 341–348.
- © The Author 2008. Published by Oxford University Press. All rights reserved. For permissions, please e-mail: journals.permissions@oxfordjournals.org.

## REFERENCES

1. Wise R, Hart T, Cars O, et al. Antimicrobial resistance: is a major threat to public health. *BMJ. 1998;317*:609–610.
2. Standing Medical Advisory Committee. *The Path of Least Resistance.* London: Department of Health; 1998.
3. Glasziou PP, Del Mar CB, Sanders SL, Hayem M. Antibiotics for acute otitis media in children. *Cochrane Database of Systematic Reviews 2003, Issue 4. Art. No.: CD000219. 2002.* doi: 10.1002/14651858.CD000219.pub2.
4. Del Mar CB, Glasziou PP, Spinks AB. *The Cochrane Library, Issue 2 2004.* Chichester, UK: John Wiley & Sons, Ltd; Antibiotics for sore throat *(Cochrane Review).*
5. Fahey T, Smucny J, Becker L, Glazier R. *Cochrane Database of Systematic Reviews. 2004.* Antibiotics for acute bronchitis. *Issue 3. Art. No.: CD000245.* doi: 10.1002/14651858 .CD000245.pub2.
6. Coenen S, Van Royen P, Vermeire E, Hermann I, Denekens J. Antibiotics for coughing in general practice: a qualitative decision analysis. *Fam Pract. 2000;*17:380–385.
7. Macfarlane J, Holmes W, Macfarlane R, Britten N. Influence of patients' expectations on antibiotic management of acute lower respiratory tract illness in general practice: questionnaire study. *BMJ. 1997;315*:1211–1214.
8. Britten N, Ukoumunne O. The influence of patients' hopes of receiving a prescription on doctors' perceptions and the decision to prescribe: a questionnaire survey [see comments]. *BMJ. 1997;315*:1506–1510.
9. Linder JA, Singer DE. Desire for antibiotics and antibiotic prescribing for adults with upper respiratory tract infections. *J Gen Intern Med. 2003;18*:795–801.
10. Altiner A, Knauf A, Moebes J, Sielk M, Wilm S. Acute cough: a qualitative analysis of how GPs manage the consultation when patients explicitly or implicitly expect antibiotic prescriptions. *Fam Pract. 2004;21*:500–506.
11. Butler CC, Rollnick S, Pill R, Maggs-Rapport F, Stott N. Understanding the culture of prescribing: qualitative study of general practitioners' and patients' perceptions of antibiotics for sore throats. *BMJ. 1998;317*:637–642.
12. Stivers T. Parent resistance to physicians' treatment recommendations: one resource for initiating a negotiation of the treatment decision. *Health Commun. 2005;18*(1):41–74.
13. Butler CC, Kinnersley P, Prout H, Rollnick S, Edwards A, Elwyn G. Antibiotics and shared decision-making in primary care. *J Antimicrob Chemother. 2001;48*(3):435–440.

14. Madle G, Kostkova P, Mani-Saada J, Weinberg J, Williams P. Changing public attitudes to antibiotic prescribing: can the internet help? *Inform Prim Care.* *2004;12*:19–26.

15. Health Education Board. Not all Bugs Need Drugs—a Guide to the Safe Use of Antibiotics. 2005. Health Education Board for Scotland.

16. Hawkings NJ, Wood F, Butler CC. Public attitudes towards bacterial resistance: a qualitative study. *J Antimicrob Chemother. 2007;59*(6):1155–1160.

17. Darzi AV. Our NHS Our Future: NHS Next Stage Review Interim Report. London: Department of Health; 2007.

18. Gill J, Kumar R, Todd J, Wiskin C. Methicillin-resistant Staphylococcus aureus: awareness and perceptions. *J Hosp Infect. 2006;62*(3):333–337.

19. Hamour SM, O'Bichere A, Peters JL, McDonald PJ. Patient perceptions of MRSA. *Ann R Coll Surg Engl. 2003;85*(2):123–125.

20. Newton JT, Constable D, Senior V. Patients' perceptions of methicillin-resistant Staphylococcus aureus and source isolation: a qualitative analysis of source-isolated patients. *J Hosp Infect. 2001;48*(4):275–280.

21. Ritchie J, Spencer L, O'Connor W. *Qualitative Research Practice: A Guide for Social Science Students and Researchers.* London: Sage; 2003.

22. Kumar S, Little P, Britten N. Why do general practitioners prescribe antibiotics for sore throat? Grounded theory interview study. *BMJ. 2003;326*:138.

23. Emslie MJ, Bond CM. Public knowledge, attitudes and behaviour regarding antibiotics—a survey of patients in general practice. *Eur J Gen Pract. 2003;9*:84–90.

24. McNulty CAM, Boyle P, Nichols T, Clappison P, Davey P. Don't wear me out—the public's knowledge of and attitudes to antibiotic use. *J Antimicrob Chemother. 2007;59*(4):727–738.

25. Criddle P, Potter J. Exploring patients' views on colonisation with meticillin-resistant Staphylococcus aureus. *Br J Infect Control. 2006;7*:24–28.

26. Duncan CP, Dealey C. Patients' feelings about hand washing, MRSA status and patient information. *Br J Nurs. 2007;16*:34–38.

27. Perz JF, Craig AS, Coffey CS, et al. Changes in antibiotic prescribing for children after a community-wide campaign. *JAMA. 2002;287*:3103–3109.

28. Bauchner H, Osganian S, Smith K, Triant R. Improving parent knowledge about antibiotics: a video intervention. *Pediatrics. 2001;108*(4):845–850.

29. Wheeler JG, Fair M, Simpson PM, Rowlands LA, Aitken ME, Jacobs RF. Impact of a waiting room videotape message on parent attitudes toward pediatric antibiotic use. *Pediatrics. 2001;108*(3):591–596.

30. Department of Health. *Getting Better Without Antibiotics.* London: DH Publications; 2008.

31. Kelley HH, Michela JL. Attribution theory and research. *Annu Rev Psychol. 1980;31*: 457–501.

32. Weiner B. *An Attribution Theory of Motivation and Emotion.* New York: Springer; 1986.

33. Weiner B. *Judgements of Responsibility.* New York: Guildford Press; 1995.

34. Campbell M, Fitzpatrick R, Haines A, et al. Framework for design and evaluation of complex interventions to improve health. *BMJ. 2000;321*:694–696.

# CHAPTER ACTIVITY QUESTIONS

**1.** What were the four "themes" or reasons attributed to the development of MRSA?

**2.** How did these compare to the reasons you identified during your brainstorming session?

**3.** Which of the Attribution Theory constructs explain the cause of MRSA?

# CHAPTER REFERENCES

Carpenter, K.M., Hasin, D.S., Allsion, D.B., & Faith, M.S. (2000). Relationships between obesity and DSM-IV major depressive disorder, suicide ideation, and suicide attempts: Results from a general population study. *American Journal of Public Health, 90*(2), 251–257.

Crandall, C.S., & Schiffauer, K.L. (1998). Anti-fat prejudice: Beliefs, values and American culture. *Obesity Research, 6*, 458–460.

Graham, S. (2006). Peer victimization in school. *Current Directions in Psychological Science, 15*(6), 317–321.

Kearsley, G. (2006). Attribution Theory. In *Explorations in Learning & Instruction: The Theory into Practice Database*. Retrieved December 8, 2007, from http://tip.psychology.org/weiner.html.

Kneckt, M.C., & Knuuttila, M.L.E. (2000). Attributions to dental and diabetes health outcomes. *Journal of Clinical Periodontics, 27*, 205–211.

Levenson, H. (1974). Activism and powerful others: Distinctions within the concept of internal-external control. *Journal of Personality Assessment, 38*, 377–383.

McDonell, J.R. (1993). Judgments of personal responsibility for HIV infection: An attributional analysis. *Social Work, 38*(4), 403–410.

Newall, N.E., Chipperfield, J.G., Clifton, R.A., Perry, R.P. & Swift, A.U. (2009). Causal beliefs, social participation, and loneliness among older adults: A longitudinal study. *Journal of Social and Personal Relationships, 26*(2-3), 273–290.

Puhl, R., & Brownell, K.D. (2001). Obesity, bias and discrimination. *Obesity Research, 9*, 788–805.

Puhl, R., & Brownell, K.D. (2003). Psychosocial origins of obesity stigma: Toward changing a powerful and pervasive bias. *Obesity Reviews, 4*, 213–227.

Robert, R. (1982, November 24). Malavasi questions character of some, says coaching is tough. *Los Angeles Times*, Pt. 3, p. 3.

Rosenbaum, R.M. (1972). *A Dimensional Analysis of the Perceived Causes of Success and Failure*. Doctoral dissertation, University of California, Los Angeles.

Rotter, J.B. (1966). Generalized expectancies for internal versus external control of reinforcement. *Psychological Monograph, 80*, 1–28.

Rotter, J.B. (1993). Expectancies. In C.E. Walker (Ed.), *The History of Clinical Psychology in Autobiography* (Vol. II, pp. 273–284). Pacific Grove, CA: Brooks/Cole.

Seneviratne, H., & Saunders, B. (2000). An investigation of alcohol dependent respondents' attributions for their own and "others" relapses. *Addiction Research*, 8(5), 439–453.

Strickland, B.R. (Ed.). (2006). Fritz Heider. In *Encyclopedia of Psychology* (2nd ed.). Retrieved December 7, 2007, from http://www.enotes.com/gale-psychology-encyclopedia/fritz-heider.

Wang, S. (2001). Motivation: General overview of theories. In M. Orey (Ed.), *Emerging Perspectives on Learning, Teaching, and Technology*. Retrieved November 27, 2005, from http://www.coe.uga.edu/epltt/Motivation.htm.

Weiner, B. (1985). An attributional theory of achievement motivation and emotion. *Psychological Review*, 92(4), 548–573.

Weiner, B. (2010). The development of an attribution-based theory of motivation: A history of ideas. *Educational Psychologist*, 45(1), 28–36.

Wiegmann, S.M., & Berven, N.L. (1998). Health locus-of-control beliefs and improvement in physical functioning in a work-hardening, return-to-work program. *Rehabilitation Psychology*, 43(2), 83–100.

# Transtheoretical Model

## STUDENT LEARNING OUTCOMES

At the end of this chapter the student will be able to:

- Explain the conceptual basis of the Transtheoretical Model.
- Describe the five different stages of change.
- Explain the ten processes of change.
- Analyze decisional balance.
- Use the theory to explain the adoption of a common health behavior.

## THEORY ESSENCE SENTENCE

Behavior change is a process that occurs in stages.

---

**Transtheoretical Model Constructs Chart**

---

**Stages of change:**
Pre-contemplation, contemplation, preparation, action, maintenance

**Decisional balance:**
Weighting the pros and cons of the change

**Processes of change:**
Consciousness raising, dramatic relief or emotional arousal, environmental reevaluation, social liberation, self-reevaluation, stimulus control, helping relationships, counter conditioning, reinforcement management, and self-liberation

**Self-efficacy:**
One's belief in one's own ability to do something

---

# IN THE BEGINNING

The Transtheoretical Model (TTM) was developed in the early 1980s as a way to understand how people change their behavior—in particular, change associated with addictive behaviors such as smoking, drug use, and alcohol abuse. Research consistently showed that people were successful in changing behaviors not only through therapeutic intervention (psychotherapy), but also by themselves (self-change) (Prochaska, DiClemente, & Norcross, 1992).

Although there was ample research documenting the effectiveness of both therapeutic intervention and self-change, the research did not show *how* the changes occurred – that is, the process by which these changes occurred was not understood. Thus, the transtheoretical model/stages of change sought to answer the following question, "Because successful change of complex addictions can be demonstrated in both psychotherapy and self-change, are there basic common principles that can reveal the structure of change occurring with and without psychotherapy?" (Prochaska, Diclemente, & Norcross, 1992, p. 1102). Research conducted to answer this revealed that there were commonalities in how people went about changing regardless of the behavior being changed or the method used. This resulted in identification of 10 processes of change that answered the question of *how* change occurs as people progress through the different stages of change (Prochaska, Diclemente, & Norcross, 1992).

# THEORETICAL CONCEPT

The Transtheoretical Model proposes that behavior change is a process that occurs in stages. As people attempt to change their behavior, they move through a variety of stages using different processes to help them get from one stage to the next until the desired behavior is attained. Thus, the theory is also known as Stages of Change.

# THEORETICAL CONSTRUCTS

The constructs of the theory include not only the stages of change, but also the processes of change and self-efficacy. Analyzing behavior change from these perspectives is helpful when trying to understand why some people are successful at changing behavior and others are not.

## STAGES OF CHANGE

There are five stages of change: pre-contemplation, contemplation, preparation, action, and maintenance. Each has its own distinct characteristics and timeframe and builds upon the preceding stage.

### Pre-contemplation

The first stage of change is pre-contemplation. People are in this stage from 6 months prior to the point they begin thinking about making a change in their behavior to when they actually begin thinking about changing. People in this "pre-thinking stage" either don't recognize they have a behavior needing change or are just not ready to change a behavior they know they should (Prochaska, DiClemente, & Norcross, 1992).

Among the possible reasons for people being in the pre-contemplation stage are being uninformed or underinformed about the negative consequence of continuing a behavior or about the benefits of changing the behavior (Cancer Prevention Research Center [CPRC], n.d.; Velicer et al., 1998). We see this with older adults and exercise behavior. Some older adults view exercise as a behavior for the young and believe it is not good for people with certain health conditions (Lach, Everard, Highstein, & Brownson, 2004). Clearly, this is a case where being uninformed explains why change to a healthy behavior, exercise, is avoided. A change in this behavior will not begin until the uninformed are informed that exercise is beneficial at any age and is not restricted by most health conditions.

Another reason why people are in the pre-contemplation stage is past experience. People who have tried in the past but failed to change a behavior give no thought to changing the behavior again. This is often the case with cigarette smokers, who say, "Quitting is easy, I've done it a million times before," or with people who have lost weight only to regain it.

Knowing why people might be in the pre-contemplation stage is useful when trying to understand why unhealthy behaviors are not changed. The goal is to take this information and assist them in moving forward from not thinking about changing their behavior to contemplating, or thinking about, changing.

## Contemplation

When people move from pre-contemplation to contemplation it means they recognize there is a problem and they are starting to think about changing. A myriad of things can get people to start thinking about changing their behavior. Examples include newspapers, magazines, TV, Internet, Twitter, news reports, family, friends, health care professionals, and so on.

In order to move out of the "thinking" mode, a decision has to be made to either proceed with the change or not. This is *decisional balance*, the process of weighing the perceived pros and cons or costs and benefits of the new behavior against the old (Prochaska, 1994). Since the weight or strength of the pros and cons is determined by individual assessment, the length of time needed to make a decision varies, and can be prolonged. In the case of cigarette smokers, for instance, some remain in this decisional stage for as long as 2 years (DiClemente & Prochaska, 1985). In the case of domestic abuse, decisional balance can result in a woman deciding to remain in an abusive situation. This happens when the cons of leaving are stronger than the pros (Burke, Denison, Gielen, McDonnell, & O'Campo, 2004). The cons, or reasons for not leaving, may include not wanting to lose the relationship (even though it is abusive), financial dependency, emotional need, or low self-esteem. Often, it is only after the safety of her children is factored in as a reason for leaving (pro) that the woman is able to leave (Burke et al., 2004).

Typically, we want to explain how people change behavior from one that hinders health to one that enhances health; for example, from smoking to quitting smoking, from not exercising to exercising, from not practicing safer sex to using condoms correctly and consistently. The decisional balance in these situations weighs the pros of changing to the "healthier" behavior against the cons of changing to the new behavior, or continuing in the old behavior. Unfortunately, not all health behavior change is a change to a healthier behavior. For example, the same stages of change and decisional balance can be applied to the behavior change that results in androgenic-anabolic steroid use. The decisional balance here is to weigh the pros of *using* androgenic-anabolic steroids against the cons of using them. Pros (of using them) might be increased strength, power, and self-confidence (Leone, Gray, Rossi, & Colandreo, 2008). The cons of using them might be side effects, cost, and illegality.

Typically, once people start thinking about changing their behavior, they usually make a decision and plan to make the change within 6 months. However, this does not hold true for everyone in all situations. Some people get stuck in "thinking" mode for extended periods of time—some for years—without being able to make a decision about changing their behavior. (DiClemente, Schlundt, & Gemmell, 2004; Prochaska, DiClemente, & Norcross, 1992). When it takes more than 6 months to make a decision, this is behavioral procrastination or chronic contemplation (CPRC, n.d.; Velicer et al., 1998).

## Preparation

The preparation stage begins once the decision to change the behavior is made. Preparation is a short stage, lasting only about 1 month, since once people decide to change a behavior, they are often anxious to get started. This preparation time is used to make a plan, obtain any tools needed, learn new skills (CPRC, n.d.; Velicer et al., 1998), acquire resources of money or support, housing, and whatever else is necessary for the change to occur.

In the case of a smoker, preparation may mean setting a quit date, obtaining a prescription for a nicotine patch, or signing up for a smoking cessation program (**Figure 6–1**). For a woman at risk of osteoporosis, preparation may mean

**FIGURE 6–1** Preparation includes setting a quit date

learning exercises to prevent bone loss, attending a lecture on new treatments (Lach et al., 2004), buying weights or new sneakers, or developing an exercise plan. For the student who wants to eat healthier, it may mean buying a cookbook, developing a weekly menu, and going grocery shopping.

The preparation stage for the athlete who decides to use anabolic steroids includes talking to others who already take steroids (to find a source of steroids [a dealer]), getting supplies (Leone, Gray, Rossi, & Colandreo 2008), and if they are injectable, learning how to administer them.

## Action

Once preparation is complete, the action stage begins. This is when the plan is put into action. However, just because there is action does not necessarily mean the behavior will change. Action and change are not the same thing (Prochaska, DiClemente, & Norcross, 1992). Action is when people are in the active process of modifying their behavior to address the problem they identified in earlier stages. These modifications tend to be observable changes and to be recognized and rewarded by others (Prochaska, DiClemente, & Norcross, 1992).

In order for action to be successful, it needs to be measured against criteria previously determined to reduce the risk of disease. For example, in the case of the smoker, the change that needs to be accomplished is quitting; switching to a low-tar cigarette or cutting down by half is not enough (CPRC, n.d.; Prochaska, DiClemente, & Norcross, 1992). For the woman at risk of osteoporosis, the change that needs to be accomplished is improvement in bone density measurements. For the student who wants to eat healthier, it is the daily consumption of meals that follow My Plate recommendations.

## Maintenance

Maintenance is the final stage of change. During this stage, people work (and sometimes struggle) to prevent relapsing to the old behavior. In general, maintenance begins after 6 months of being in the active stage of changing and continues for at least 6 months. With some behavior changes, maintenance goes on for years (Prochaska, DiClemente, & Norcross, 1992), as is the case with recovering alcoholics.

For some behaviors, such as diet and exercise changes implemented for weight loss, maintaining change is extremely difficult. Although most people who participate in a weight loss program are successful in losing weight (i.e., they make it through the action), almost all regain the weight lost within 5 years (Thomas,

1995); that is, they relapse to their old diet and sedentary behaviors. Therefore, while changing may be difficult, permanently incorporating the new behavior, or the change, into one's lifestyle is the most difficult phase.

## SELF-EFFICACY

The second construct of the TTM is self-efficacy. Self-efficacy plays a major role in how successful people are in changing their behavior and maintaining the change. Remember, self-efficacy is one's confidence in one's own ability to do something. In the context of maintaining a behavior change, it has to do with one's confidence in coping with situations in which there is a high risk of relapse. For example, an ex-smoker would need a great deal of self-efficacy to avoid relapsing to smoking in social situations where alcohol is served or when under financial stress (Borland, 1990; Dijkstra & Borland, 2003; Siahpush & Carlin, 2006). For a disabled person who wants to maintain a change to an active life-style, self-efficacy means having confidence in the ability to overcome barriers to physical activity (Kosma, Gardner, Cardinal, Bauer, & McCubbin, 2006), which may include negotiating public transportation to an exercise facility or park, for example, or wheelchair-inaccessible dressing rooms. For elderly women wanting to maintain physical activity, self-efficacy may mean having confidence in their ability to overcome a lack of energy, motivation, or discomfort with body image (Aubertin-Leheudre, Rousseau, Melancon, Chaput, & Dionne, 2005).

Among college students, self-efficacy is predictive of successful exercise behavior change. It seems that students with greater levels of self-efficacy at the start of an exercise change process are able to maintain their increased exercise levels, while students with less self-efficacy relapse to their old sedentary ways (Sullum, Clark, & King, 2000).

## PROCESSES OF CHANGE

While the stages of change help us understand *when* people change their behavior, the processes of change help us understand *how* change occurs (Prochaska & DiClemente, 1982). There are ten processes of change: consciousness raising, dramatic relief or emotional arousal, environmental reevaluation, social liberation, self-reevaluation, stimulus control, helping relationships, counter conditioning, reinforcement management, and self-liberation (Prochaska & DiClemente, 1983; Prochaska et al., 1988; Velicer et al., 1998).

The ten processes are divided into two groups: cognitive processes and behavioral processes. Consciousness raising, dramatic relief, self-reevaluation, environmental reevaluation, and social liberation are cognitive and stimulus control; helping relationships, counter conditioning, reinforcement management, and self-liberation are behavioral (Prochaska et al., 1988).

## Consciousness Raising

Consciousness raising is the process whereby people obtain information about themselves and the problem behavior. It is the process of becoming aware of the problem and the causes and consequences of continuing a particular behavior (Prochaska, DiClemente, & Norcross, 1992; Velicer et al., 1998). Using fast food as an example, consciousness raising might be evidenced by a person saying, "I didn't realize fast food was so bad for me until I saw *Super Size Me* and *Fast Food Nation*." This awareness may help move a person from pre-contemplation to contemplation. Or, it may have been the nutrition course a student took that provided new insight into his or her poor eating habits.

## Dramatic Relief

Dramatic relief, also referred to as emotional arousal, is being able to express feelings about or react emotionally to the behavior in question (Prochaska, DiClemente, & Norcross, 1992; Velicer et al., 1998) and the possible solutions (Cancer Prevention Research Center, 2004).

For the smoker trying to quit, this process may mean talking about how much one loathes quitting (Andersen & Keller, 2002); for the person who eats fast food, it might be feeling disgusted when viewing fast food commercials on TV.

For some overweight women, being able to talk about their weight problem and their plans for change is what moves them from preparation to action (Hoke & Timmerman, 2011).

## Environmental Reevaluation

The process of environmental reevaluation is looking at the behavior being changed (old behavior) in light of its impact or effect on the physical and social environments (Prochaska, DiClemente, & Norcross, 1992; Velicer et al., 1998). Examples of this process for the smoker who wants to quit smoking is understanding the environmental effects of secondhand smoke (Andersen & Keller,

2002), for the conventional farmer who wants to change to organic farm practices, the environmental damage caused by continued pesticide use, or for the college student who drinks water from plastic bottles but wants to change to a refillable bottle, the environmental impact of using plastic water bottles.

An example of reevaluation of the social environment in light of a behavior change is when the older diabetic woman works to have better control over her blood sugar so her children will worry less about her living alone (Ruggiero, 2000). Or, when sedentary African-American women take into consideration how their lack of physical activity affects the people around them—family, friends (the social environment), and because of this put more effort into being active (Martin et al., 2008).

## Social Liberation

Social liberation is the process whereby options or alternatives are sought that support the new behavior (Prochaska, DiClemente, & Norcross, 1992; Velicer et al., 1998). For the smoker trying to quit, social liberation would be sitting in the nonsmoking section of a restaurant (Andersen & Keller, 2002). For the person who regularly eats fast food, it would mean ordering a salad at a fast food restaurant or, for the former couch potato, planning a vacation at a resort with a gym.

## Self-Reevaluation

Self-reevaluation is the process in which people look at themselves with and without the problem behavior and assess the differences in their self-esteem (Prochaska, DiClemente, & Norcross, 1992; Velicer et al., 1998). For smokers, this process means thinking about themselves as smokers and comparing it to how they feel about themselves as nonsmokers (Andersen & Keller, 2002). For those who regularly eat fast food it means asking "If I stopped eating fast foods, would I be healthier and happier, and would I like myself better?" For sedentary people it may mean evaluating how they would feel about themselves if they exercised, if they would be proud of themselves for adopting a healthier habit.

## Stimulus Control

Stimulus control is when people remove the cues or triggers for the problem behavior from their environment (Prochaska, DiClemente, & Norcross, 1992;

**FIGURE 6–2** Stimulus control may mean avoiding the dessert table at a buffet

Velicer et al., 1998). The person who eats fast food might drive to work on back roads rather than the highway in order to avoid passing fast food restaurants (**Figure 6–2**). The smoker might avoid drinking coffee after dinner and switch to drinking tea, since coffee is a trigger for many smokers. The overeater might stop buying the half-gallon carton of ice cream and switch to the pint-size fruit sorbet instead.

## Helping Relationships

Helping relationships are relationships with people who act as a support system for changing the unwanted, unhealthy behavior (Prochaska, DiClemente, & Norcross, 1992; Velicer et al., 1998). This might be the roommate who agrees to keep only fruit to snack on in the room, or the sponsor in a 12-step program for alcoholics who is there whenever the urge for a drink hits. It can be a neighbor who calls another neighbor at 7 a.m. to confirm they are meeting for their morning walk.

## Counter Conditioning

In counter conditioning, a healthier behavior is substituted for the unhealthy one (Prochaska, DiClemente, & Norcross, 1992; Velicer et al., 1998). Using this process, the person trying to change fast food consumption might bring fruit to eat in the car on the way home from campus, instead of stopping for fries and a soda. The smoker might doodle when talking on the phone rather than smoke a cigarette. The person wanting to add more activity to his or her daily routine might use the stairs rather than the elevator whenever possible.

## Reinforcement Management

The process of reinforcement management has to do with rewards and punishments. Although unwanted behavior can be changed through the fear of punishment or negative consequences (as any child will tell you), rewards for engaging in the targeted behavior are more natural. The reward can be from the person to himself or herself, or from someone else (Prochaska, DiClemente, & Norcross, 1992; Velicer et al., 1998). For example, a reward for not eating fast food during the week might be dinner at a nice restaurant with friends. For the woman who quits smoking, a reward from a significant other might be a bouquet of fresh flowers at the end of every week she doesn't smoke. For the exerciser, it might be a new exercise outfit or sneakers.

## Self-Liberation

When using the process of self-liberation, people choose to change their behavior, believe they can, and commit to making the change (Andersen & Keller, 2002; Burke et al., 2004; Prochaska, DiClemente, & Norcross, 1992). In self-liberation, people free themselves from a behavior in which they no longer choose to engage.

This process is what enables women in abusive relationships to do something about changing their situation. The behavior they choose to change is remaining in an abusive relationship. The commitment they make is to a different lifestyle, one that does not rely on violence as an expression of love (Burke et al., 2004). For the person with chronic obstructive pulmonary disease (COPD), self-liberation is frequently used to change from being inactive to exercising (walking) (Yang & Chen, 2005). For a college student, self-liberation might mean choosing not to drink every night.

## STAGES OF CHANGE AND PROCESSES OF CHANGE

The processes of change help move people through the stages of change. Thus, different processes are used during different stages (**Table 6–1**). The research to

**Table 6–1** Moving Through the Stages of Change

| Transition Between Stages | Processes Used | Possible Intervention Methods |
|---|---|---|
| From pre-contemplation to contemplation | Consciousness raising | Dissemination of reading material that raises awareness of the problem, media campaigns |
| | Seeks new information and gains an understanding of the problem behavior | |
| | Dramatic relief | Psychodrama, encourage grieving for loss of old behavior, role playing, providing opportunities for discussion |
| | Expressing feelings about the problem behavior and potential solutions | |
| | Environmental reevaluation | Empathy training, developing or showing documentaries, role modeling of healthy behavior |
| | Considering how the problem behavior affects the physical and social environment | |
| | Social liberation | Developing advocacy and policy interventions that support the new behavior |
| | Acceptance of the problem-free lifestyle | |
| | Counter conditioning | Developing positive self-statements, stress management programs to minimize stress of change, desensitization activities |
| | Substitutes alternative behaviors for the problem behavior | |
| From contemplation to preparation | Helping relationships | Establishing support or buddy systems, identifying significant "helping" others, including those "helping others" in the program |
| | Accepting the support of caring others while changing the problem behavior | |
| | Self-reevaluation | Conducting value clarification exercises, using imagery, identifying role models |
| | Reappraisal of personal values with respect to the problem behavior and seeing one's self with and without the problem behavior | |
| | Social liberation | Developing advocacy and policy interventions that support the new behavior |
| | Committing to changing the problem behavior, and believing in the ability to change | |

**Table 6–1** (*Continued*)

| Transition Between Stages | Processes Used | Possible Intervention Methods |
|---|---|---|
| | Dramatic relief | Psychodrama, encourage grieving for loss of old behavior, role playing, providing opportunities for discussion |
| | Expressing feelings about the problem behavior and potential solutions | |
| From preparation to action | Self-liberation | Developing behavior change plans, setting goals, making a commitment/contract to change |
| | Committing to changing the problem behavior, and believing in the ability to change | |
| Maintenance | Counter conditioning | Encouraging the use of positive self-statements, stress management programs to minimize stress of change, desensitization activities |
| | Substitutes alternative behaviors for the problem behavior | |
| | Helping relationships | Establishing support or buddy systems, identifying significant "helping" others, including those "helping others" in the program |
| | Accepting the support of caring others while changing the problem behavior | |
| | Reinforcement management | Identifying meaningful rewards. making contracts that lead to rewards |
| | Rewarding oneself or being rewarded by others for making changes | |
| | Stimulus control | Establishing self-help groups, avoidance training, environmental restructuring to support the new behavior and diminish or eliminate the old behavior triggers |
| | Control of situations and other causes which trigger the problem behavior | |

Adapted from the Cancer Prevention Center (2004). *Process of Change*. Available at: http://www.uri.edu/research/cprc/TTM/ProcessesOfChange.htm. Accessed February 11, 2013.

identify the processes used in each stage was originally conducted on smokers and may or may not hold true for all behavior changes (DiClemente et al., 1991; Prochaska, DiClemente, & Norcross, 1992; Fava, Velicer, & Prochaska, 1995).

People in pre-contemplation use processes of change the least as they move from pre-contemplation to contemplation (DiClemente et al., 1991). When processes of change are used, consciousness raising, dramatic relief, and environmental reevaluation (Prochaska, DiClemente, & Norcross, 1992), social liberation (Andersen & Keller, 2002; Marcus, Ross, Selby, Niaura, & Abrams, 1992), and counter conditioning (Andersen & Keller, 2002) are used more than the others. These processes increase awareness of a behavior as being a problem, including talking about the behavior as a problem and looking at how the behavior affects others in the environment.

All of the processes are used as people move through contemplation to preparation, although helping relationships, self-reevaluation, social liberation, and dramatic relief are the ones most associated with this stage (Andersen & Keller, 2002; DiClemente et al., 1991). Using these processes helps people talk with others and express feelings about the change, to look at themselves with respect to the problem behavior, and to look at or evaluate the types of support they have available in their social environments.

In moving from preparation to action, self-liberation is the most important process (Andersen & Keller, 2002; DiClemente et al., 1991; Marcus et al., 1992). Self-liberation makes sense in this stage because this is the point at which people are ready to actually do something about changing their behavior. Logically, they need to make a commitment to act before they take action.

In maintenance, the processes of counter conditioning, helping relationships, reinforcement management, and stimulus control are used most often (DiClemente et al., 1991). These enable people to sustain the new behaviors, have supportive people available, avoid triggers for the problem behavior that may cause relapse, and be rewarded for changing.

In summary, according to the Transtheoretical Model, behavior change occurs in stages with specific processes moving the change along.

# THEORY IN ACTION—CLASS ACTIVITY

In a small group, make a list of the modifiable risk factors for cardiovascular disease you learned in previous classes. Then, think about your own behavior in relation to these risk factors. Which one are you in the process of changing or would you like to change? Share your answer with the others in the group. At what stage of change are you each in relative to changing the risk factor behavior? Thinking about the stages of change, what would you need to move you along in the stages of change?

Now read the following article and answer the questions at the end.

# Chapter 6 Article: Change for Life/ *Cambia tu vida:* A Health Promotion Program Based on the Stages of Change Model for African Descendent and Latino Adults in New Hampshire[1]

*Ryan, A; Smith, C.*

## Abstract

Studies have shown that diabetes and cardiovascular disease can be controlled and prevented through the modification of behavioral risk factors. The transtheoretical model of behavior change, also known as the *stages of change* model, offers promise for designing behavior change interventions. However, this model has rarely been applied in group settings with minority communities. To address racial and ethnic disparities related to the risk for diabetes and cardiovascular disease, the New Hampshire REACH 2010 Initiative has designed and implemented Change for Life/ *Cambia tu vida*, a health promotion program based on the stages of change model for African descendent and Latino residents of southern New Hampshire. The program guides participants through the five stages of change and provides resources to support healthy behavior change. We also sponsor periodic class reunions that help program graduates to maintain these healthy habits. This article describes curriculum development, participant feedback, and early pretest and posttest evaluation results from a standardized assessment.

## REDUCING RISK FACTORS FOR DIABETES AND CARDIOVASCULAR DISEASE AMONG MINORITY POPULATIONS

Diabetes and cardiovascular disease and the complications resulting from these diseases disproportionately affect racial and ethnic minority populations, particularly

[1] Reproduced from Ryan, A. & Smith, C. (2006). Change for life/*Cambia tu vida*: A health promotion program based on the stages of change model for African descendent and Latino adults in New Hampshire. *Preventing Chronic Disease*, 3(3), available from http://www.cdc .gov/pcd/issues/2006/jul/05_0218.htm. Accessed February 11, 2013.

blacks and Latinos. The Racial and Ethnic Approaches to Community Health (REACH) 2010 Risk Factor Survey, conducted in 21 minority communities in the United States, showed that median prevalence rates of diabetes were 12.5% among blacks and 11.4% among Hispanics, compared with 6.1% among the general population in the United States (1). Similarly, median prevalence rates of cardiovascular disease were 9.4% among blacks and 8.3% among Latinos, compared with 7.6% among the general population (1).

Although diabetes and cardiovascular disease pose serious health risks, several studies have shown that these diseases can be controlled and prevented through modification of risk factors (2-4). The Diabetes Prevention Program established that modification of eating and exercise habits decreases the probability that individuals with impaired glucose tolerance will develop type 2 diabetes (2). Similarly, evidence from the Framingham Heart Study indicates that overweight, smoking, lack of exercise, and unhealthy eating habits are all related to the development of heart disease (3) and that the modification of these risk factors can reduce mortality rates from heart disease (4).

As the relationship between modifiable risk factors and the onset and progression of these diseases has become increasingly clear, the transtheoretical model of behavior change, more commonly known as the *stages of change* model (5), has been seen as a promising theoretical framework for behavior change interventions. The model posits that successful behavior change results when an individual progresses through five stages of change that culminate in the ability to maintain the desired behavior for the long term. Each of the following five stages in the model is defined in relation to when an individual plans to take action to change a behavior: 1) precontemplation—not intending to take action in the next 6 months; 2) contemplation—intending to take action in the next 6 months; 3) preparation—intending to take action in the next 30 days; 4) action—has made overt changes for less than 6 months; and 5) maintenance—has made overt changes for more than 6 months (6). Individuals may move sequentially through the stages or, as is more common, may revert to an earlier stage one or more times during the process. The model also includes 10 *processes of change* that people use to move through the stages. There are five *experiential* processes (e.g., consciousness raising, self-reevaluation) that are used primarily in earlier stages and five *behavioral* processes (e.g., helping relationships, stimulus control) that are used primarily in later stages (5,6).

The stages of change model has broad applications for improving behavioral risk factors for both diabetes and hypertension. It can help participants both to acquire new healthy behaviors, such as exercise (7), stress management (8), and better diet (9), and to stop unhealthy habits such as smoking (10) and substance abuse (11). However, most interventions based on the model have been conducted in a clinical setting or, occasionally, through a home-based approach in which an intervention is tailored to an individual based on responses to an assessment tool (12). Very few interventions have been implemented in group settings in the community. Although the model has been used with African Americans and Latinos (13-15), the authors found only three studies of a group-based behavioral intervention using the stages of change model with minority participants (16-18). One evaluated a community-based program that was individually tailored to the stages of change of African American women and found that they were more likely to have reduced their fat intake three months later than were those in a randomly assigned control group (16).

The New Hampshire (NH) Minority Health Coalition, through its REACH 2010 Initiative, has designed a program that implements the stages of change model as a group-based intervention. Change for Life, or *Cambia tu vida*, is designed to help participants from minority communities modify behaviors that may put them at risk for diabetes and cardiovascular disease. Sponsored by the Centers for Disease Control and Prevention and first implemented in 2002, it is one of several programs offered by the NH REACH 2010 Initiative to address racial and ethnic health disparities in New Hampshire. (More information about the NH REACH 2010 Initiative is available from www.nhhealthequity.org/pro _reach.html.)

## CONTEXT

The Change for Life program serves the growing black and Latino population of Hillsborough County in southern New Hampshire. Hillsborough County includes Manchester and Nashua, the two largest cities in the state. The county's population is culturally diverse. An increasing number of residents are recent immigrants from Africa and the Caribbean, including Sudan, Nigeria, and Haiti. The REACH 2010 Initiative uses the term *African descendent* to acknowledge and welcome these participants in addition to African Americans. The Latino population is also diverse, with individuals from other U.S. states, Puerto Rico, the Dominican Republic, Mexico, Colombia (19), and other Latin American countries.

The REACH 2010 Risk Factor Survey (20) in 2004 documented economic and health disparities among blacks and Latinos in Hillsborough County as compared with New Hampshire overall. Although less than 20% of non-Hispanic white New Hampshire residents earned less than $25,000 per year according to the NH Behavioral Risk Factor Surveillance System (BRFSS) (21), 44% of blacks and 54% of Latinos in Hillsborough County were in that income category in the REACH 2010 survey. Similarly, only 7% of non-Hispanic white New Hampshire residents had not finished their high school education, compared with 14% of blacks and 43% of Latinos in Hillsborough County. Fewer blacks (34%) or Latinos (37%) were in the normal weight range (based on body mass index) than the 43% of New Hampshire respondents to the BRFSS. Minorities were also less physically active, with 18% of blacks and 27% of Latinos reporting no moderate or vigorous activity in a usual week compared with 10% of all New Hampshire residents (20,21). Although prevalence rates of hypertension and diabetes are comparable among populations, blacks and Latinos who have been diagnosed with either condition are less likely to receive treatment. Among adults with diagnosed hypertension, 55% of blacks and Latinos in Hillsborough County take antihypertensive medication, compared with 77% of New Hampshire overall (21). Similarly, 55% of black and Latino respondents with diagnosed diabetes in the REACH 2010 survey reported having had a hemoglobin A1c test in the past year, compared with nearly 90% of New Hampshire BRFSS respondents.

The physical environment may contribute to health disparities. The neighborhoods in Manchester and Nashua with predominantly black or Latino residents lack access to healthy foods. Although there are two large supermarkets in Manchester and one in Nashua, they are not easily accessible to many low-income residents who do not drive or own vehicles. Instead, neighborhood markets or "superettes" are more common, and they tend to have more expensive food and a limited selection of fresh fruits and vegetables. Several studies have linked access to food stores to fruit and vegetable consumption (22,23) and have shown that lack of access can disproportionately affect minority communities (24). In addition, the long, dark New Hampshire winters and the lack of affordable recreational facilities for low-income residents can discourage physical activity, as has been shown among older adults in minority populations (25).

These economic and health disparities are occurring in minority populations that are much younger than the rest of New Hampshire. According to the 2000 U.S. census, the median age of New Hampshire's non-Hispanic whites is 37.6 years, compared with 28.3 years among blacks and 24.2 years among Latinos. More than 60% of black and Latino respondents in the REACH 2010 survey were younger than 40 years, compared with 30% of New Hampshire BRFSS respondents (20,21). Disparities in rates of chronic disease and the risk factors that lead to these diseases are likely to increase as New Hampshire's younger minority communities age.

# PROGRAM DEVELOPMENT AND IMPLEMENTATION

The Change for Life/*Cambia tu vida* program was developed to reduce health disparities by addressing the increased risk of developing diabetes and hypertension among African descendent and Latino residents of Hillsborough County. **Table 1** provides the timeline for designing, pilot testing, implementing, and evaluating the program.

## CURRICULUM

The NH REACH 2010 Initiative team designed the curriculum for Change for Life based on the stages of change model described in the book by Prochaska et al, *Changing for Good* (5). The team also reviewed health promotion programs identified by Pro-Change Behavior Systems, Inc (West Kingston, RI) on its Web site (6). The stages of change model was adapted in several ways to be culturally

**Table 1** Timeline of Change for Life/*Cambia tu vida* Program, New Hamphsire Racial and Ethnic Approaches to Community Health (REACH) 2010 Initiative

| Date | Activity |
|---|---|
| Spring 2002 | Program curriculum developed based on stages of change model (5) |
| Summer 2002 | Draft of curriculum reviewed by cultural advisors and piloted with community members |
| Fall 2002 | Staff facilitators trained |
| November 2002 | First Change for Life class conducted with African descendent participants |
| January 2003 | First *Cambia tu vida* class conducted with Latino participants |
| June 2003 | Train-the-trainers program begun to train community facilitators to teach classes |
| October 2003 | Before/after evaluation design implemented with participants and community comparison group |

appropriate for Latino and African descendant participants. For example, instead of emphasizing independent self-help, Change for Life/*Cambia tu vida* was designed to provide group support for individual change. The program also encourages participants to choose which health behaviors to change rather than counseling them about what they should change about their behavior. Finally, the program educates participants about the stages of change so that they are able to apply the model in the future to other aspects of their lives.

After the curriculum was drafted, it was reviewed by NH REACH 2010 cultural advisors from the targeted communities. They recommended adding graphics to the materials and revising some of the language, not only to reach low-literacy participants but also to include more culturally relevant examples in the curriculum. After these changes were made, the curriculum and class materials were translated into Spanish. Both the Spanish and English curricula were then reviewed by health literacy experts. The facilitator's manual was revised to a sixth-grade reading level, and the participant workbook was written at a fourth-grade reading level. The curriculum was then pilot tested in both communities and revised again based on the results.

## INTERVENTION

The Change for Life program consists of six 2-hour classes held weekly, followed by periodic group support meetings after the series of classes is completed. The first Change for Life class series began in November 2002, and the *Cambia tu vida* classes began in January 2003. *Cambia tu vida* is facilitated by a native speaker of Spanish. At the beginning of each class series, participants are required to choose at least one of the modifiable risk factors for diabetes and cardiovascular disease that they would like to change. Participants focusing on different modifiable risk factors and in different stages of change are often included in the same class to help participants learn from each other how to use the stages of change model.

In each class, the facilitator teaches participants about one or two of the five stages of change. **Figure 1** shows a handout summarizing the curriculum for participants. The curriculum includes group exercises tailored to the stage being discussed that encourage facilitators and participants to share their experiences with current and previous efforts at behavior change. Participants are taught how to identify their triggers for the unhealthy habit they want to change, recognize the barriers to change, and solicit the support they need to begin to make the change. Participants set realistic goals for their behavior change and reward themselves for their progress in taking

## THE STAGES OF CHANGE

### STAGE ONE: NOT READY TO TAKE ACTION
In this stage you think you don't have a problem or you have tried to change and think you can't do it. It helps to think about the benefits of a healthy change and also the barriers to making the change.

### STAGE TWO: THINKING ABOUT TAKING ACTION
When you are in this stage, you think about changing but are not ready to change. It helps to learn more about why the change is needed and to learn about a healthy habit to adopt.

### STAGE THREE: GETTING READY TO TAKE ACTION
This is an exciting stage. You make specific plans to change. It helps to make a detailed plan and to set a starting date.

### STAGE FOUR: TAKING ACTION
Finally, after all this work, you make the change! It is helpful to avoid situations that would tempt you back to the unhealthy habit. It is important to have a reward for every small success. This stage lasts at least 6 months.

### STAGE FIVE: STAYING HEALTHY
When you get here, you feel like the healthy habit is part of you. You still have to work on your health but you can celebrate your success. It helps in this stage to have the support of friends to stay healthy.

A program of the NH Minority Health Coalition's NH REACH 2010 Initiative

**FIGURE 1** Handout summarizing the curriculum for participants in the Change for Life program, New Hampshire Racial and Ethnic Approaches to Community Health (REACH) 2010 Initiative. (Please visit the online version of this article to download a full-size copy of this handout.)

overt actions in their change plan. Each week they are also encouraged to track their progress through the stages of change by using a decision tree (**Figure 2**). The decision tree is also used in the participant workbook and in evaluation assessments.

## FACILITATOR TRAINING

For the first year, the Change for Life and *Cambia tu vida* classes were facilitated by NH REACH 2010 staff. After that, the program shifted to a train-the-trainer model, and community members were trained to facilitate the classes. Facilitator

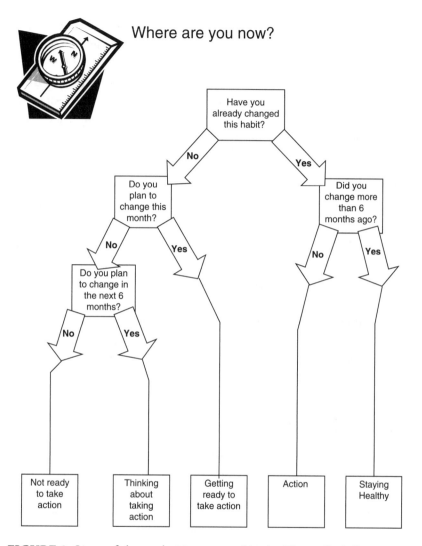

**FIGURE 2** Stages of change decision tree used in the Change for Life program, New Hampshire Racial and Ethnic Approaches to Community Health (REACH) 2010 Initiative. (Please visit the online version of this article to download a full-size copy of this handout.)

training is conducted in a single 4-hour session that includes a review of the curriculum and instruction on group facilitation techniques. Community facilitators receive a facilitator's manual, designed and tested by NH REACH 2010 staff, with information on leading the groups as well as detailed lesson plans for each session.

Facilitators are paid to organize and teach Change for Life or *Cambia tu vida* classes in their communities. NH REACH 2010 provides facilitators with mentoring and support to recruit participants, conduct the classes, and collect data for the evaluation. Series taught by community facilitators are usually held at the homes of facilitators or participants. To date, four train-the-trainer sessions have been held, two in each community; 11 Latino and 16 African descendent community members have been trained to teach these classes.

## RECRUITMENT

The first participants in the program were recruited from other NH REACH 2010 Initiative interventions. Later, as the train-the-trainer model was implemented, participants were also recruited by community facilitators, through staff community outreach, from referrals by partner organizations, and by word of mouth, frequently from program graduates. Classes are held in both Manchester and Nashua, with transportation and childcare provided.

From November 2002 through May 2005, 46 African descendents and 127 Latinos attended Change for Life or *Cambia tu vida* classes. Thirty-four of the African descendent participants and 91 of the Latino participants completed the program, for a completion rate of 72%.

## EVALUATION AND DATA ANALYSIS

A quasi-experimental design for evaluation was implemented in October 2003. Participants were asked to report their stage of change at baseline, immediately after the last class, and 3 months after the last class using the decision tree (Figure 2). The nonparametric Wilcoxon matched-pairs signed rank test was used to test whether there was significant advancement through the stages of change by participants. The matched-pair comparisons were performed among all participants who had completed both of the assessments (i.e., baseline and last class or baseline and 3-month follow-up).

Qualitative information was obtained through semistructured interviews with NH REACH 2010 program coordinators and group discussions with participants at the close of the final session of the class. Staff were asked about how the intervention was developed and implemented, their perceptions of the impact of the class on participants' behavior change, and their perceptions of the factors that contributed to the strengths and weaknesses of the intervention. Participants were asked to provide general feedback about the program and how it might be improved in the future.

# CONSEQUENCES

## DESCRIPTION OF PARTICIPANTS

From October 2003 through May 2005, 18 African descendent participants and 74 Latino participants responded to the baseline assessment. Of these 92 participants, 88 completed the class. Eleven African descendent participants and 40 Latino participants (total = 51) completed the 3-month follow-up assessment in time to be included for this article, for a preliminary follow-up rate among those who had graduated before March 2005 of 93% for African descendent graduates and 71% for Latino graduates.

Most of the participants who responded to the baseline assessment were women younger than 40 years (**Table 2**). Most were immigrants from Latin American countries such as Mexico and the Dominican Republic, although more than half of the participants had been born in the United States or had been in the United States for 5 or more years. Half of the participants had annual household incomes less than $25,000, and about 30% had not graduated from high school. Approximately 16% had been diagnosed with diabetes, and 24% had hypertension. Most chose diet (77%), exercise (52%), or both as the health habits they wanted to change by participating in the program. A few participants (14%) focused on reducing their cigarette smoking or alcohol consumption.

## CHANGE AMONG PROGRAM PARTICIPANTS

**Table 3** shows matched-pair comparisons of participant stage of change status at baseline compared with the last class and at baseline compared with the 3-month follow-up. Forty-nine participants who were trying to improve their diets responded to the baseline and last class assessments. Of the participants who chose diet as their focus, 37% were in the first two stages (precontemplation or contemplation) at baseline, 39% were in the preparation stage, and 24% reported they were already taking action at baseline. These participants were significantly more likely to be in a more advanced stage of change after completing the class series than they had been before. For the 35 participants who also completed the 3-month follow-up assessment, responses on the stages of change measures reveal that participants

**Table 2** Description of Change for Life Program/*Cambia tu vida* Participants (N = 88) From Baseline Assessments, New Hampshire, October 2003– May 2005

| Characteristic | No. of Participants (%) |
| --- | --- |
| **Sex** | |
| Male | 22 (25) |
| Female | 66 (75) |
| **Age, y** | |
| 18-24 | 13 (14.8) |
| 25-39 | 35 (39.8) |
| 40-64 | 38 (43.2) |
| ≥65 | 2 (2.3) |
| **Ethnic group** | |
| African American | 9 (10.2) |
| African immigrant or refugee | 9 (10.2) |
| Latino | 70 (79.5) |
| **Years in United States** | |
| Born in U.S. | 11 (12.5) |
| Less than 1 | 3 (3.4) |
| 1 or more but less than 5 | 30 (34.1) |
| 5-10 | 16 (18.2) |
| More than 10 | 28 (31.8) |
| **Annual income, $** | |
| <10,000 | 9 (10.2) |
| 10,000-24,999 | 35 (39.8) |
| 25,000-49,999 | 19 (21.6) |
| ≥50,000 | 11 (12.5) |
| Don't know or refused | 14 (15.9) |
| **Education** | |
| Less than 9th grade | 16 (18.2) |
| Some high school (≥9th grade) | 10 (11.4) |
| High school diploma or graduate equivalency degree | 22 (25.0) |
| Some college | 27 (30.7) |
| College graduate or more | 13 (14.8) |
| **Chronic disease** | |
| Diabetes | 14 (15.9) |
| Hypertension | 21 (23.9) |
| **Area of focus at baseline**[a] | |
| Smoking | 10 (11.4) |
| Alcohol consumption | 2 (2.3) |
| Diet | 68 (77.3) |
| Exercise | 46 (52.3) |
| Stress | 36 (40.9) |

[a]Participants could choose more than one area for change.

**Table 3** Pair-Comparison of the Distribution of Stages of Change Among Participants in Change for Life/*Cambia tu vida* Program at Baseline and Follow-up Assessments, New Hampshire, October 2003–May 2005

| Area of Focus and Stage of Change | Baseline and at Last Class (N = 67)[a] | | | Baseline and at 3-Month Follow-up (N = 46)[b] | | |
|---|---|---|---|---|---|---|
| | Baseline No. (%) | Follow-up No. (%) | P Value[c] | Baseline No. % | Follow-up No. (%) | P value[c] |
| **Diet** | | | | | | |
| Precontemplation | 2 (4.1) | 0 | <.001 | 1 (2.9) | 0 | .002 |
| Contemplation | 16 (32.7) | 3 (6.1) | | 13 (37.1) | 9 (25.7) | |
| Preparation | 19 (38.8) | 15 (30.6) | | 13 (37.1) | 2 (5.7) | |
| Action | 9 (18.4) | 29 (59.2) | | 7 (20.0) | 20 (57.1) | |
| Maintenance | 3 (6.1) | 2 (4.1) | | 1 (2.9) | 4 (11.4) | |
| **Exercise** | | | | | | |
| Precontemplation | 0 | 0 | .04 | 1 (4.5) | 1(4.5) | .06 |
| Contemplation | 6 (27.3) | 2 (9.1) | | 9 (40.9) | 6 (27.3) | |
| Preparation | 10 (45.5) | 9 (40.9) | | 5 (22.7) | 4 (18.2) | |
| Action | 4 (18.2) | 10 (45.5) | | 5 (22.7) | 7 (31.8) | |
| Maintenance | 2 (9.1) | 1 (4.5) | | 2 (9.1) | 4 (18.2) | |
| **Stress** | | | | | | |
| Precontemplation | 0 | 0 | <.001 | 0 | 0 | .06 |
| Contemplation | 7 (33.3) | 3 (14.3) | | 4 (33.3) | 4 (33.3) | |
| Preparation | 12 (57.1) | 4 (19.0) | | 6 (50.0) | 0 | |
| Action | 2 (9.5) | 13 (61.9) | | 2 (16.7) | 6 (50.0) | |
| Maintenance | 0 | 1 (4.8) | | 0 | 2 (16.7) | |
| **All areas** | | | | | | |
| Precontemplation | 2 (3.0) | 0 | <.001 | 1 (2.2) | 0 | <.001 |
| Contemplation | 22 (32.8) | 6 (8.6) | | 16 (34.8) | 11 (23.9) | |
| Preparation | 26 (38.8) | 20 (28.6) | | 18 (39.1) | 3 (6.5) | |
| Action | 13 (19.4) | 40 (57.1) | | 9 (19.6) | 21 (45.7) | |
| Maintenance | 4 (6.0) | 4 (5.7) | | 2 (4.3) | 11 (23.9) | |

[a]For diet, n = 49; for exercise, n = 22; for stress, n = 21. Participants could choose more than one area for change.
[b]For diet, n = 35; for exercise, n = 22; for stress, n = 12. Participants could choose more than one area for change.
[c]Test of statistical significance was one-tailed Wilcoxon matched pair signed rank test.

continued their advances. The reported stages of change for the participants who wanted to exercise more were similarly distributed at baseline. Similar advances through the stages of change were reported by participants who focused on exercise or stress, although changes for these behaviors reported at 3-month follow-up are not statistically significant. When considered together, program participants showed significant progress to later stages of change at the last class and at 3-month follow-up.

## PARTICIPANT FEEDBACK

**Table 4** summarizes perceptions at the end of class and at the 3-month follow-up. Most participants who completed the assessment at the end of the last class reported that the program had been helpful. More than half of participants reported that they had made progress toward changing their health habits in the 3-month follow-up assessment. Discussions at the end of the class indicated that participants had benefited from the program. Participants reported becoming more aware of unhealthy behavior. For example, one participant explained:

> Since I've been coming to this group, . . .I can honestly say that I'm seeing things from a different perspective. Now when I'm doing something, no matter what it is, I get this awareness about this meeting. . . .[I now feel] I am accountable for the decisions and the actions that I make.

Participants also indicated the importance of support for behavior change. Another participant said:

> I think that I have changed a lot because I used to eat a lot of things that I shouldn't eat. . . .Because of my [diabetes], I have to eat different foods and I wouldn't [before the class]. I would go and buy cake, and cake was bad for me, but I would eat it anyway, and I would eat the whole thing because since I don't have anyone to share it with or to give it to, I would eat it all. But I thank God, and thank you guys for all your help because you guys give these terrific classes that do so much good and help so many people, and I hope that this is not the last time that you guys give these classes because it does a lot of people very good.

Participant feedback also indicated a desire for continued support after the intervention. During the 3-month follow-up assessments, some participants reported having lost their momentum for behavior change once the class was over.

**Table 4** Change for Life/*Cambia tu vida* Participants' Perceptions of Intervention at the End of Class and at 3-Month Follow-up, New Hampshire, October 2003–May 2005

| Indicator | No. (%) |
|---|---|
| **End of class** | |
| Helpfulness of the class (n = 72) | |
|     Not helpful or somewhat helpful | 6 (8.3) |
|     Quite helpful | 15 (20.8) |
|     Very helpful | 51 (70.8) |
| Helpfulness of the intervention workbook (n = 70) | |
|     Not helpful or somewhat helpful | 3 (4.3) |
|     Quite helpful | 23 (32.9) |
|     Very helpful | 44 (62.9) |
| **3-Month follow-up** | |
| Progress made toward changing behavior (n = 48) | |
|     No progress or some progress | 19 (39.6) |
|     Quite a bit of progress | 20 (41.7) |
|     A lot of progress | 9 (18.8) |
| Frequency of reading workbook (n = 49) | |
|     Never | 6 (12.2) |
|     Rarely | 10 (20.4) |
|     Sometimes | 30 (61.2) |
|     Often | 3 (6.1) |

# INTERPRETATION

Early evaluation results indicate that the Change for Life/*Cambia tu vida* intervention helped participants to make progress toward their goals of behavior change and created a better awareness of personal behavior in a fun, supportive, and culturally appropriate setting. In addition, the train-the-trainer program helped to empower participants to take an active role in improving the health of their communities. To respond to participant requests for continued support after the intervention, NH REACH 2010 staff sponsor class reunions that offer advice on nutrition and enlist the help of local fitness centers to provide reduced rates to program graduates.

The Change for Life/*Cambia tu vida* program has been more readily implemented among Latinos than among African descendents in New Hampshire. The home-based, group support model appears to be more appealing to Latino residents, especially women. A faith-based approach has been found to be more appealing to African descendents. One of the most successful facilitators of the Change for Life classes is an African American minister whose church serves a predominantly black neighborhood in a city center of Hillsborough County.

When Change for Life was first implemented, the program evaluation was exclusively qualitative and aimed primarily at collecting information about participant satisfaction. Several months later, a quasi-experimental evaluation design was implemented to strengthen the outcome evaluation. The newer evaluation uses a pretest–posttest design with a comparison group of community members who are not randomly assigned but who have chosen not to participate in the program. Both participants in the intervention and members of the comparison group are administered assessments during the course of a year and are weighed and have their blood pressure taken each time. The assessments for both groups are conducted at baseline, 3 months later, and 1 year after baseline. The intervention and this evaluation are expected to continue through spring 2007. Our early findings indicate that African descendant and Latino participants are reporting progress toward their goals. Self-reported advancement through the stages of change suggest that participants have learned about the model and are applying it to their health behavior. Subsequent analysis will compare their self-reports with those of the comparison group to evaluate whether these behavioral intentions have resulted in the adoption of healthier habits in the months following participants' completion of the Change for Life/ *Cambia tu vida* program.

## ACKNOWLEDGMENTS

This study was supported by the Centers for Disease Control and Prevention, grant number U50-CCU122162.

We express our appreciation to the staff of the New Hampshire Minority Health Coalition for their commitment to identifying populations in the state that encounter barriers to accessing health care, advocating for adequate and appropriate services, and empowering these populations to be active participants in their health care. As the umbrella agency for the NH REACH 2010 Initiative of New Hampshire, the Coalition has fostered the spirit of innovation that sparked the Change for Life program. We also thank our colleagues who provided critical reviews of drafts of this manuscript: Jeanie Holt, RN, MS, Youlian Liao, MD, Sonia Parra, Nancy Ryan, MEd, and Mandy Smith, PhD. (http://www.ncbi.nlm.nih.gov/pmc/articles/PMC1637793/-ui-ncbiinpagenav-2)

## FOOTNOTES

The opinions expressed by authors contributing to this journal do not necessarily reflect the opinions of the U.S. Department of Health and Human Services, the Public Health Service, Centers for Disease Control and Prevention, or the authors' affiliated institutions. Use of trade names is for identification only and does not imply endorsement by any of the groups named above.

*Suggested citation for this article:* Ryan A, Smith C. Change for Life/Cambia tu vida: a health promotion program based on the stages of change model for African descendent and Latino adults in New Hampshire. Prev Chronic Dis [serial online] 2006 Jul [date cited]. Available from: URL: http://www.cdc.gov/pcd/issues/2006/jul/05_0218.htm

## CONTRIBUTOR INFORMATION

Chris Smith, New Hampshire Minority Health Coalition. 25 Lowell St, 3rd Floor, Manchester, NH 03105, Phone: 603-627-7703, Email: chris@nhhealthequity.org.

Andrew Ryan, Heller School for Social Policy and Management, Brandeis University, Waltham, Mass. At the time this work was done, Mr Ryan was with the Research and Evaluation Group, New Hampshire Minority Health Coalition, Manchester, NH.

## REFERENCES

1. Liao Y, Tucker P, Giles WH. Health status among REACH 2010 communities, 2001–2002. *Ethn Dis.* 2004;*14*(3 suppl 1):S9–13.
2. Knowler WC, Barrett-Connor E, Fowler SE, Hamman RF, Lachin JM, Walker EA, et al. Reduction in the incidence of type 2 diabetes with lifestyle intervention or metformin. *N Engl J Med.* 2002;*346*(6):393–403.
3. Kannel WB. New Perspectives on cardiovascular risk factors. *Am Heart J.* 1987;*114*(1 Pt 2):213–219.
4. Multiple risk factor intervention trial. Risk factor changes and mortality results. Multiple Risk Factor Intervention Trial Research Group. *JAMA.* 1982;*248*(12):1465–1477.
5. Prochaska JO, Norcross JC, DiClemente CC. *Changing for good.* Morrow; New York (NY): 1994. p. 304.
6. Pro-Change Behavior Systems, Inc. Transtheoretical Model [Internet] West Kingston (RI): Pro-Change Behavior Systems, Inc.; [cited 7 Mar 2006]. Available from: URL: http://www.prochange.com/company/ttm.html.

7. Marcus BH, Banspach SW, Lefebvre RC, Rossi JS, Carleton RA, Abrams DB. Using the stages of change model to increase the adoption of physical activity among community participants. *Am J Health Promot.* 1992;*6*(6):424–429.

8. Evers KE, Johnson JL, Mauriello LM, Padula JA, Prochaska JO, Prochaska JM. A randomized clinical trial of a population based stress management intervention: 18-month outcomes. Conference proceeding from the Annual Scientific Sessions of the Society of Behavioral Medicine. 2003 Mar 19–22; Salt Lake City, UT.

9. Greene GW, Rossi SR, Rossi JS, Velicer WF, Fava JL, Prochaska JO. Dietary applications of the stages of change model. *J Am Diet Assoc.* 1999;*99*(6):673–678.

10. Velicer WF, Prochaska JO. An expert system intervention for smoking cessation. *Patient Educ Couns.* 1999;*36*(2):119–129.

11. Velasquez MM, Maurer GG, Crouch C, DiClemente CC. *Group treatment for substance abuse: a stages-of-change therapy manual.* New York (NY): The Guilford Press; 2001. p. 222.

12. Prochaska JO, Velicer WF, Redding C, Rossi JS, Goldstein M, DePue J, et al. Stage-based expert systems to guide a population of primary care patients to quit smoking, eat healthier, prevent skin cancer, and receive regular mammograms. *Prev Med.* 2005;*41*(2):406–416.

13. Bull FC, Eyler AA, King AC, Brownson RC. Stage of readiness to exercise in ethnically diverse women: a U.S. survey. *Med Sci Sports Exerc.* 2001;*33*(7):1147–1156.

14. Block G, Wakimoto P, Metz D, Fujii ML, Feldman N, Mandel R, et al. A randomized trial of the Little by Little CD-ROM: demonstrated effectiveness in increasing fruit and vegetable intake in a low-income population. *Prev Chronic Dis.* 2004 Jul;*1*(3) Available from: URL: http://www.cdc.gov/pcd/issues/2004/jul/04_0016.htm.

15. Jantz C, Anderson J, Gould SM. Using computer-based assessments to evaluate interactive multimedia nutrition education among low-income predominantly Hispanic participants. *J Nutr Educ Behav.* 2002;*34*(5):252–260.

16. Auslander W, Haire-Joshu D, Houston C, Rhee CW, Williams JH. A controlled evaluation of staging dietary patterns to reduce the risk of diabetes in African-American women. *Diabetes Care.* 2002;*25*(5):809–814.

17. Collins R, Lee RE, Albright CL, King AC. Ready to be physically active? The effects of a course preparing low-income multiethnic women to be more physically active. *Health Educ Behav.* 2004;*31*(1):47–64.

18. Taylor T, Serrano E, Anderson J, Kendall P. Knowledge, skills, and behavior improvements on peer educators and low-income Hispanic participants after a stage of change-based bilingual nutrition education program. *J Community Health.* 2000; *25*(3):241–262.

19. Camayd-Freixas Y, Karush G, Lejter N. Latinos in New Hampshire: enclaves, diasporas, and an emerging middle class. In: Torres A, editor. *Latinos in New England: yesterday's newcomers, tomorrow's mainstream?* Temple University Press; Philadelphia (PA): 2005.

20. Centers for Disease Control and Prevention. REACH 2010 Risk Factor Survey: Year 1 data report for New Hampshire Minority Health Coalition. Atlanta (GA): National Center for Chronic Disease Prevention and Health Promotion; 2004.

21. Centers for Disease Control and Prevention. Behavioral Risk Factor Surveillance System Survey Data [Internet] Atlanta (GA): U.S. Department of Health and Human Services, Centers for Disease Control and Prevention; 2003. Available from: URL: http://www.cdc.gov/brfss/technical_infodata/surveydata/2003.htm.
22. Rose D, Richards R. Food store access and household fruit and vegetable use among participants in the US Food Stamp Program. *Public Health Nutr.* 2004;*7*(8):1081–1088.
23. Morland K, Wing S, Diez Roux., A. The contextual effect of the local food environment on residents' diets: the atherosclerosis risk in communities study. *Am J Public Health.* 2002;*92*(11):1761–1767.
24. Zenk SN, Schulz AJ, Israel BA, James SA, Bao S, Wilson ML. Neighborhood racial composition, neighborhood poverty, and the spatial accessibility of supermarkets in metropolitan Detroit. *Am J Public Health.* 2005;*95*(4):660–667.
25. Belza B, Walwick J, Shiu-Thornton S, Schwartz S, Taylor M, LoGerfo J. Older adult perspectives on physical activity and exercise: voices from multiple cultures. *Prev Chronic Dis.* 2004 Oct;*1*(4):A09. Available from: URL: http://www.cdc.gov/pcd/issues/2004/oct/04_0028.htm.

# CHAPTER ACTIVITY QUESTIONS

1. How was the stages of change model adapted in this program and why?
2. Which, if any, of these adaptations did you identify as something that would be helpful in moving you through the stages of change?
3. Why were program participants at different stages of change in the same class sessions and how does this support one of the adaptations made to the model?
4. What was done to provide support to the participants to maintain the changes made?

# CHAPTER REFERENCES

Andersen, S., & Keller, C. (2002). Examination of the Transtheoretical Model in current smokers. *Western Journal of Nursing Research, 24*(3), 282–294.
Aubertin-Leheudre, M., Rousseau, S., Melancon, M.O., Chaput, J., & Dionne, I.J. (2005). Barriers to physical activity participation in North American elderly women: A literature review. *American Journal of Recreation Therapy, 4*(1), 21–30.

Borland, R. (1990). Slip-ups, and relapse in attempts to quit smoking. *Addictive Behavior*, *15*(3), 235–245.

Burke, J.G., Denison, J.A., Gielen, A.C., McDonnell, K.A., & O'Campo, P. (2004). Ending intimate partner violence: An application of the Transtheoretical Model. *American Journal of Health Behavior*, *28*(2), 122–133.

Cancer Prevention Center Center (2004). Process of change. Retrieved April 1, 2013 from http://www.uri.edu/research/cprc/TTM/ProcessesOfChange.htm.

DiClemente, C.C., & Prochaska, J.O. (1985). Processes and stages of change: Coping and competence in smoking behavior change. In S. Shiffman & T.A. Wills (Eds.), *Coping and Substance Abuse* (pp. 319–343). San Diego: Academic Press.

DiClemente, C.C., Prochaska, J.O., Fairhurst, S.K., Velicer, W.F., Velasquez, M.M., & Rossi, J.S. (1991). The process of smoking cessation: An analysis of precontemplation, contemplation, and preparation stages of change. *Journal of Consulting and Clinical Psychology*, *59*(2), 295–304.

DiClemente, C.C., Schlundt, D., & Gemmell, L. (2004). Readiness and stages of change in addiction treatment. *American Journal of Addiction*, *13*, 103–119.

Dijkstra, A., & Borland, R. (2003). Residual outcome expectations and relapse in ex-smokers. *Health Psychology*, *23*(4), 340–346.

Fava, J.L., Velicer, W.F., & Prochaska, J.O. (1995). Applying the transtheoretical model to a representative sample of smokers. *Addictive Behaviors*, *20*(2), 189–201.

Hoke, M.M. & Timmerman, G.M. (2011). Transtheoretical model: Potential usefulness with overweight rural Mexian-American women. *Hispanic Health Care International*, *9*(1), 41-49. DOI: 10.1891/1540–4153.9.1.41.

Kosma, M., Gardner, R.E., Cardinal, B.J., Bauer, J.J., & McCubbin, J.A. (2006). Psychosocial determinants of stages of change and physical activity among adults with physical disabilities. *Adapted Physical Activity Quarterly*, *23*, 49–64.

Lach, H.W., Everard, K.M., Highstein, G., & Brownson, C.A. (2004). Application of the Transtheoretical Model to health education for older adults. *Health Promotion Practice*, *5*(1), 88–93.

Leone, J.E., Gray, K.A., Rossi, J.M., & Colandreo, R.M. (2008). Using the Transtheoretical Model to explain androgenic-anabolic steroid use in adolescents, and young adults: Part one. *Strength and Conditioning Journal*, *30*(6), 47–54.

Marcus, H., Ross, J., Selby, V., Niaura, R., & Abrams, D. (1992). The stages and processes of exercise adoption and maintenance in a worksite sample. *Health Psychology*, *11*(6), 386–395.

Martin, M.Y, Person, S.D., Kratt, P., Prayor-Patterspon, H., Kim, Y., Salas, M., & Pisu, M. (2008). Relationship of health behavior theories with self-efficacy among insufficiently active hypertensive African-American women. *Patient Education and Counseling*, *72*(1), 137–145.

Prochaska, J.O. (1994). Strong and weak principles for progressing from precontemplation to action on the basis of twelve problem behaviors. *Health Psychology*, *13*, 47–51.

Prochaska, J.O., & DiClemente, C.C. (1982). Transtheoretical therapy: Toward a more integrative model of change. *Psychotherapy: Theory, Research and Practice*, *20*, 161–173.

Prochaska, J.O., & DiClemente, C.C. (1983). Stages and processes of self-change of smoking: Toward an integrative model of change. *Journal of Consulting and Clinical Psychology*, *51*, 390–395.

Prochaska, J.O., DiClemente, C.C., & Norcross, J.C. (1992). In search of how people change: Applications to addictive behaviors. *American Psychologist, 47*(9), 1102–1114.

Prochaska, J.O., Velicer, W.F., DiClemente, C.C., & Fava, J.L. (1988). Measuring the processes of change: Applications to the cessation of smoking. *Journal of Consulting and Clinical Psychology, 56*, 520–528.

Ruggiero, L. (2000). Helping people with diabetes change behavior: From theory to practice. *Diabetes Spectrum, 13*(3), 125.

Siahpush, M., & Carlin, J. (2006). Financial stress, smoking cessation and relapse: Results from a prospective study of Australian national sample. *Addiction, 101*(1), 121–127.

Sullum, J., Clark, M.M., & King, T.K. (2000). Predictors of exercise relapse in a college population. *American Journal of College Health, 48*(4), 175–180.

Thomas, P.R. (Ed), Committee to Develop Criteria for Evaluating the Outcomes of Approaches to Prevent and Treat Obesity. (1995). *Weighing the Options: Criteria for Evaluating the Weight-Management Programs.* Institute of Medicine. Retrieved February 19, 2008, from www.nap.edu/catalog/4756.html.

Velicer, W.F, Prochaska, J.O., Fava, J.L., Norman, G.J., & Redding, C.A. (1998). Smoking cessation and stress management: Applications of the Transtheoretical Model of behavior change. *Homeostasis, 38*, 216–233.

Yang, P., & Chen, C. (2005). Exercise and process of change in patients with chronic obstructive pulmonary disease. *Journal of Nursing Research, 13*(2), 97–104.

# Social Cognitive Theory

## STUDENT LEARNING OUTCOMES

After reading this chapter the student will be able to:

- Explain the concept of reciprocal determinism.
- Differentiate among the many constructs of the Social Cognitive Theory.
- Explain how each of the constructs influences health behavior.
- Use the theory to analyze at least one behavior.

## THEORY ESSENCE SENTENCE

Behavior, personal factors, and environmental factors interact with each other, and changing one changes them all.

---

### Social Cognitive Theory Constructs Chart

**Self-efficacy**
One's own estimation of one's personal ability to do something

**Observational learning (modeling)**
Learning by watching others

**Expectations**
The likely outcome of a particular behavior

**Expectancies**
The value placed on the outcome of the behavior

**Emotional arousal**
The emotional reaction to a situation and its resulting behavior

**Behavioral capability**
The knowledge and skills needed to engage in a particular behavior

**Reinforcement**
The rewards or punishments for doing something

**Locus of control**
One's belief regarding one's personal power over life events

---

# IN THE BEGINNING

Social cognitive theory has its roots in Albert Bandura's research on observation, social learning, and aggressive behavior dating back to the late 1950s. During this time, the prevailing theory about behavior acquisition was rooted in behaviorism—that is, behavior is the result of environmental stimuli, consequences, rewards, and punishments (Pajares, 2004).

In keeping with this, Bandura's early research explored the influence of observation and modeling on behavior acquisition, that is, people learn by watching and copying others. Early on he looked at aggressive behavior in boys. He found boys were aggressive even when they were from homes in which aggressive behavior was not condoned (not rewarded). Although this type of behavior was unacceptable in the home, the parents of these boys nonetheless expected their sons to be tough and settle disputes with other children physically (aggressively), if necessary. He found the parents themselves were aggressive toward the school system and toward other children they felt were giving their sons a hard time. From this Bandura concluded that the boys learned aggressive behavior by copying or modeling their parents—thus demonstrating the power of observational learning (Bandura & Walters, 1959; Pajares, 2004).

Bandura and his colleagues continued researching the impact of modeling on social behavior in 1961 with the now famous Bobo doll experiments. (The Bobo doll was a 5 foot inflated clown.) Children were separated into groups, with one group observing an adult (model) playing with toys in a room ignoring the Bobo doll in the corner. The other group watched as the adult (model) began playing with toys in the room, then start hitting and beating on the Bobo doll. The children from both groups were then individually left alone with the Bobo doll and other toys. Children who observed the aggressive adults (models) imitated almost identically much of the physical and verbal aggression they witnessed. In contrast, the children who saw the nonaggressive models only rarely interacted with the Bobo doll in an aggressive manner (Bandura, Ross, & Ross, 1961).

With modeling and observational learning (environmental factors) as the foundation, research continued into personal factors that contribute to behavior including self-reward, self-regulation, self-efficacy, self-directedness, and self-reflection, which furthered the idea that behavior is more than just a result of the consequences of one's actions (Pajares, 2004). The inter-relation between environmental factors, personal factors, and behavior is acknowledged in the Social Cognitive Theory (Grusec, 1992).

## THEORETICAL CONCEPT

Social Cognitive Theory (SCT) is based on the concept of *reciprocal determinism*, that is, the dynamic interplay among personal factors, the environment, and behavior (Bandura, 1977). The way in which people interpret their environment, and their personal factors, affect their behavior (Parjares, 2004), their behavior affects their personal factors, which can affect their environment, and so on. The point being that changing one of these three factors, changes all of them, and therefore changes behavior.

An example of this interaction can been seen when we look at bottled water use. It is impossible to walk on a campus today and not see students and faculty alike toting water bottles. They are ubiquitous. However, the plastic disposable bottles have quickly become an environmental problem in addition to a potential health hazard from the leaching of plastic chemicals into the water. Armed with this information (personal factor—knowledge) campuses across the country are beginning to install water stations or hydration stations (environment). These new and improved "water fountains" filter the water and are constructed purposely for refilling reusable water bottles. Students are filling up their reusable bottles (behavior) rather than buying bottles of water thus, helping to eliminate pollution and are using water as a healthy alternative to soda or other sweetened beverages.

# THEORETICAL CONSTRUCTS

The factors of reciprocal determinism—personal, environmental, and behavioral—are affected by the many constructs of SCT. These include self-efficacy, expectations, observational learning (modeling), expectancies, emotional arousal, behavioral capability, reinforcement, and locus of control.

## SELF-EFFICACY

Of all the constructs of SCT, self-efficacy is probably the single most important determinant of behavior. This construct forms the basis of Self-Efficacy Theory, and plays a role in the Health Belief Model and the Transtheoretical Model as well. As we know, even when people have the skills and knowledge to accomplish a task, it is their belief in their ability to use them that enables people to actually perform the task (Bandura, 1993). That is, people will only do what they believe they can do.

## EXPECTATIONS

Behavior is influenced by expectations. This construct suggests that people behave in certain ways because of the results they expect. A man uses a condom because he expects to be protected from sexually transmitted infections and fatherhood. An obese woman begins exercising because she expects to lose weight. Students drink because they expect to be accepted as part of the group.

Our expectations of the outcome of a behavior can also cause us to avoid the behavior. For example, women who worry that cancer will be found if they have a mammogram tend not to have mammograms (Rawl, Champion, Menon, & Foster, 2000). It is the expectation of worry that deters them from having this important screening test done.

Similar behavior is seen relative to influenza vaccination. People who expect to get sick from the flu vaccine won't be vaccinated. This same avoidance is also found with digital rectal examinations for prostate cancer. If a man expects that he will be embarrassed having this examination performed, then he probably will not go for the screening (Shelton, Weinrich, & Reynolds, 1999).

Our expectations of outcomes are influenced by any number of things, including our past experiences in similar situations, observing others or hearing about others in a similar situation, and by the emotional or physical response that occurs as a result of the behavior. For example, because of my past experience playing badminton, there is an expectation that I can play tennis. Because the women's figure skating champions are the same age as me, there is an expectation that I can also skate. Because quitting smoking increases appetite, I expect to gain weight.

## SELF-REGULATION

Meshing the previous two constructs, self-efficacy and expectations, and adding goal setting gives rise to the construct of self-regulation. Self-regulation occurs when people form beliefs about what they can do, anticipate the likely outcome of their actions, set goals, and plan a course of action that will result in the expected outcome (Bandura, 1991).

In an effort to understand how it is possible that even though the U.S. population has access to healthier foods, the overall diet of the population has not improved, self-regulation was found to be the best predictor of nutrition of all the SCT constructs. People who plan and track their eating, plan different strategies to increase fruit, vegetable, and fiber consumption, and to decrease fat, have healthier diets (Anderson, Winett, & Wojcik, 2007).

## OBSERVATIONAL LEARNING

Observational learning (or modeling) is learning by watching others and copying their behavior. Think back to when you were a child. How did you learn to brush your teeth, tie your shoes, ride a bike, color within the lines, bake cookies, hammer a nail, and get dressed? In addition to learning basic life skills through observation, we adopt observed mannerisms, interpersonal communication style, leadership style, and health practices, to name a few. So much of our behavior results from observational learning that the list might be endless.

As a result, the construct of observational learning can be very useful in explaining why people behave the way they do. Unfortunately, it does not always lead to healthy behaviors. For example, we have known for some time that if a parent (role model) smokes, it is more likely that the child will also smoke. Children learn and do what they see.

The strength of observational learning depends on how much attention is given to the person who is modeling the behavior. This degree of attention is influenced by a number of things, among them the attractiveness of the model, the circumstances under which the model is being observed, what is motivating the person to learn the behavior, how important it is that the behavior be learned, and the complexity of the behavior (Bandura, 1977, 1986; Grusec, 1992).

Observational learning is most useful when the model is considered to be a powerful person, is well respected, or is someone to whom the observer can relate (NCI, 2003). This is why companies use celebrity endorsements to sell their products. Think of the athlete who makes it onto the cereal box. An Olympic gold medalist is a role model for many children. Having this person's picture on the cereal box implies that the athlete eats the cereal in the box. If the child eats the cereal, he or she will be like this athlete. The child's desire to be like the role model may be one explanation for why he or she eats the cereal, which is what the food company hopes.

We pay more attention to a model when we need to learn the behavior and when the behavior is complex. For example, the person newly diagnosed with Type I diabetes needs to learn how to inject insulin, a complex task that is essential for survival. This person is likely to be more attentive when observing how to inject insulin than he or she is when observing how to measure a cup of food.

## EXPECTANCIES

While expectations are the anticipated or expected outcomes of a particular behavior, *expectancies* are the values we place on those outcomes. A certain behavior is more likely to occur when the expectancy, or value placed on its outcome, maximizes a positive result and minimizes a negative one. Returning to the mammogram example used earlier, for the woman who worries that the mammogram will show cancer, the outcome (expectation) of the behavior (having a mammogram) is seen as being negative, something to be avoided. In this case, the negative expectancy (diagnosis of cancer) is another way to explain why she avoids having the mammogram in the first place. On the other hand, if a woman viewed early diagnosis of breast cancer as something that would increase her chance of cure (positive expectancy), this could explain why she *would* have an annual mammogram.

## EMOTIONAL AROUSAL

The construct of emotional arousal suggests that in certain situations people become fearful and, when this happens, their behavior becomes defensive in an effort to reduce the fear (Bandura, 1977). The possibility of having unprotected sex with a new partner leads to the fear of contracting the human immunodeficiency virus (HIV). To reduce the fear, abstinence is practiced until HIV testing is done or condoms are used, or both. In this situation, emotional arousal leads to a more positive health behavior, namely, HIV risk reduction.

However, emotional arousal may also hinder good health practices. For some people, going to the dentist causes intense fear and anxiety. To reduce the fear and anxiety, people avoid going to the dentist. Thus, their dental health is compromised.

## BEHAVIORAL CAPABILITY

The construct of behavioral capability tells us that if people are to perform a certain behavior, they must have knowledge of the behavior and the skills to perform it. Simply put, before doing something, you have to know what it is you're going to do and know how to do it.

When we look at the 2010 Dietary Guidelines for Americans, one of the recommendations for a healthy diet is that it is low in saturated fats, trans fats, cholesterol, salt, and added sugars (U.S. Department of Health and Human Services & U.S. Department of Agriculture, 2010). According to the construct of behavioral capability, in order for people to follow this recommendation, they must choose foods that are low in saturated fats, but in order to do so, they must know what saturated fats are, what foods are low in saturated fats, and have the ability (skill) to make the better choices (**Figure 7–1**).

## REINFORCEMENT

Reinforcement is a construct in the SCT with which you may be familiar, because it is also the basis for operant conditioning and behavior modification. In general, reinforcement is a system of rewards (positive reinforcement) and punishments (negative reinforcements) in response to behavior. Behavior occurs because people either want the reward or want to avoid the punishment.

© Diego Cervo/Shutterstock, Inc.

**FIGURE 7–1** Knowledge and skills are needed to make better choices

A common example of this can be found with children. If a child eats all of the vegetables on his plate, he is rewarded with a favorite dessert; thus, the behavior (eating vegetables) is repeated so the reward (dessert) can be obtained again.

Reinforcement might be discontinuing medication for Type II diabetes because dietary changes and exercise have it under control. It could be new clothes in a smaller size because of weight loss, or the "runner's high" one gets after exercising. All of these are rewards or positive reinforcements that would support continuation of the new behavior. What would a positive reinforcement be for you? (See **Figure 7–2.**)

Behavior resulting in a negative reinforcement or punishment tends not to be repeated. A child who refuses to eat her vegetables is denied dessert, and watches as everyone else eats. To avoid this punishment, she eats her vegetables the next time, unless, of course, she doesn't like what is being served for dessert. To avoid being arrested again for DUI, a group of friends designates a driver when they go out drinking.

## LOCUS OF CONTROL

Although most of the constructs in the SCT explain behavior by the influence of external or social forces, the construct of locus of control is a bit different. This construct explains behavior based on the idea that people have varying degrees of

© Warren Goldswain/Shutterstock, Inc.

**FIGURE 7–2** Positive reinforcement supports continuation of new behavior

belief in their ability to control what happens to them. This belief in the extent of personal control has an impact on health decisions, and thus on health behavior.

Locus of control works on a continuum from internal to external. Internally controlled people believe that everything that happens to them is a result of their own decisions and behaviors. They believe they have control over all aspects of their lives and their destiny. Externally controlled people believe that forces outside of their control, such as fate, God's will, or important or powerful others, govern all aspects of their lives (Levenson, 1974).

Internality or externality has a strong influence on our health decision making. In the case of breast cancer, for example, women who are more externally controlled are not likely to have mammograms unless their physicians (important or powerful others) tell them to have one. In contrast, women who are more

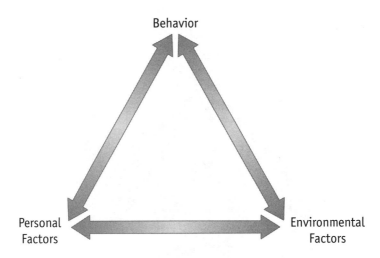

**FIGURE 7–3** Social Cognitive Theory

*Source:* Pajares, F. (2002). Overview of social cognitive theory and of self-efficacy. Retrieved from http://www.emory.edu/EDUCATION/mfp/eff.html. Reprinted with permission.

internally controlled will have mammograms regardless of whether their physicians recommend them or not (Borrayo & Guarnaccia, 2002). In young adults, internality is associated with greater odds of engaging in healthy behaviors, specifically, eating fiber, exercising, and low salt and fat consumption (Steptoe & Wardle, 2001).

Where people fall on the continuum of internality and externality may change depending upon the situation. Some people are very internal when it comes to changing unhealthy behaviors, such as weight loss or stress management, for example. Yet these same people do not wear seatbelts, for instance, because "What will be, will be" or "If it's my time to go, there is nothing I can do about it."

In summary, according to Social Cognitive Theory, personal factors, the environment, and behavior interact with each other; therefore, changing one of them changes all of them (**Figure 7–3**).

## THEORY IN ACTION—CLASS ACTIVITY

Think back to when, where, and how you first learned about HIV prevention and the impact this had on your own behavior. Share your responses with your classmates. Then, read the following article and answer the questions that follow.

# Chapter 7 Article: Reducing HIV and AIDS through Prevention (RHAP): A Theoretically Based Approach for Teaching HIV Prevention to Adolescents through an Exploration of Popular Music[1]

*Carla Boutin-Foster; Nadine McLaughlin; Angela Gray; Anthony Ogedegbe; Ivan Hageman; Courtney Knowlton; Anna Rodriguez; and Ann Beeder*

[1] Weill Medical College, Cornell University, 525 East 68th Street, Room F1421, Box 46, New York, NY 10021 USA
[2] The East Harlem School, 309 East 103rd Street, New York, NY 10029 USA
Carla Boutin-Foster, Email: cboutin@med.cornell.edu.
Corresponding author.

## Abstract

Using popular culture to engage students in discussions of HIV prevention is a nontraditional approach that may complement current prevention efforts and enhance the ability to reach youth who are at high risk of contracting HIV and other sexually transmitted infections. Hip-hop or rap music is the dominant genre of music among adolescents, especially Black and Latino youth who are disproportionately impacted by HIV and AIDS. This paper describes the rationale and development of the Reducing HIV and AIDS through Prevention (RHAP) program, a school-based program that uses hip-hop/rap music as a vehicle for raising awareness among adolescents about HIV/AIDS. Constructs from the Social Cognitive Theory and the Sexual Script Theory were used in developing the program. It was piloted and evaluated among 26 middle school students in East Harlem, New York. The lessons learned from a formative evaluation of the program and the implications for developing other programs targeting public health problems are discussed. The RHAP program challenges the traditional

---

[1] Reproduced from Boutin-Foster, C., McLaughlin, N., Gray, A. Ogedegbe, A., Hageman, I., Knowlton, C., Rodriguez, A., et al. (2010). Reducing HIV and AIDS through prevention (RHAP): A theoretically based approach for teaching HIV prevention to adolescents through an exploration of popular music. *Journal of Urban Health*, *87*(3), 440–451.

pedagogue–student paradigm and provides an alternative approach to teaching about HIV prevention and awareness.

**Keywords:** HIV prevention, Adolescents, Hip-hop music, Sexual scripts, Social cognitive theory

# INTRODUCTION

Despite national efforts targeted at educating the youth about the prevention of HIV infection and the morbidity and mortality associated with HIV/AIDS, the number of teens and adolescents who are sexually active and who engage in unprotected sexual activity remains high. Youths between the ages of 3–19 account for approximately 10–15% of new HIV infections.[1] According to the Youth Risk Behavior Surveillance Survey, in New York City (NYC), nearly one half of public high school teenagers reported being sexually active. Of these, only 63% said that they used a condom. One in three was sexually active within 3 months of completing the survey and one in five reported having had four or more sex partners in their lifetime. Given that 10% of respondents reported having sex before the age of 13, educating young adolescents about HIV transmission is a public health imperative.[2]

NYC surveillance data on HIV among youth and young adults showed that in 2006 approximately 3,000 adolescents, ages 13–19 years, had a diagnosis of HIV.[3] Black and Latino adolescents living in areas that have less socioeconomic resources such as Bedford Stuyvesant, Brooklyn, East and Central Harlem, Manhattan, and the South Bronx are at a greater risk of becoming infected with HIV than those residing in other parts of NYC. Teens and adolescents residing in these communities are more likely to be sexually active than those residing in other communities in NYC, up to 45% compared to 29%. Other factors that increase the risk of contracting HIV and other sexually transmitted infections (STIs) are the earlier initiation of sexual activity, concurrent use of drugs or alcohol, and a greater number of sexual partners.[4] Therefore, programs that are culturally tailored to address the needs of Black and Latino youth in these communities are necessary.

## Music as a Learning Tool

In order to develop effective health messages and interventions that raise awareness about HIV among the youth, there must be an understanding of the factors that inform sexual perceptions and dictate sexual behaviors. HIV awareness programs must also use approaches that match the unique characteristics of the target population.[5] When speaking with urban youth, understanding the dynamic social factors that influence their behaviors can facilitate the development of appropriate messages that are framed in a culturally familiar manner. The use of popular art forms, such as music, has been advocated as one way to reach adolescents.[6,7] Music is a form of socialization that can provide cues to understanding what is considered as normative values, what gender-specific behaviors are, and what drives expectations. Thus, music can serve as an informal learning tool.[8] Music plays a pivotal role in the socialization of adolescents; an average adolescent may listen to approximately three or more hours of music daily. Music has been used as a device for self-reflection and self-regulation, in helping individuals to gain insight into a problem, to stimulate discussions, to communicate values, and to develop awareness and solutions.[9,10] For example, the exploration of lyrics from rock music has been used to discuss drug use among adolescents in a substance abuse program.[9] With the advent of technology such as MP3 players or the ability to download music from the internet instantaneously, the opportunities for listening and sharing music and its potential for education are great.[10]

## THE CULTURE OF HIP-HOP

Among Black and Latino youth, hip-hop music is the dominant form of music. The hip-hop culture is a movement that emerged among inner-city youth in the 1970s. The primary elements of the hip-hop culture include the stylized form of art (graffiti art) and dancing (break dancing). Hip-hop culture also includes a unique style of dress and colloquial language. Hip-hop or rap music has become by far the most widely celebrated expression of the hip-hop culture that transcends race, ethnicity, and gender.[11] Hip-hop/rap music is a fusion of jazz and rhythm and blues. The lyrics of the songs are presented as repetitive and rhythmic bursts of words. The content and message of these songs are diverse, ranging from those that raise social or political consciousness, or those that are spiritually based to those that contain sexually explicit lyrics that degrade women, glorify drug use, or violence.[12] These lyrics are not unique to hip-hop/rap music; however, for the purpose of this program, hip-hop/rap music was selected because it is the most common genre of music listened to by urban Black and Latino youth.

A Kaiser Foundation study on music in the lives of 8 to 18 year olds found that, among seventh to 12th graders who listened to music in a typical day, 65% listened to rap music. When examined by race and ethnicity, among 7th to 12th graders who listened to hip-hop/rap music, 60% were Caucasian, 70% were

Latino youth, and 80% were Black youth.[10] Studies have shown that youth as young as 10–12 years old have a general understanding of the message of hip-hop/rap songs, which is a cause for concern since many of these songs contain sexually explicit lyrics.[13]

## THE ASSOCIATION BETWEEN EXPOSURE TO SEXUALLY EXPLICIT MUSIC AND UNHEALTHY SEXUAL BEHAVIOR

The type of media that youth are exposed to has tremendous public health implications. Approximately, 40% of music listened to by early adolescents' have been found to contain sexually explicit content. For example, approximately 50% of hip-hop/rap music or R&B has been found to contain sexually explicit content.[14] Focusing on the role of music in framing health behaviors is important because exposure to sexually explicit music has been linked to risky behaviors. Media exposure has been documented as a social antecedent to sexual behavior, both current activity and intention for future sexual behavior.[15] In one study, adolescents who had greater exposure to hip-hop/rap music videos were almost twice as likely to have had multiple sexual partners and more than 1.5 times as likely to have acquired a new sexually transmitted disease over the 12-month follow-up period.[16]

Exposure to music containing more degrading sexual content has also been linked to initiation of intercourse and progression to more advanced levels of noncoital sexual activity. In a prospective study, Martino found that among youth ages 12 to 17, there was a significant association between listening to sexually degrading song lyrics and engaging in sexual activity.[8] Viewing videos which featured hip-hop/rap music with sexually explicit lyrics and violent images has been linked to a greater likelihood of violent interactions at school and being arrested, having multiple sexual partners, and having a new laboratory-confirmed sexually transmitted disease.[16,17] These music videos were most often viewed at home with siblings or friends. This observation that the music is shared and readily accessible makes it a powerful and sustainable vehicle for education.

The pervasiveness of hip-hop/rap music in the culture of youth makes it a tremendous resource for communication and may provide a culturally relevant and innovative medium for health education. Several studies have used hip-hop/rap music in youth prevention programs. Tyson used hip-hop/rap songs among at-risk youth who had been incarcerated, homeless, or abused to engage them in an exercise of self-exploration.[18] Allen has also explored the use of hip-hop/rap in "hip-hop therapy" which entails the analysis of hip-hop music lyrics as a strategy to stimu-late discussion and promote self-examination of life struggles and experiences.[19] Stephens and Few used images depicted in hip-hop/rap music as a framework in preadolescents for understanding their perceptions on physical attractiveness and sexuality.[20] Stokes and colleagues have explored the use of hip-hop culture as a tool for empowering female urban youth.[21] There have been no programs that use hip-hop/rap music in a school-based classroom setting. Therefore, among a cohort of adolescents attending an urban middle school, the objective was to determine the feasibility of using hip-hop/rap music as a method of teaching students about HIV and AIDS awareness and prevention in a structured classroom setting.

## THEORETICAL CONSTRUCT

In developing this program, two theoretical perspectives on health behavior were explored: Social Cognitive Theory (SCT) and Sexual Script Theory. SCT explains human behavior as a function of reciprocal interactions between the individual and their environment.[22] Major constructs of SCT include expecta-tions, observational learning, reinforcements, and self-efficacy. Expectations are the anticipated outcomes of a behavior. Several of the music lyrics that glorify sex may be highlighting unrealistic positive outcomes of sexual promiscuity such as enhanced popularity and fame. Another construct of SCT is observational learn-ing which is highlighted by some rap music videos. They provide visual displays of young, attractive, popular artists who are often viewed as role models. This may influence beliefs about norms and expectations about engaging in sexual intercourse. Reinforcements refer to factors that will either increase or decrease the likelihood of the behavior. The glorification of money, luxurious cars, and palatial homes may serve as a positive reinforcement for such sexually gratuitous behavior. Self-efficacy is also a construct of SCT that describes the confidence to achieve a goal. The lyrics in rap music and the artists in the accompanying videos most often give the impression of being in control or having an exaggerated sense of self-efficacy. This may give the illusion that these behaviors are associated with confidence or a sense of "machismo" or that this type of behavior results in get-ting the goal, which is often a female object or sex.

Inherent within the development of this program is the notion of reciprocal determinism or the belief that there is a dynamic and reciprocal relationship between individuals, their behavior, and their environment. Hip-hop/rap music creates a social environment in which music is shared by individuals and thus provides opportunities for sharing of misconceptions and the perpetuation of unrealistic perceptions that may influence sexual behaviors. In this model, the individual, the behaviors, and the environment are all interdependent and determinants of each other.[23]

The Sexual Script Theory provides a framework for conceptualizing how different perspectives on sexuality and sexual interactions are formed. This theory describes the social and cognitive process that guides social and sexual interactions and processes by which meaning is given to sexuality. Sexual scripts can be visual or behavioral cues that dictate beliefs about sexual interactions, set normative values, form attitudes toward sexual interactions, and drive expectations.[24] Sexual scripts can be conveyed through written narrative, television, or music. Hip-hop/rap music may provide "sexual scripts" or a conceptual schema that informs views of sexual norms.[22,25]

Viewed within the contexts of SCT and Sexual Script Theory, hip-hop/rap music serves as a powerful medium for engaging youth in discussions about behaviors that places them at risk for contracting HIV and other sexually transmitted diseases. Some of the sexually explicit and at times misogynist lyrics of rap music make it an effective and creative tool for engaging youth in these discussions. This paper describes a model using popular culture for delivering HIV/AIDS prevention messages to adolescents in a classroom setting.

# METHODS

## TARGET POPULATION

The target population for the Reducing HIV and AIDS Through Prevention (RHAP) program were adolescents residing in communities that are most impacted by HIV/AIDS. The program was piloted at a local middle school in East Harlem, NYC, a predominantly Black and Latino community that is disproportionately impacted by poverty, lower rates of high school graduation, and violence. Approximately one in eleven residents in this community report participating in behaviors that increase the risk of acquiring sexually transmitted diseases such as using injection drugs, having unprotected anal intercourse, and exchanging sex or drugs for money. Therefore, in order to prevent adverse health outcomes, raising awareness about high-risk sexual behaviors in this community at an early age is important.[26]

## Methods Used in Program Development

The Institutional Review Board office at the Academic Medical College reviewed the RHAP protocol as an educational program. In order to gain access to middle schools that were located in East Harlem, telephone calls were made to a random sample of schools. The middle school in which the program was actually piloted was a school that was located near the Academic Medical Center and one with which a facilitator of the program had some familiarity. In order to pilot the RHAP program, there were several meetings with the principal and other faculty at the school prior to meeting or talking with any of the students.

In developing the RHAP program, content material was selected from the New York City Department of Education's HIV/AIDS curriculum for students in kindergarten through the 12th grade.[27] The curriculum for students in kindergarten through grade 3 stresses the importance of health and introduces the concept of making healthy choices and avoiding unhealthy choices. The curriculum for students in grades 4 to 12 introduces more specific behaviors and personal choices such as abstinence and avoiding drug use as methods of prevention. A main emphasis of the curriculum is on teaching students to make developmentally appropriate health behavior choices that can protect them from HIV infection. Select items from the seventh and eighth grade curriculum were integrated into a multisession program that had the overall goal of raising awareness about high-risk behaviors and prevention as well as encouraging abstinence.

In an effort to make the content of the program appropriate and consistent with the learning environment and philosophy of the school, the curriculum was reviewed with the administrative faculty before it was implemented. The faculty at the school was supportive of the concept of using hip-hop/rap music as a teaching tool because they recognized that it was the most popular form of music listened to by their students. The faculty at the school also recommended including a session where students could become aware of resources for finding information on HIV. After reviewing the overall curriculum with the school faculty, the program concepts were introduced to four seventh and eighth graders who were identified by the school faculty as students who could help guide further development of the program. These students provided a list of popular songs that described behaviors that increased the risk of HIV and other STIs such as songs that contained lyrics that described the use of drugs, sexual behavior, or that discussed intimate relationships. The songs themselves were purchased via online music sources and their lyrics were also retrieved from free and publically available web-based sources.

## Methods Used in Program Implementation

The RHAP program was implemented during regular school hours thereby avoiding the need for students and teachers to stay after school. It was integrated during the last period where students generally would be doing their homework or independent study. The program was delivered by two health professionals; a teacher from the school was often present in the classroom. The format of the program included 10–15 mins of introduction during which the goals of the sessions were described. This was followed by 25–30 min of an interactive discussion on a key topic. This was an interactive session during which students were asked questions that helped to stimulate discussion. This exercise was followed by an approximately 30-min period during which groups of three to four students analyzed the lyrical content of select songs. During this exercise, students listened to a song twice. The first time the song was played, they were asked to listen. The second time it was played, the lyrics were distributed and students were asked to read the lyrics and identify words or phrases that were relevant to the topic of HIV/AIDS. During this exercise, the lyrics were all viewed as sexual scripts to which the SCT framework was applied in an effort to stimulate discussion. **Table 1** describes how constructs of SCT were incorporated in classroom discussions and in the analysis of music. Using the SCT as a framework, the following questions were asked of students:

- What is the behavior or behaviors described in this song that increases the risk or chance of becoming infected with HIV/AIDS?
- What are some bad or negative results of the behavior(s) described in this song?
- What are some of the lyrics which make this behavior seem desirable or may make someone want to repeat this behavior or what does the artist say that makes you want to do what he/she is talking about?
- How confident does the artist seem to be?
- What is the artist saying that gives the impression that he/she is confident?

During a given session, two to three songs were usually discussed in this format. In the last 5 min of the session, the main points of the class were reviewed and students were told the topic that was going to be discussed during the following session and were asked to suggest songs that would be useful in discussing the next topic.

**Table 1** Construct of SCT Incorporated in Classroom Discussions and in the Analysis of Music

| SCT construct | Definition of constructs | Topics for discussion |
|---|---|---|
| Expectations | Anticipatory outcomes of a behavior | Discuss the serious and negative consequences of sexually risky behaviors such as teen pregnancy and sexually transmitted diseases |
| Observational learning | The behavioral acquisition that occurs by watching the actions and outcomes of other's behavior | Discuss the risky behaviors described by the artist such as drinking and having sex |
| Reinforcement | Responses to a person's behavior that increases or decreases the likelihood of reoccurrence | Discuss the illusion of money and cars as rewards of sexually risky behavior that is often described in the songs |
| Self-efficacy | Confidence in performing a particular behavior | Discuss the illusion of self-efficacy or over confidence that are often described in some songs |

## METHODS USED IN PROGRAM EVALUATION

A formative evaluation was done in order to determine student's satisfaction with the program and to inform its further development. The school faculty suggested gauging students understanding by asking them to describe the goals of the program. Students were also asked to describe what they liked the most about the sessions, what they disliked, and what they would like to improve.[28] Students were also asked whether participation in the program affected the way in which they listened to music. The responses were evaluated using qualitative analysis. Each response was analyzed line-by-line to generate preliminary concepts. Similar concepts were grouped to form larger categories, which were then examined for their properties and dimensions. Categories that shared similar properties and dimensions were grouped into larger themes.[29]

## THE FINAL PROGRAM (RHAP)

The RHAP program was piloted during five consecutive weekly sessions that lasted 1h and 15min. The first session focused on the concept of making general healthy choices. This session focused on healthy eating, physical activity, and reducing risk of chronic conditions such as diabetes. These general health items were included because the school faculty felt that a discussion of sexual behavior should be placed in the context of overall health. Sessions 2 through 4 focused on abstinence, sexual health, making healthy decisions about sex, HIV prevention and risks, HIV testing, and the impact of drugs on making health decisions regarding sex.

The fifth session and final session was conducted at the medical college from which the facilitators came. Permission to bring the students out of their school for the final session was obtained from the school faculty. Parents were invited to come, and a teacher from the school accompanied students to and from the medical college. During this, students learned how to do an online search about HIV and were asked to do a 5-min presentation on what they learned. Students also completed evaluations during this last session.

The core content of the HIV awareness and prevention program was delivered in sessions 2 through 4 which will be the basis of the remainder of the paper. During session 2, the key topics discussed were the immune system and the distinction between HIV and AIDS. The discussion on how HIV impairs the immune system was adopted from the seventh and eighth grade curriculum. Students in the RHAP program were introduced to vocabulary from among the list provided in the seventh and eighth grade curriculum such as the *antigen, B cell, CD4 count, T cell, lymphokines, macrophages, deficiency, opportunistic,* and *susceptible.* In addition, the magnitude of HIV in the world and locally in their community was also discussed. Data from the New York City Department of Health and Mental Hygiene was used to describe the impact of HIV and AIDS in East Harlem compared to the rest of NYC.

Session 3 focused on modes of transmission and methods of HIV prevention. Specifically, the discussion on transmission through bodily fluids (blood, semen, preseminal fluid, vaginal fluid, menstrual blood, and breast milk) that was described in the seventh and eighth grade curriculum was also integrated into the RHAP program. This session also included a discussion on other categories of STIs and strategies to remain abstinent.

Session 4 focused on the impact of drugs and alcohol on decision-making capacity. The goal of this session was used to describe how the use of these substances can impair one's ability to make healthy choices about sex. Both the seventh and eighth grade curriculum included a discussion on the role of alcohol and other drugs and unsafe sexual behavior. The eighth grade curriculum contained guidelines on stages of alcohol and other drug use which was integrated in the discussion on alcohol and drugs. These stages included abstinence from alcohol or drug use, experimental use, regular use, daily preoccupation, and dependency. The eighth grade curriculum also provided examples of drugs that were discussed such as marijuana, cocaine, PCP, crystal methamphetamine, and heroin. In addition, tobacco, steroids, and prescription pills were also discussed as "gateway drugs."

# RESULTS

## EVALUATIONS

In total, 26 students in the sixth and seventh grade participated; there were 12 girls and 14 boys, their ages ranged from 12 to 13. In general, students related the goals of the program to HIV prevention. In response to the question that asked students to describe the goals of the program, categories of responses included: to teach and raise awareness about HIV, to provide education on making healthy sexual choices, and to use hip-hop as an approach to HIV education. For example, one student said "The goal of the program was to bring awareness to HIV/AIDS." Another student stated that the goal was "to learn and understand HIV/AIDS."

Students' responses also suggested that they understood that the goal of the programs was to enable them to make healthy choices in addition to knowing about HIV. For example, one student said "The goal of the program was to educate students about HIV and AIDS and also to make right choices." Another student said "The goal was to teach us about HIV/AIDS and teach us to make healthy choices."

Students also understood that listening to hip-hop was the approach used for teaching. One student described the goal as "to use hip-hop to educate children about HIV/AIDS." Another student stated "to learn more about HIV/AIDS and to make it fun." Some students also viewed the goal of the program as helping to spread the word about HIV/AIDS. An example of this response was "The goals of the program were to spread and bring awareness to HIV/AIDS and also to help us pass on the information." Another example is "The goals were to send a message that HIV/AIDS is a serious and dangerous disease."

When asked to describe what they liked about the program, categories of responses included: learning about HIV and listening to music. One of the students reported, "I thought this program was great because we learned a lot and it was fun because we got to listen to music that we enjoyed." Other responses were "I liked listening to the music, talking about leaders, choices, and making presentation about HIV/AIDS" and "I really enjoyed learning about HIV/AIDS and listening and understanding the music we listened to."

While most students enjoyed the program, there were aspects of the program that some students wanted to improve such as the duration of the program and having more interactive sessions. Several students felt that the program was too brief, "we should have more interactive activities like plays" or "we can improve the program if we make the time longer." Other recommendations included more field trips and playing more music.

When asked to describe the impact that this had on how they listened to music, students did not imply that they would stop listening to hip-hop or rap. However, based on their responses, they stated that the program raised the awareness of the content of the lyrics. For example, students stated "Now when I listen to music, I do not just listen to the beats, I listen to the words too." Another response was "I learned to listen to motivational songs that are positive," "It taught me how to analyze the music that I listen to every day," and "It taught me about the bad messages the songs send to people about sex."

## DISCUSSION

In spite of educational efforts targeted at sex education, the number of sexually active adolescents continues to increase and, not surprisingly, the prevalence of HIV also continues to soar. These trends beg for a new approach that can complement existing methods of HIV education. The RHAP project represents a new approach to addressing the problem of HIV/AIDS. It is based on constructs of SCT and Sexual Script Theory and uses hip-hop/rap music as mechanisms for teaching HIV awareness and prevention. The lyrics of hip-hop/rap music and other forms of popular music are often controversial and contain misogynous lyrics about drugs, sex, and money. This fact makes hip-hop music an inexpensive yet powerful tool for discussing HIV/AIDS and the social factors that contribute to its spread. These lyrics also provide a forum for discussing images of women in the media and the power dynamics with which adolescents, especially girls, must often contend.

Studies have found that, on average, adolescent's exposure to sexually explicit rap videos can be as much as 14 h/week.[16] Public health advocates need to understand the degree to which this music can penetrate and influence the lives of urban youth. The RHAP program enabled students to listen to popular hip-hop/rap music, analyze their lyrics, and discuss their relevance to HIV prevention. Much of the discussions were stimulated by student comments and their interpretation of the lyrics. The appeal of this approach is that the songs are created by familiar artists of the same racial and ethnic background who may be regarded as respectable peers and, therefore, may serve to establish expectations and norms of sexual behavior.

The objective of the RHAP program was to determine whether it was feasible to use hip-hop/rap music as a method of teaching students about HIV and AIDS awareness and prevention. Based on our experience, it was feasible to engage students in this program. Formative discussions with the faculty revealed that they too recognized the depth to which the hip-hop culture had penetrated the lives of the students. Formative discussions with students also revealed that most of them listened to hip-hop/rap music on a daily basis.

The student evaluations revealed that students understood that the goals of the program were to teach and raise awareness about HIV/AIDS. While listening to music was described as enjoyable, they also viewed this exercise as being educational and one in which they learned about HIV/AIDS. The goal of the program was to use hip-hop to teach about HIV/AIDS and not to persuade students to stop listening to this music but rather to be more aware of what they listened to and understand that the lyrics may be antithetical to tenets of HIV prevention. Some students stated that, as a result of their participation in this program, they have become more aware of the content of the music and how it relates to behaviors that increase the risk of HIV/AIDS.

The intention of the RHAP program was not to portray all hip-hop as "bad." This genre of music represents a diverse body of music, some of which has positive and motivational content that has been used to raise social and political consciousness. The use of this music challenges the traditional pedagogue–student paradigm and provides an alternative to the pedantic approach to teaching about HIV. It is entertaining and familiar to students. Students knew more about the songs which may have supported a sense of ownership and greater involvement.

This was a preliminary evaluation of the RHAP program and, therefore, there are limitations. The program was not tested against other methods of HIV/AIDS education nor was the long-term impact of this program in terms of future sexual behavior assessed. It is also not known whether students who participate in this program will be less likely to engage in risky behaviors such as early initiation of sexual behavior, use of condoms, and avoidance of drugs and alcohol. It is also unknown whether this approach, when used with other HIV prevention methods, reduces the rate of pregnancy or STIs. Although the music is often shared and discussed with their peers, it is also unknown whether students who participated in this program were more comfortable in discussing HIV/AIDS awareness and prevention with their peers than those who did not. In order to answer some of these questions, we are in the process of developing a proposal in order to test in a randomized trial the effectiveness of the RHAP program on short-term outcomes, such as knowledge, as well as long-term sexual behaviors and rates of STIs.

Hip-hop culture and music has become an influential entity among youth especially those in urban and inner-city environments. There is ample literature that describes the links between listening to music with degrading and sexually explicit content to risky sexual behavior. There is also the opportunity to use this as a teaching modality. Parents, educators, and health care providers should understand the impact that this music may have on adolescents. Parents and teachers may wish to ask their children to describe the content of the songs that they are listening to and take this opportunity to discuss the messages in the context of HIV and other STI prevention. Health care providers may wish to engage their patients in discussions about the content of the songs they listen to and use the opportunity to also provide counseling on prevention.

Based on formative evaluations, the RHAP program is a feasible program that addresses an important public health issue and can be implemented to complement current educational programs on sexual health. It engages students to reflect on their health and choices that they may make. The use of music is also sustainable since students will listen to these songs outside of the classroom setting. There is also greater opportunity for dissemination to other peers through sharing. The program can be supplemented with other forms of popular culture such as television and books or art. This approach is widely applicable and can be replicated in other populations and used to address other public health issues such as intimate partner violence, substance use, and gang-related violence. RHAP provides an opportunity to create greater synergy between popular culture and health promotion.

## REFERENCES

1. New York City Department of Mental Health and Hygiene. The health of Brooklyn. Available at: http://www.nyc.gov/health. Accessed December 3, 2008.
2. New York City Department of Health and Mental Hygiene. *Vital Signs: A Report of from the New York City Youth Risk Behavior Survey*, vol. 6 issue 3; 2007.

3. Hygiene NYCDoMHa. *Surveillance and Epidemiology Reports: NYC Pediatric/Adolescent HIV/AIDS Surveillance*; 2007.

4. Hygiene NYCDoHaM. Youth risk behavior survey: health behaviors among youth in East and Central Harlem, Bedford-Stuyvesant and Bushwick, and the South Bronx. Available at: http://www.nyc.gov/html/doh/html/episrv/episrv. Accessed December 3, 2008.

5. Resnicow K, Baranowski T, Ahluwalia JS, Braithwaite RL. Cultural sensitivity in public health: defined and demystified. *Ethn Dis*. 1999;*9*(1):10–21.

6. Stephens T, Braithwaite RL, Taylor SE. Model for using hip-hop music for small group HIV/AIDS prevention counseling with African American adolescents and young adults. *Patient Educ Couns*. 1998;*35*(2):127–137. doi: 10.1016/S0738-3991(98)00050-0.

7. Tyson EH. Hip hop therapy: an exploratory study of a rap music intervention with at-risk and delinquent youth. *J Poet Ther*. 2002;*15*(32002):131–144. doi: 10.1023/A:1019795911358.

8. Martino SC, Collins RL, Elliott MN, Strachman A, Kanouse DE, Berry SH. Exposure to degrading versus nondegrading music lyrics and sexual behavior among youth. *Pediatrics*. 2006;*118*(2):e430–e441. doi: 10.1542/peds.2006-0131.

9. Mark A. Adolescents discuss themselves and drugs through music. *J Subst Abuse Treat*. 1986;*3*(4):243–249. doi: 10.1016/0740-5472(86)90035-8.

10. Roberts DF, Foehr UG, Rideout V. Generation M: Media in the Lives of 8–18 Year-Olds. Menlo Park: Henry J. Kaiser Foundation; 2003.

11. Leach A. One day it'll all make sense: hop-hop and rap resources for music librarians. Available at: http://muse.jhu.edu/. Accessed December 3, 2008.

12. Guo J, Chung IJ, Hill KG, Hawkins JD, Catalano RF, Abbott RD. Developmental relationships between adolescent substance use and risky sexual behavior in young adulthood. *J Adolesc Health*. 2002;*31*(4):354–362. doi: 10.1016/S1054-139X(02)00402-0.

13. Hall PD. The relationship between types of rap music and memory in African American children. *J Black Stud*. 1998;*28*(6):802–814. doi: 10.1177/002193479802800607.

14. Pardun CJ, Ladin L'Engle K, Brown JD. Linking exposure to outcomes: early adolescents' consumption of sexual content in six media. *Mass Commun Soc*. 2005;*8*(8):75–91. doi: 10.1207/s15327825mcs0802_1.

15. Brown JD, L'Engle KL, Pardun CJ, Guo G, Kenneavy K, Jackson C. Sexy media matter: exposure to sexual content in music, movies, television, and magazines predicts black and white adolescents' sexual behavior. *Pediatrics*. 2006;*117*(4):1018–1027. doi: 10.1542/peds.2005-1406.

16. Wingood GM, DiClemente RJ, Bernhardt JM, et al. A prospective study of exposure to rap music videos and African American female adolescents' health. *Am J Public Health*. 2003;*93*(3):437–439. doi:.10.2105/AJPH.93.3.437.

17. Peterson SH, Wingood GM, DiClemente RJ, Harrington K, Davies S. Images of sexual stereotypes in rap videos and the health of African American female adolescents. *J Womens Health (Larchmt)* 2007;*16*(8):1157–1164. doi: 10.1089/jwh.2007.0429.

18. Tyson EH. Hip hop therapy: an exploratory study of a rap music intervention with at-risk and delinquent youth. *J Poet Ther*. 2002;*15*(3):1567–2344.

19. Allen NMT. Exploring hip-hop therapy with high-risk youth. Available at: http://www.luc.edu/socialwork/praxis/pdfs/praxis_article4.pdf; 2005. Accessed December 3, 2008.

20. Stephens DP, Few Al. The effects of images of African American women in hip hop on early adolescents' attitudes toward physical attractiveness and interpersonal relationships. *Sex Roles*. 2007;*56*:251–264. doi: 10.1007/s11199-006-9145-5.

21. Stokes CE, Gant LM. Turning the tables on the HIV/AIDS epidemic: hip hop as a tool for reaching African-American adolescent girls. *Afr Am Res Perspect*. 2002;8:70–81.

22. Glanz K, Lewis FM, Rimer BK. *Health Behavior and Health Education: Theory, Research, and Practice*. San Francisco: Jossey-Bass; 1997.

23. Wingood GM, DiClemente RJ. The use of psychosocial models for guiding the design and implementation of HIV prevention interventions. Translating theory into practice. In: Gibney L, DiClemente RJ, Vermund SH, editors. *Preventing HIV in Developing Countries Biomedical and Behavioral Approaches*. New York: Kluwer Academic; 1999. pp. 187–204.

24. Simon W, Gagnon JH. Sexual scripts: origins, influences and changes. *Qual Sociol*. 2003;*26*(4):1573–7837. doi: 10.1023/B:QUAS.0000005053.99846.e5.

25. Stokes CE. Representin' in cyberspace: sexual scripts, self-definition, and hip hop culture in Black American adolescent girls' home pages. *Cult Health Sex*. 2007;*9*(2):169–184. doi: 10.1080/13691050601017512.

26. New York City Department of Health and Mental Hygiene. *Community Health Profiles*. 2006.

27. New York City Department of Education. *HIV/AIDS Curriculum. A Supplement to a Comprehensive Health Curriculum*.

28. Brush T. The effects on student achievement and attitudes when using integrated learning systems with cooperative pairs. *Education Tech Research Dev*. 1997;*45*(1):1556–6501. doi: 10.1007/BF02299612.

29. Morse JM, Field PA, et al. *Qualitative Research Methods for Health Professionals*. Thousand Oaks: Sage; 1995.

# CHAPTER ACTIVITY QUESTIONS

1. Which constructs of the SCT were used as the basis of the RHAP intervention and why?

2. What is the explanation the authors provide for why the theoretical concept of Reciprocal Determinism is applicable to the RHAP approach for HIV prevention?   .

3. Identify one other construct that may be consistent with the approach used in this program, and explain why.

# CHAPTER REFERENCES

Anderson, E.S., Winett, R.A., & Wojkcik, J.R. (2007). *Annals of Behavioral Medicine, 34*(3), 304–312.

Bandura, A., & Walters, R.H. (1959). *Adolescent Aggression.* Ronald Press: New York.

Bandura, A., Ross, D., & Ross, S.A (1961). Transmission of aggression through imitation of aggressive models. *The Journal of Abnormal and Social Psychology, 63*(3), 575–582.

Bandura, A. (1977). *Social Learning Theory.* Englewood Cliffs, NJ: Prentice-Hall.

Bandura, A. (1986). *Social Foundations of Thought and Action: A Social Cognitive Theory.* Englewood Cliffs, NJ: Prentice-Hall.

Bandura, A. (1991). Social cognitive theory of self-regulation. *Organizational Behavior, 50,* 248–287.

Bandura, A. (1993). Perceived self-efficacy in cognitive development and functioning. *Educational Psychologist, 28*(2), 117–148.

Borrayo, E.A., & Guarnaccia, C.A. (2002). Differences in Mexican-born and U.S.-born women of Mexican descent regarding factors related to breast cancer screening behaviors. *Health Care for Women International, 21*(7), 599–614.

Grusec, J.E. (1992). Social learning theory and developmental psychology: The legacies of Robert Sears and Albert Bandura. *Developmental Psychology, 28*(5), 776–786.

Levenson, H. (1974). Activism and powerful others: Distinctions within the concept of internal-external control. *Journal of Personality Assessment, 38,* 377–383.

Rawl, S.M., Champion, V.L., Menon, U., & Foster, J.L. (2000). The impact of age and race on mammography practices. *Health Care for Women International, 21*(7), 583–598.

Shelton, P., Weinrich, S., & Reynolds, W.A. (1999). Barriers to prostate cancer screening in African-American men. *Journal of National Black Nurses Association, 10*(2), 14–28.

Steptoe, A., & Wardle, J. (2001). Locus of control and health behaviour revisited: A multivariate analysis of young adults from 18 countries. *British Journal of Psychology, 92,* 659–672.

U.S. Department of Health and Human Services & U.S. Department of Agriculture. (2010). Choosemyplate.gov. Website. Washington, DC, Dietary Guidelines. Accessed, October 18, 2012. http://www.choosemyplate.gov/dietary-guidelines.html.

# Diffusion of Innovation

## STUDENT LEARNING OUTCOMES

After reading this chapter the student will be able to:

- Explain the concepts of Diffusion Theory.
- Discuss the characteristics of an innovation.
- Discuss the components of time relative to innovation adoption.
- Identify communication channels used in diffusion.
- Identify social systems through which innovations diffuse.
- Use the theory to explain the adoption of one health behavior.

## THEORY ESSENCE SENTENCE

Behavior changes as innovations are adopted.

**Diffusion of Innovation Constructs Chart**

**Innovation**
The new idea, product, process, etc.

**Communication channels**
Methods through which the innovation is made known to the members of the social system

**Time**
How much time it takes for the innovation-decision process to occur, and the rate at which different segments of the social system adopt the innovation

**Social system**
The group structure into which the innovation is being introduced

# IN THE BEGINNING

Diffusion of innovation is a communication theory with its roots in rural sociology (Valentine & Rogers, 1995). In the 1920s, research supported by the U.S. Department of Agriculture was conducted to determine the effectiveness of the different methods used to inform farmers of new (innovative) farming practices (Wilson, 1927). This type of research continued into the 1930s with studies being done to determine how the introduction of other new practices (innovations) were shared and eventually accepted, such as postage stamps, limits on municipal taxation rates, and compulsory school law (Pemberton, 1936; Valente & Rogers, 1995).

Building on this, research done in 1943 on the diffusion of hybrid corn seed by Ryan and Gross laid the foundation for understanding how new practices (innovation) were spread into society, that is, the diffusion of innovation. What prompted Ryan and Gross's research was the unexpected reaction of farmers to hybrid corn seed. Since the hybrid seed increased crop yield and produced hardier, drought-resistant corn, farmers were expected to quickly switch to the new seed. However, this is not what happened. On average, it took seven years for a farmer to go from trying the hybrid seed to planting 100% of his land with it. Obviously, something other than economics was at the root of this seemingly irrational behavior (Rogers, 2004; Ryan & Gross, 1943). What Ryan and Gross (1943; Valente & Rogers, 1995) found was that the spread of the hybrid corn innovation was a *social* process that resulted from interpersonal communication – that is, one farmer tried it because another farmer told him he had already tried it and liked it. Diffusion of innovation provided the explanation for the farmers' slow adoption of the new type of seed. From this research came the four main aspects of diffusion: the innovation-decision process, the role and source of the communication channel, the normal distribution curve or the rate of adoption, and the characteristics of people who adopt an innovation at the various rates (Valente & Rogers, 1995).

# THEORETICAL CONCEPT

Diffusion of innovation is the process by which new ideas (innovations) are disseminated (diffused) and adopted by a society. As new ideas are adopted and integrated into the society—that is, they become the norm—behavior changes.

# THEORETICAL CONSTRUCTS

How a new idea spreads through a society, and why some become part of the social fabric and others do not, can be explained by the four main constructs of this theory: the innovation, the channels through which it is communicated, time, and the social system. Diffusion is the process by which this takes place (Rogers, 2003).

## INNOVATION

An innovation is something new, or novel, whether it is a device, a practice, or an idea (National Cancer Institute [NCI], 2005). Diffusion and ultimate adoption (or rejection) of an innovation is affected by certain characteristics of the innovation itself. These characteristics include having an advantage over what is already available, compatibility with social norms and values, trial on a limited basis, ease of use, and having observable results. Innovations with these characteristics will be adopted more rapidly than those without these characteristics (Rogers, 2003; Rogers & Scott, 1997) (**Figure 8–1**).

### Relative Advantage

An innovation has a greater chance of being adopted if it is better than what is already out there, or if it fills a void where nothing else similar exists. In either case, the innovation has a relative advantage over what is currently available.

An example of a product having a relative advantage is the female condom. When this product was introduced in 1993, it had a decided advantage over

**FIGURE 8–1** Innovation

what was already available because no other product like it existed. Although its adoption has not been as great as anticipated for a number of reasons, relative advantage is not one of them.

Another example is "candy" calcium supplements. Standard calcium supplements are relatively large pills that must be taken, on average, two to three times a day. Changing the calcium delivery system from a large pill to a candy-like formulation was an innovation with a relative advantage. Eating a piece of chocolate "candy" twice a day is much more appealing than swallowing a bunch of large pills.

While restaurants serving locally grown foods would not have been viewed as an innovation 100 years ago, this is an innovation today. The advantages of using locally grown foods over foods sourced from large scale agri-businesses include: better taste, freshness, variety, and sometimes price (Inwood, Sharp, Moore, & Stinner, 2009).

With so much attention being given to the adoption of environmentally sustainable practices, the advantages to adoption of these has not been lost on the hotel and resort industry. While the relative advantage may not always be directly related to health, anything that supports good environmental stewardship is welcomed. In this case, the relative advantage of environmental sustainable practices is avoidance of regulatory penalties. Hotels are required to follow practices that minimize negative environmental impact. The fines associated with not following these regulations are expected to increase in the years to come, thus adoption of environmentally sustainable practices would go a long way in avoiding these (Smerecnik & Andersen, 2011).

## Trialability

It is advantageous if an innovation can be used on a trial basis or limited scale. If people can try something new without making a major commitment to it in terms of time, money, or effort, there is a better chance of it being adopted. This is why companies make trial sizes of new products and offer coupons.

Take vision correction, for example. If you decide to switch from glasses to contact lenses, there is a trial period before you make a commitment to using contacts and buy a supply of them. Even then, you can switch back and forth between the contacts and glasses. On the other hand, Lasik vision correction cannot be tried or used on a limited scale because Lasik is corrective surgery that permanently changes the shape of the cornea (Food and Drug Administration [FDA], 2004).

A classic example of trialability is the practice of pharmaceutical companies giving physicians free samples. Free samples promote physician adoption of medication, and, when samples are given to patients, it promotes their adoption as well (Kane & Mittman, 2002).

## Complexity

An innovation's complexity will also affect its likelihood of adoption. The more complex it is to understand and use, the less likely it is to be adopted or even tried. For example, female condoms are not easy to use the first time (Piot, 1998). They require proper placement before and during sex and careful removal afterwards. Unless a woman feels she can insert the condom, keep it in place, and remove it correctly, the odds of her using it again after the first time are not good nor are the chances of it being adopted (Hollander, 2004).

In contrast, the nicotine patch is relatively simple to use. Choose an area of skin on the upper body that is free from hair, intact, and dry. Open the package, peel the protective covering off the patch, and apply it to the skin. Pretty simple.

The Centers for Disease Control and Prevention is encouraging people to adopt an innovative technique to reduce disease transmission through droplet infection. It calls for people to sneeze and cough into their upper sleeve instead of into their hands or into the air (Centers for Disease Control and Prevention [CDC], 2007; Lounsbury, 2006). This is an easy-to-use innovation that anyone can adopt. It requires no special training, equipment, or practice.

Adoption of sustainable practices at hotels and ski resorts is predicated on their ease of implementation. In fact, ease of implementing sustainable practices is the most significantly related variable in the prediction of adoption of sustainable practices (Smerecnik & Andersen, 2011). The easier it is to put the innovation in place, the greater the likelihood that it will be implemented (**Figure 8–2**).

## Compatibility

To be adopted, an innovation needs to be compatible with the existing values and needs of the people, culture, or social environment (Rogers, 2003). Certainly in the case of the female condom, its adoption would not likely occur among women whose culture considers touching one's own genitals taboo or whose religious beliefs prohibit contraception.

Incompatibility with social norms is one of the issues at the heart of HIV/ AIDS prevention in Tanzania, a country with one of the highest rates of AIDS

©doglikehorse/Shutterstock, Inc.

**FIGURE 8–2** Complexity affects adoption

in the world. Although most infections are transmitted horizontally (adult to adult) through heterosexual intercourse, a substantial number of infants are infected through vertical transmission (from infected mother to child). Consequently, one of the interventions being tried is aimed at preventing transmission of HIV through breast milk (Burke, 2004; Israel-Ballard et al., 2005).

Although the solution to this problem seems obvious—just have mothers use formula—it is not that easy. The majority of Tanzanian women breastfeed their children until 2 years of age because it is expected of them. Even HIV-positive women are expected to breastfeed. Consequently, women who do not breastfeed are stigmatized. However, there is a way to reduce the risk of HIV transmission in breast milk, namely, by heat treating. Heat treating destroys HIV in breast milk without significantly changing its nutrient content (Burke, 2004; Israel-Ballard et al., 2005). But heat treating breast milk requires the mother to express her milk and then heat it using one of two simple methods. Although heat treating is effective, simple to do, and still allows the mother to feed her child breast milk, expressing breast milk is taboo and incompatible with local practices and beliefs (Burke, 2004).

Although originally introduced in the 1980s, hand sanitizers were not considered socially acceptable at the time. If a business provided them for its customers, questions were raised about the cleanliness of the establishment. Times have changed, and people are now more germ phobic. Today, if a business offers hand sanitizers, customers are grateful (Yee, 2007). Hand sanitizers are now available in a host of places—from supermarkets (to wipe off cart handles) to fast food restaurants and children's playgrounds. People are carrying small, personal-size containers of sanitizer in their purses, briefcases, and backpacks. It is almost to the point now where *not* using a hand sanitizer is socially unacceptable.

## Observability

If the results of using an innovation can be seen by other people, it is more likely to be adopted. Think about the rate of adoption of breast augmentation, tattoos, and body piercing. Observability may explain why these have become so widely adopted. Observability drives the diet industry. People try new diets because, if they work, the results are noticeable.

Observability has affected health care as well. Early on, chiropractic care was something novel, an innovation. It was a different way to treat illness. Its adoption was largely based on word of mouth and the improvement observed by others (McCarthy & Milus, 2000). The same situation occurred with acupuncture.

While it was first seen as something novel (although it dates back 2,500 years in China), it is now an accepted treatment option, especially for chronic pain management. Its results are observable (Eshkevari & Heath, 2005) in that many people who had limited mobility prior to treatment are active after.

## Communication Channel

Diffusion is the active sharing or communication of information among people. It is a social process: people talking to one another about a new idea, product, tool, food, or so on (Haider & Kreps, 2004; Rogers, 2003). The communication channel is how word of an innovation spreads.

The most effective and rapid means of communicating something new is through mass media—the television, newspapers, radio, and the Internet. Mass media channels can reach a huge audience very quickly, making a large portion of a society readily aware of a new product or idea.

As appealing as this method is to get the message out, it is often not the best means of ensuring adoption of an innovation. Sometimes, one-on-one conversation is more effective. For example, one person tries a new product, and she talks with a friend about it, who then talks to another friend, and so on. This is demonstrative of diffusion as a social process that relies on interpersonal communication (Rogers, 2003).

Interpersonal communication and the transfer of information about ideas occur most frequently between two people who are the same, *homophilius*, meaning they share the same beliefs, education level, or socioeconomic level, to name but a few characteristics (Rogers, 2003). A friend talking to friends would have a greater impact on the latter trying something new that the former has already tried (**Figure 8–3**). Thus, the likelihood of an innovation being adopted also depends on how people find out about it, and from whom.

Restaurants implementing the "innovation" of local food sourcing utilize the wait staff as an integral component of the communication channel. They are the ones who interact with consumers and can educate them, one-on-one, about the restaurant's use of local foods and can encourage them to try meals prepared with these ingredients (Inwood, Sharp, Moore, & Stinner, 2009).

## Time

The adoption or rejection of an innovation is the result of the innovation-decision process. This process takes time because it follows a sequence of steps that

**FIGURE 8-3** Friends talking with friends is an effective means of diffusing information about an innovation

includes knowledge, persuasion, decision, implementation, and confirmation (Rogers, 2003) (In the past, these steps were identified as awareness, interest, trial, decision, and adoption.)

## The Innovation-Decision Process

### Knowledge

Common sense tells us that before people can adopt an innovation, they have to know it exists. Knowledge of an innovation is where the communication channels come into play, as discussed previously. Think about how the general public was made aware of the pharmaceutical innovation for erectile dysfunction. Advertisements in magazines, newspapers, TV, direct mail, and disclosure by well-known public figures were all used to inform us about a pharmaceutical innovation to treat a problem many people didn't even know existed.

In 2006, a vaccine against human papillomavirus (HPV) that protects against cervical cancer was introduced for girls and young women aged 9 to 26. Prior to its release, the pharmaceutical company that developed the vaccine began a multimedia "Tell Someone" disease awareness campaign. The campaign was designed to raise awareness of the relationship between HPV and cervical cancer, preparing the U.S. market for the vaccine's release (O'Malley, 2006). Once parents, teens, and young women were made aware of the vaccine's availability, they were able to decide if they would adopt the innovation, that is, be vaccinated. (Unfortunately, the campaign failed to mention that HPV is a sexually transmitted infection and that there are other ways to prevent or reduce infection [O'Malley, 2006].)

### Persuasion

During the persuasion stage, people develop an attitude (either positive or negative) about the innovation (Haider & Kreps, 2004; Rogers, 2003). This comes from having knowledge of or information about the innovation and then mentally applying it to a present or future situation. It is a thought process people go through that helps them formulate a perception of the innovation (Rogers, 2003). It's like trying the innovation on, so to speak.

Persuasion was used when a hospital administration tried to implement an innovative screening program for domestic violence in a postpartum clinic. The clinic staff had to be persuaded of the benefits and appropriateness of the program. They had to be given information that would help them develop a positive attitude toward asking new mothers questions about domestic violence right after they delivered their babies. This was accomplished by having staff engage in training activities that made domestic violence real to them through dialogue with survivors, sharing their own stories, and clinical storytelling (Janssen, Holt, & Sugg, 2002).

Sometimes, opinion leaders are the ones who need to be persuaded about the benefits of an innovation in order to gain access to the people who would be helped most by the innovation. This is what happened in rural Haiti when HIV/AIDS education was introduced. The trusted, influential opinion leaders among this population were voodoo practitioners. They had to be persuaded that preventing HIV/AIDS was easier than trying to cure it. Once these influential people adopted the idea of prevention, they made people in the rural villages accessible, and the message of HIV/AIDS prevention was passed along. (Unfortunately, funding for this project was terminated because "the U.S. government objected to the involvement of voodoo practitioners in the project" [Barker, 2004, p. 133]).

### Decision

Once people have knowledge of an innovation and have developed an attitude toward it, they are ready to make a decision about using it. It is during this stage that people engage in activities that result in a decision to adopt or reject an innovation (Rogers, 2003). This is similar to decisional balance in the Transtheoretical Model.

To support adoption of the postpartum violence program discussed earlier, the program developers provided opportunities for the staff to observe assessments being conducted. Watching new mothers respond in a positive, nonjudgmental way to questions about domestic violence (Janssen, Holt, & Sugg, 2002) helped the staff decide to adopt the violence assessment.

Let's look at "candy" calcium supplements. Before this method of delivery can be adopted, people need to know about this innovative way to take a mineral supplement and they need a good attitude about eating candy. Trying the supplements would be the activity that would result in the decision to adopt or reject the innovation.

Sometimes, however, even if people decide that an innovation is a good idea, they still decide not to adopt it. Reasons for rejection of an innovation that clearly is beneficial might be cost, conflict with values and beliefs, logistics, or lack of skill needed to use the innovation. For example, even though taking calcium in candy form might be seen as a terrific idea, especially after trying it, it still may not be adopted because it is much more expensive than taking calcium in pill form.

## Implementation

The implementation stage occurs when the innovation is tried. Obviously, before people adopt something new, they have to try it to see if they like it. You may have decided that a hybrid car is a terrific innovation, and that you'd like one. But, before you buy a hybrid, you'll take one for a test drive.

Sometimes, even though people decide an innovation is good, they don't try it and consequently don't adopt it. For example, Internet-based cardiac recovery (rehabilitation) interventions are a new way to serve the needs of those who cannot, or who choose not to, attend in-person programs. However, some cardiac clients will not try it, even though they may have decided the idea is good. The reasons are many, including lack of access to the necessary computer equipment, inability to operate a keyboard, and inadequate health literacy (Nguygen, Carrieri-Kohlman, Rankin, Slaughter, & Stubarg, 2004).

The implementation stage results in the adoption, rejection, or reinvention of the innovation. If the trial implementation results are positive, adoption takes place, which means the innovation becomes integrated into the individual's lifestyle.

If the trial implementation results in unacceptable outcomes or the innovation is too costly, culturally inconsistent, or logistically not feasible, it will be rejected. In the example of HIV/AIDS in rural Haiti discussed earlier, if the voodoo practitioners had not been persuaded that prevention was easier than curing, then promoting HIV/AIDS prevention in the villages would not have been possible.

However, sometimes the trial implementation results in the need to modify the innovation before it can be adopted. In the domestic violence program discussed

previously, a modification would have been to have the new mothers complete a questionnaire rather than be interviewed (Rogers, 2003).

## Confirmation

Sometimes the innovation-decision process is completed once the decision is made to either adopt or reject the innovation. Other times, when the decision is made to adopt, people need reinforcement or confirmation from others that it was a good decision. Conflicting messages about the goodness of their decision causes dissonance, or an uncomfortable state of mind (Rogers, 2003) that comes from having made a decision that continues to be questioned or evaluated. We have all done this at one time or another: we make a decision and then continue to question ourselves and others as to whether the decision was a good one or not.

There are times when the decision to adopt is not supported by others, leading to discontinuance or rejection of the innovation. People also discontinue the use of something that was previously adopted when a better "something" comes along to replace it, or if they are dissatisfied with its performance or outcome (Rogers, 2003). Sometimes, instead of discontinuing use of the innovation in these situations, the innovation is reinvented or modified.

A prime example of discontinuance or rejection of a previously adopted innovation is Project DARE (Drug Abuse Resistance Education). Project DARE was implemented in the late 1980s as a way to decrease or eliminate drug use among children and adolescents. Its innovation was having uniformed police officers teach children about the perils of drug use. There was tremendous interest in and adoption of this way to address a growing drug problem. As it turned out, the program was not effective (Dukes, Ullman, & Stein, 1996; Dukes, Stein, & Ullman, 1997; Lynam et al., 1999). Consequently, some schools have modified (reinvented) the program by having only certain lessons taught by a uniformed police officer, whereas others have discontinued its use altogether (Roger, 2003).

## Adoption Curve

In addition to the innovation-decision process, adoption occurs at different rates by different segments of the population. The rate of adoption follows an adoption curve, a bell-shaped curve that sorts people into the following five categories or segments: innovators, early adopters, early majority, late majority, and laggards (**Figure 8–4**).

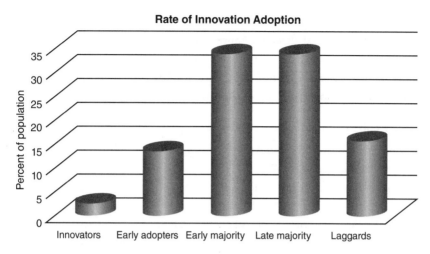

**FIGURE 8–4** Rogers' Adoption/Innovation Curve

*Source:* Adapted from www.12manage.com. Accessed February 25, 2013.

These segments reflect the amount of time it takes to adopt an innovation. Placement on the curve depends on a number of characteristics, such as comfort with risk taking, socioeconomic status, extent of social networks, and leadership. Where one falls on the adoption curve may differ depending on the innovation.

### Innovators

People in the first segment on the curve are the innovators. Innovators represent that small fraction of the population who like to take chances. Innovators are risk takers. They have the financial resources to absorb possible loss from an unprofitable innovation. They are technologically savvy in that they understand and can apply complex technical knowledge, and they can cope with the unpredictability of an innovation (Rogers, 2003).

Innovators are the people who try everything as soon as it is available. They were the first ones to buy an iPod and plasma screen TV, to drive a hybrid, have acupuncture, use solar power, recycle, and eat organic. Innovators tend to be independent, change-oriented risk takers who are inclined to interact with others like themselves rather than a broad cross section of the population. In fact, going back to the Lasik example used earlier, people who are risk takers are considered good candidates for this procedure (FDA, 2004).

Sometimes the innovators are unexpected people. In the case of restaurant use of locally produced food, the innovators were celebrity chefs. They started using locally grown foods in their own restaurants and because of their notoriety, greatly influenced others in the culinary community leading to follow their lead (Inwood, Sharp, Moore, & Stinner, 2009).

### Early Adopters

Early adopters make up the next segment on the adoption curve. They represent a slightly larger portion of the population than do the innovators. Early adopters tend to be the opinion leaders in a community. They are well respected and are often seen as role models. They have a powerful influence over others because they are often the people others like to emulate. They usually have high self-esteem and complex communication networks. They talk to and know a lot of different people and therefore have a broad influence in the community (Rogers, 2003).

### Early Majority

The early majority represents one of the largest segments of the population. On the bell curve, they are part of the inclining side of the bell. They are greatly influenced by opinion leaders and mass media. Although they do adopt new things, they do so over time. But, given their sheer number, when they begin to adopt, the innovation becomes mainstream (Rogers, 2003).

### Late Majority

The late majority is on the downward side of the bell curve. These people tend to question change, choosing to wait until an innovation is an established norm or for it to become a social or economic necessity. They tend to have more modest financial resources and to be greatly influenced by their peers (Rogers, 2003). These are the people who only recently bought a cell phone and a DVD player.

### Laggards

The last group on the curve is the laggards. Laggards tend to be conservative and traditional, have lower self-esteem, have less education, are suspicious of innovation, and are adverse to risk taking. They also tend to be geographically mobile and detached from the social environment. Laggards are the last group of people to adopt an innovation. They wait until very late, even when it's obvious that the innovation is advantageous (Rogers, 2003). These would be the people who just bought their first computer.

## SOCIAL SYSTEM

The fourth construct in diffusion of innovation is the social system. A social system can be individuals, an informal or formal group of people, or organizations that are interrelated and engaged in solving a joint problem to accomplish a goal (Backer & Rogers, 1998; Rogers, 2003). Examples of social systems are the physicians in a hospital, the families in a community, or consumers in the United States. All units in a social system, whether they are individuals (such as the physicians in the hospital) or a collective entity (such as each family in a community), cooperate with each other to reach a common goal. It is the common goal that holds them together (Rogers, 2003). Social systems are essentially different groupings of people. As such, they also include the norms, values, beliefs, attitudes, and other common characteristics of the people who comprise the system. Diffusion takes place within these social systems (Rogers, 2003).

Diffusion of an innovation through a social system is exemplified by the CDC's Business Responds to AIDS (BRTA) program. BRTA was a way to bring HIV/AIDS prevention education to the workplace and, through this effort, prevent discrimination against people with HIV/AIDS at work.

The social system through which this program was diffused included all private companies in the United States (Backer & Rogers, 1998).

The Kitchen Garden Project in the South Central Asian country of Nepal is another example of diffusion of an innovation through a social system. The social system used here was neighborhoods. The project was implemented to combat the country's high infant and maternal mortality rates, which were due mostly to inadequate vitamin A intake. The innovation was to have individual households in neighborhoods plant gardens to grow their own high vitamin A–containing fruits and vegetables (Barker, 2004).

In summary, according to Diffusion of Innovation, the characteristics of an innovation – how it is made known, how long it takes for a decision to be made about it, and the group structure into which it is being introduced – all affect its adoption and, therefore, behavior (**Figure 8–5**).

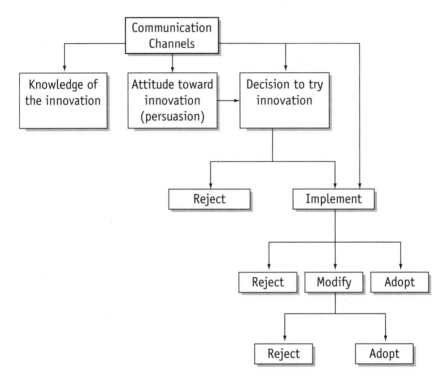

**FIGURE 8–5**  Diffusion of Innovation

*Source:* Adapted from Rogers, E. (1962). *Diffusion of Innovation,* Fifth Edition. Free Press, Simon & Schuster Adult Publishing Group.

# THEORY IN ACTION—CLASS ACTIVITY

Colon cancer is the second leading cause of cancer death in the United States. One non-invasive screening method used for early detection of this treatable cancer is the *fecal-occult blood test (FOBT),* which detects hidden blood in the stool—one of the first signs of colon cancer. The actual test itself requires nothing more than the healthcare provider putting a drop of a chemical reagent on a stool sample that has been smeared on a special collection card by the individual. The difficulty lies in getting people to correctly collect the samples at home. Done correctly, the stool sample is collected *before* it comes in contact with the water in the toilet using a small wooden spatula (about 6–8 inches long). The sample is then smeared on a special collection card. The sample has to dry before the card can be closed. Multiple samples are collected over a few days and then returned (often via mail) to the healthcare provider. In addition to this, there are dietary restrictions for 3 days prior and during stool collection. Red meats, certain vitamins, and medication (aspirin) must be avoided. With this background and using the characteristics of an innovation, what would an innovative method of testing for fecal occult blood look like? When you have finished, read the following article and answer the questions.

# Chapter 8 Article: Exploring Perceptions of Colorectal Cancer and Fecal Immunochemical Testing Among African Americans in a North Carolina Community[1]

*Harden, Elizabeth; Moore, Alexis; Melvin, Cathy.*

## Abstract

### Introduction

African Americans have a lower colorectal cancer screening rate than whites and higher disease incidence and mortality. Despite wide acceptance of colonoscopy for accurate screening, increasing promotion of high-sensitivity stool test screening, such as the fecal immunochemical test (FIT), may narrow racial, ethnic, and socioeconomic disparities in screening. This study provides formative research data to develop an intervention to increase colorectal cancer screening among underinsured and uninsured African Americans in central North Carolina.

### Methods

We held 4 focus groups to explore knowledge, beliefs, and attitudes about colorectal cancer screening, particularly FIT. Participants (n = 28) were African American adults recruited from neighborhoods with high levels of poverty and unemployment. Constructs from the diffusion of innovation theory were used to develop the discussion guide.

### Results

In all groups, participants noted that lack of knowledge about colorectal cancer contributes to low screening use. Attitudes about FIT sorted into 4 categories of "innovation characteristics": *relative advantage* of FIT compared with no screening and with other screening tests; *compatibility* with personal beliefs and values;

---

[1] Reproduced from Harden, E., Moore, A., & Melvin, C. (2011). Exploring perceptions of colorectal cancer and fecal immunochemical testing among African Americans in North Carolina Community. *Preventing Chronic Disease, 8*(6), available at www.cdc.gov/pcd/issues/2011/nov/10_0234.htm.

test *complexity*; and test *trialability*. A perceived barrier to FIT and other stool tests was risk of incurring costs for diagnostic follow-up.

## Conclusion

Community-based FIT screening interventions should include provider recommendation, patient education to correctly perform FIT, modified FIT design to address negative attitudes about stool tests, and assurance of affordable follow-up for positive FIT results.

# INTRODUCTION

Screening for colorectal cancer (CRC), the second leading cause of cancer death in the United States, leads to increased early detection and treatment of this disease (1). Although 62% of the US population reports following recommended CRC screening guidelines, screening rates are lower for those with lower incomes and those without health insurance (2). Rates are also thought to be lower among African Americans, who are more likely than other ethnic groups to be diagnosed with late-stage CRC (2) and 40% more likely than whites to die of CRC (3).

Adults at average risk for CRC may choose from several screening options. Until recently, organizations that develop and issue guidelines were generally in consensus about which tests to endorse. The US Preventive Services Task Force (USPSTF) recommends that patients choose from among yearly high-sensitivity fecal occult blood test (FOBT) or high-sensitivity fecal immunochemical test (FIT), flexible sigmoidoscopy every 5 years, or colonoscopy every 10 years. Each screening regimen is clinically effective for reducing mortality (4,5).

In 2008, the American Cancer Society (ACS), in collaboration with the US Multi-Society Task Force on Colorectal Cancer and the American College of Radiology, issued a slightly diverging set of recommendations, adding stool DNA and computed tomographic colonoscopy tests. The ACS guidelines also categorize tests according to their potential to detect versus prevent CRC. The first category includes FOBT and FIT. The second category includes screening tests that produce visual images of the colon and, therefore, can detect and guide removal of adenomatous polyps, a benign precursor of most colorectal cancers, thereby preventing them from developing into cancer (6).

With either set of guidelines, patients must choose a test that most closely aligns with their needs and values. Each test conveys distinct benefits and limitations related to test frequency, cost, invasiveness, sensitivity, specificity, convenience, and regional availability. For lay and professional audiences alike, determining the relative advantage of the various screening tests is a complex issue.

FOBT and FIT are the least expensive options and do not require access to endoscopy facilities. Some types of FIT are increasingly preferred over FOBT because the tests are specific to human hemoglobin and have a similarly high or higher sensitivity (7). Vitamins, foods, and drugs do not alter FIT accuracy, and patients may find it easier to use. Improving access to FIT has potential to increase screening by reducing costs and removing some structural barriers, such as geographically distant endoscopy facilities (8–12).

The objective of this study was to provide formative research data for an intervention to increase CRC screening in a target population of underinsured and uninsured African Americans living in a metropolitan area in central North Carolina. We conducted focus groups with members of the target population to explore knowledge, beliefs, and attitudes about CRC screening, particularly FIT. Focus group data are being used to inform the design of a FIT screening intervention.

# METHODS

## THEORETICAL FRAMEWORK: DIFFUSION OF INNOVATIONS

The diffusion of innovations theory describes the adoption of new practices or products (innovations) and the factors that accelerate or impede their spread throughout a community. Application of this theory during intervention planning can help cancer prevention and control practitioners develop dissemination strategies specific to different CRC screening tests and populations.

The theory posits that perceptions of an innovation's characteristics affect how quickly and widely the innovation is adopted. Five attributes that explain 49% to 87% of variance in adoption rates are *relative advantage, compatibility, complexity, trialability,* and *observability* (13). Relative advantage is the degree to which a potential user perceives the innovation as superior to the practice that it supersedes. Compatibility refers to the beliefs about whether the innovation is consistent with personal values. Complexity is the extent to which the user perceives the innovation as difficult to use. Trialability is the degree to which someone can experiment with the innovation before adopting it. Potential users can also conduct a vicarious trial by observing and learning from someone else's experimentation (13). Observability is the extent to which results of adopting an innovation are visible to others. Modifying FIT in ways that affect perceptions of these 5 attributes in the target population can enhance or diminish its diffusion potential. Intervention planning also requires audience and community assessment research to understand how an innovation is likely to interact with individual and environmental characteristics. Elements in the diffusion of innovation theory guided the organization and presentation of the focus group results.

## PROCEDURES

Starting in January 2007, a local community research advisory board, a standing group that advises about research projects in several North Carolina counties, reviewed the research protocol, recommended appropriate honoraria for participants, and guided the research team in disseminating results locally. The institutional review board of the University of North Carolina at Chapel Hill also approved this study. Community organizations assisted in early spring 2007 by posting flyers and allowing study staff to attend their outreach events to recruit and enroll participants. Potential participants contacted research staff in person at these events or by telephone after seeing recruitment materials. Two study staff administered brief eligibility surveys and enrolled participants.

Eligible participants were African Americans aged 50 years or older who were not at elevated risk for CRC because of a family history of CRC in a first-degree relative or a personal history of the disease. Those screened by FOBT or FIT within the past year or by any endoscopy method or contrast barium enema within the past 5 years were excluded. Of 51 people who completed eligibility screening, 16 were ineligible because of age or recent screening. Thirty-five eligible people received assignment to a male or female focus group session (there were 2 of each), a confirmation letter, and a reminder letter and telephone call. Of those, 28 attended 1 of 4 two-hour focus groups and completed a brief demographic questionnaire in March 2007. Focus groups of 5 to 9 people were conducted at 2 African American churches of different denominations and at a community resource center. The churches and the resource center were recommended as neutral sites that were likely to be familiar and geographically accessible to participants. Eligible participants chose to attend either a weekend morning or weekday evening focus group. The study covered taxi costs for participants without transportation. All participants received a $30 gift certificate.

Focus group members gave written consent for their participation. A trained African American facilitator of the same sex as participants moderated the focus groups. All groups were tape recorded. Facilitators followed a semistructured guide with preset probes (Appendix) to ensure conversation depth. The moderator began with questions about participants' knowledge and attitudes about CRC and screening. After distributing a 3-sample Hemoccult ICT packet, an FIT manufactured and donated by Beckman Coulter, Inc (Brea, CA), the moderator asked participants to examine the packet and share opinions about its design, packaging, instructions, and usability. The moderator also asked participants questions about community characteristics and local health services, and participants were able to ask questions or raise topics that they thought were important but had not been addressed.

## ANALYSIS

Verbatim transcription of audio recordings produced 191 pages of text. The first author used Atlas.ti software (Atlas.ti Scientific Software Development GmbH, Berlin, Germany) to conduct a content analysis followed by thematic analysis. Content analysis examined the degree of consensus in responses to questions and generated a list of codes that defined overarching themes. The analyst coded and ranked each comment from most to least frequently mentioned. A second analyst also reviewed transcripts, and differences in the analyses were resolved.

Thematic analysis entailed grouping codes by themes, which were defined by elements of diffusion of innovation theory. Qualifying findings had to emerge in at least 2 groups. A finding's strength increased if it occurred in 3 or all 4 groups. To count as a finding for women, a code had to occur in both women's groups, and likewise for the men. During thematic analysis, the analyst abstracted quotes that illustrated findings.

# RESULTS

Half of study participants reported an annual income of less than $10,000 (Table). Twenty participants reported having a regular health care provider, yet only 13 had ever spoken with a provider about CRC. More women than men reported talking with a health care provider about CRC.

Themes are presented in terms of individual, innovation, and environmental characteristics that, following diffusion of innovation theory, are likely to influence FIT adoption. Comments about FIT aligned with 4 of the 5 innovation characteristics believed to predict adoption: *relative advantage* of FIT compared to no screening or other CRC screening, *compatibility* of FIT with personal beliefs and preferences, *complexity* of the FIT procedures, and strategies to enhance FIT's *trialability*. Participant comments did not directly address the innovation's *observability*; however, the low profile of CRC screening emerged as a related theme.

## INDIVIDUAL CHARACTERISTICS: AWARENESS AND KNOWLEDGE OF CRC AND CRC SCREENING

Across all groups, awareness and knowledge of CRC and screening were low. Female participants said that CRC screening is discussed less frequently than breast or cervical cancer screening.

> You know, you do tell people "I went for a mammogram" because one of the things that women do discuss when they go for a mammogram is. . . how the test felt, you know, what was done. We talk about Pap[anicolaou] smears. But I just never, ever heard anybody say anything when they go for their physical about [CRC screening]. (Woman, group C)

## INNOVATION CHARACTERISTICS: PERCEPTIONS ABOUT FIT SCREENING

### Relative advantage

Most participants noted that finding cancer early is beneficial relative to late diagnoses, and most indicated that FIT screening was preferable to other CRC screening tests. Several men said that they liked the idea of a home test for CRC.

> There was a time I was, uh, the doctors wanted to take that [colonoscopy] for me and I wouldn't allow them because that's a part of my body. I just, just can't see nobody doing what they do. So, I told them "Ain't there no other way you can test it?" (Man, group A)

When differences between FOBT and FIT were discussed, FIT was preferred because it requires no food restrictions.

### Compatibility

Negative attitudes about FIT were due mostly to perceptions of the test as "gross." Women expressed more reluctance about collecting and storing stool samples than men and noted that people may be deterred by smelly odors or embarrassment when returning the samples. All groups discussed problems associated with storing stool samples. Some recommended adding a device to hold used sample cards until they go to the lab.

> No one thinks to let it dry completely overnight. So, I guess you have to put this someplace where — I don't know — You know, because you got to let it dry completely, and you don't want to just leave it on the sink. (Man, group D)

Participants also said stool tests are a good screening option for those preferring home remedies to medical services.

Participants generally approved of the appearance of FIT packaging; however, they thought that the thin, lightweight materials could easily be overlooked or discarded.

> If I don't really have an understanding of how important it is, I'll just discard it, you know, because it looks like another piece of mail. So, it just goes in the garbage can with all my other mail. (Man, group D)

## Complexity

Although most said FIT is a simple procedure, in every group participants said FIT's multistep instructions would challenge some. Instructions in small type were acknowledged as a potential problem for low literacy patients. Not understanding the rationale for each step of the FIT procedure, which is performed over several days, bothered some participants: "Okay, you're gonna put 2 [pieces of stool] on it, 1 for the bottom, 1 for the top. Then you're going to smear [them] together. For what?" (woman, group B). Another participant said, "All the processes . . . Lift the toilet seat. Attach it to fit you. Measuring tissue. . . . You know, it's a lot to do. A lot to do for me" (man, group A).

Others shared similar concerns.

> I think before they give a person a kit like that, they just educate them on why they're doing it and what they should do, what they're going to be looking for. 'Cause if they just give it and tell them to take it home, bring their stool sample back, I mean they haven't told them nothing. (Woman, group B)

## Trialability

A few had previously tried and completed a 3-sample FOBT. One man explained that "there's nothing to it" (group D). Another participant described how a female health care provider helped him practice a test procedure before he attempted it independently.

> They went through the whole thing with me. Cause I didn't know exactly how to do it. Cause I can read and I can guess. . . . She said, "I'm gonna sit here and we'll go through the whole process." Then you know exactly what to do. (Man, group D)

In addition to hands-on instruction, video or illustrations were suggested by the participants to improve adherence to test procedures.

## Observability

The silence surrounding CRC was discussed in all groups. One woman (group C) compared the invisibility of CRC screening with other screenings: "We hear a lot about mammograms . . . we hear a lot about cervical cancer . . . and the importance of Pap[anicolaou] smears. But we don't really hear a lot about colon cancer." Although benefits of early detection or prevention of cancer are not easily observed, negative consequences of late-stage cancer diagnosis are, prompting such remarks as "a lot of people [are] afraid of taking the necessary steps as far as being examined. I guess they're scared of what they will find out" (woman, group C).

## ENVIRONMENTAL CHARACTERISTICS WITH POTENTIAL TO AFFECT FIT SCREENING

### Provider recommendation

Lack of provider recommendation appeared as a screening impediment: "If the doctor tells me this [FIT] is something I must do, or I have to do it, I just have to humble myself and get it done. But until that time, man, I'll just take my personal beliefs and use them" (man, group A). Participants described physicians as important health information sources, yet rarely discussed CRC with a doctor.

### Health care cost and access

Even if free CRC screening were available, participants said they might opt out unless affordable follow-up is assured. In the absence of diagnostic care and treatment, screening may be pointless: "The cost factor. If I do [have cancer], I can't afford to continue with the treatment or whatever is needed to be done.

Therefore, if I don't start and I don't know, I won't have to follow through" (man, group A).

## DISCUSSION

The National Commission on Prevention Priorities ranked CRC screening as the fourth most valuable clinical preventive service that medical practices can offer (14). Although some tests, particularly colonoscopy, have ardent supporters, most people agree that USPSTF- or ACS-recommended tests increase early detection of CRC (1,15) and that patients should be able to choose a test they prefer. Results from published studies indicate that patients do not unanimously favor one test over another; some studies indicate FOBT and FIT are least preferred (16,17). Others show some patients preferring stool tests over colonoscopy (9,18). Findings from our study suggest that FIT is perceived as an acceptable or preferred CRC screening test relative to other screening tests, including colonoscopy. Fisher et al (12) report that using annual stool tests for primary screening would allow 100% of the age-appropriate US population to be screened at a savings of nearly $10 billion per decade from what is currently spent to screen only half the targeted population. For cancer prevention and control planners working to extend CRC screening to underinsured and uninsured patients, our findings suggest FIT is viable for community screening. Participant comments exposed factors that could impede widespread adoption and should be taken into consideration when planning screening programs that include FIT.

Complexity of test procedures emerged as a concern. For innovations requiring acquisition of new skills, diffusion tends to be slow (13). FIT screening entails following multistep instructions over a span of several days. Other studies have found that people often lack skills and confidence to successfully complete stool tests (11,19,20). Another focus group study reported that clearer instructions about test procedures would improve participation rates (11). Similarly, participants in our study recommended adding instructions in large type and illustrations of test procedures.

Participants also recommended hands-on practice sessions using sample materials or video demonstrations. In addition to reducing complexity, these activities address the concept of trialability by allowing patients to try FIT before committing to using it at home. Three-sample FIT and FOBT are already designed with a certain degree of trialability: patients can gain confidence in doing the test as they attempt to collect a sample each day. Although test accuracy decreases with an incomplete sampling, 1 or 2 samples can still be analyzed. The next year, the patient will have another opportunity to perform the test.

Our focus group participants indicated that handling or mailing stool samples is embarrassing and mildly offensive, hence incompatible activities. Similar attitudes have been reported about FOBT (20-22). In an Australian study of FOBT use, the 2 main reasons, together accounting for almost 50% of reasons for nonadherence, were perceived unpleasantness and inconvenience (22). Participants in our study noted that merely adding a storage device to securely contain fecal samples until they are returned to the doctor may make FIT more acceptable.

In addition to the innovation characteristics of FIT screening, the public's low awareness of stool testing may impede adoption (11,19,20,23,24). The effectiveness of mass media interventions for increasing CRC screening deserves further research (25); however, the most important source of information about CRC screening is health care professionals (23,26). Although physician recommendation for screening is a leading predictor of screening adherence (23,26), only 13 of 28 participants in this study had talked with a health care provider about CRC. Physicians have reported not recommending CRC screening to uninsured patients if access to diagnostic care is lacking (11). Participants noted that FIT screening has little value unless diagnostic follow-up services are available and affordable. In regions where CRC screening programs do not fund screening and diagnostic colonoscopy for the underinsured and uninsured, adhering to CRC screening guidelines is a challenge.

Focus group data, while offering great depth and detail in response to research questions, cannot be generalized beyond the sample. In our study, convenience sampling and the small sample size further decreased generalizability of the results. Also, only 1 researcher coded the content analysis, potentially decreasing the validity of our findings.

CRC disproportionately affects the lives of African Americans, and screening rates must be increased to reduce the number of African American lives lost to the disease. Findings from our study and others indicate that FIT is a viable option for more widespread population-based CRC screening.

## ACKNOWLEDGMENTS

Research for this publication was supported by the Centers for Disease Control and Prevention and the National Cancer Institute (NCI) cooperative agreements for the Cancer Prevention and Control Research Networks at the University of North Carolina at Chapel Hill, Center for Health Promotion and Disease Prevention (5-U48-DP000059). The authors also acknowledge Andrea Meier, PhD, Allan Steckler, PhD, and Jennifer Leeman, DrPH, for consultation on this research and Jennifer Scott for administrative support. We also thank staff and community collaborators of the Carolina Community Network (CCN), an NCI Center to Reduce Cancer Health Disparities, Community Networks Program (grant no. U01CA114629). Thanks also to CCN community outreach specialist Brandolyn White, MPH, and CCN collaborators in the community, including Ms Kathy Norcott.

# Appendix

## FOCUS GROUP MODERATOR'S GUIDE

**Table.** Characteristics of Participants in a 2007 Focus Group Study Conducted With African Americans (n = 28) in Central North Carolina

| Characteristic | Women | Men | Women and Men Combined |
|---|---|---|---|
| No. of participants | 14 | 14 | 28 |
| Average age, y | 65 | 57 | 61 |
| Annual income, $10,000[a] | 7 | 7 | 14 |
| Annual income $10,000-$19,000[a] | 3 | 4 | 7 |
| Has a regular health provider | 12 | 8 | 20 |
| Has talked to provider about colorectal cancer | 9 | 4 | 13 |

[a] Data on income were missing for 1 woman and 2 men.

## FOOTNOTES

The findings and conclusions in this report are those of the authors and do not necessarily represent the official position of the Centers for Disease Control and Prevention.

*Suggested citation for this article:* Harden E, Moore A, Melvin C. Exploring perceptions of colorectal cancer and fecal immunochemical testing among African Americans in a North Carolina community. Prev Chronic Dis 2011;8(6):A134.http://www.cdc.gov/pcd/issues/2011/nov/10_0234.htm. Accessed [*date*].

## CONTRIBUTOR INFORMATION

Elizabeth Harden, University of North Carolina at Chapel Hill, Chapel Hill, North Carolina.

Alexis Moore, Lineberger Comprehensive Cancer Center, University of North Carolina at Chapel Hill. CB# 7295, Chapel Hill, NC 27599-7295, Phone: 919-843-7027, Email: alexis_moore@unc.edu.

Cathy Melvin, University of North Carolina at Chapel Hill, Chapel Hill, North Carolina.

## REFERENCES

1. Pignone M, Rich M, Teutsch SM, Berg AO, Lohr KN. Screening for colorectal cancer in adults at average risk: a summary of the evidence for the U.S. Preventive Services Task Force. *Ann Intern Med*. 2002;*137*(2):132–141.

2. Henley SJ, King JB, German RR, Richardson LC, Plescia M. Surveillance of screening-detected cancers (colon and rectum, breast, and cervix)—United States, 2004-2006. *MMWR Surveill Summ*. 2010;*59*(9):1–25.

3. Cancer facts, and Cancer facts and figures for African Americans, 2007-2008. Atlanta (GA): American Cancer Society; 2007.

4. Screening for colorectal cancer: U.S. Preventive Services Task Force recommendation statement. *Ann Intern Med*. 2008;*149*(9):627–637.

5. Whitlock EP, Lin JS, Liles E, Beil TL, Fu R. Screening for colorectal cancer: a targeted, updated systematic review for the U.S. Preventive Services Task Force. *Ann Intern Med*. 2008;*149*(9):638–658.

6. Smith RA, Cokkinides V, Brooks D, Saslow D, Brawley OW. Cancer screening in the United States, 2010: a review of current American Cancer Society guidelines and issues in cancer screening. *CA Cancer J Clin*. 2010;*60*(2):99–119.

7. Allison JE, Sakoda LC, Levin TR, Tucker JP, Tekawa IS, Cuff T, et al. Screening for colorectal neoplasms with new fecal occult blood tests: update on performance characteristics. *J Natl Cancer Inst*. 2007;*99*(19):1462–1470.

8. Church TR, Yeazel MW, Jones RM, Kochevar LK, Watt GD, Mongin SJ, et al. A randomized trial of direct mailing of fecal occult blood tests to increase colorectal cancer screening. *J Natl Cancer Inst*. 2004;*96*(10):770–780.

9. DeBourcy AC, Lichtenberger S, Felton S, Butterfield KT, Ahnen DJ, Denberg TD. Community-based preferences for stool cards versus colonoscopy in colorectal cancer screening. *J Gen Intern Med*. 2008;*23*(2):169–174.

10. Goel V, Gray R, Chart P, Fitch M, Saibil F, Zdanowicz Y. Perspectives on colorectal cancer screening: a focus group study. *Health Expect*. 2004;*7*(1):51–60.

11. O'Malley AS, Beaton E, Yabroff KR, Abramson R, Mandelblatt J. Patient and provider barriers to colorectal cancer screening in the primary care safety-net. *Prev Med.* 2004;*39*(1):56–63.

12. Fisher JA, Fikry C, Troxel AB. Cutting cost and increasing access to colorectal cancer screening: another approach to following the guidelines. *Cancer Epidemiol Biomarkers Prev.* 2006;*15*(1):108–113.

13. Rogers EM. *Diffusion of innovations.* 5th edition. New York (NY): Free Press; 2003.

14. Maciosek MV, Solberg LI, Coffield AB, Edwards NM, Goodman MJ. Colorectal cancer screening: health impact and cost effectiveness. *Am J Prev Med.* 2006;*31*(1):80–89.

15. Smith RA, Cokkinides V, Eyre HJ. Cancer screening in the United States, 2007: a review of current guidelines, practices, and prospects. *CA Cancer J Clin.* 2007;*57*(2):90–104.

16. Marshall DA, Johnson FR, Kulin NA, Ozdemir S, Walsh JM, Marshall JK, et al. How do physician assessments of patient preferences for colorectal cancer screening tests differ from actual preferences? A comparison in Canada and the United States using a stated-choice survey. *Health Econ.* 2009;*18*(12):1420–1439.

17. Imaeda A, Bender D, Fraenkel L. What is most important to patients when deciding about colorectal screening? *J Gen Intern MedI* 2010;*257*:688–693.

18. Almog R, Ezra G, Lavi I, Rennert G, Hagoel L. The public prefers fecal occult blood test over colonoscopy for colorectal cancer screening. *Eur J Cancer Prev.* 2008;*17*(5):430–437.

19. Brouse CH, Basch CE, Wolf RL, Shmukler C, Neugut AI, Shea S. Barriers to colorectal cancer screening with fecal occult blood testing in a predominantly minority urban population: a qualitative study. *Am J Public Health.* 2003;*93*(8):1268–1271.

20. Beeker C, Kraft JM, Southwell BG, Jorgensen CM. Colorectal cancer screening in older men and women: qualitative research findings and implications for intervention. *J Community Health.* 2000;*25*(3):263–278.

21. Vernon SW. Participation in colorectal cancer screening: a review. *J Natl Cancer Inst.* 1997;*89*(19):1406–1422.

22. Worthley DL, Cole SR, Esterman A, Mehaffey S, Roosa NM, Smith A, et al. Screening for colorectal cancer by faecal occult blood test: why people choose to refuse. *Intern Med J.* 2006;*36*(9):607–610.

23. Wee CC, McCarthy EP, Phillips RS. Factors associated with colon cancer screening: the role of patient factors and physician counseling. *Prev Med.* 2005;*41*(1):23–29.

24. McAlearney AS, Reeves KW, Dickinson SL, Kelly KM, Tatum C, Katz ML, Paskett ED. Racial differences in colorectal cancer screening practices and knowledge within a low-income population. *Cancer.* 2008;*112*(2):391–398.

25. Guide to Community Preventive Services. Cancer prevention and control: client-oriented screening interventions. [Accessed April 12, 2010]. http://www.thecommunityguide.org/cancer/screening/client-oriented/index.html. Last updated March 30, 2010.

26. Seeff LC, Nadel MR, Klabunde CN, Thompson T, Shapiro JA, Vernon SW, et al. Patterns and predictors of colorectal cancer test use in the adult U.S. population. *Cancer.* 2004;*100*(10):2093–2103.

# CHAPTER ACTIVITY QUESTIONS

1. How does FIT differ from FOBT in relation to the characteristics of an innovation?
2. Were these characteristics among those that your group identified?
3. What suggestions were given to increase the likelihood of FIT adoption?
4. Other than the characteristics of the innovation, what other factors were identified as being an impediment to increasing colon cancer screening?

# CHAPTER REFERENCES

Barker, K. (2004). Diffusion of Innovations: A world tour. *Journal of Health Communication, 9*, 131–137.

Backer, T.E., & Rogers, E.M. (1998). Diffusion of innovation theory and work-site AIDS programs. *Journal of Health Communication, 3*, 17–28.

Burke, J. (2004). Infant HIV infection: Acceptability of preventive strategies on Tanzania. *AIDS Education and Prevention, 16*(5), 415–425.

Centers for Disease Control and Prevention. (2007). Cover your cough. Retrieved March 30, 2013, from http://cdc.gov/flu/protect/covercough.htm.

Dukes, R.L., Stein, J.A., & Ullman, J.B. (1997). Long-term impact of Drug Abuse Resistance Education (D.A.R.E.). *Evaluation Review, 21*, 483–500.

Dukes, R.L., Ullman, J.B., & Stein, J.A. (1996). A three-year follow-up of Drug Abuse Resistance Education (D.A.R.E.). *Evaluation Review, 20*, 49–66.

Eshkevari, L., & Heath, J. (2005). Use of acupuncture for chronic pain. *Holistic Nursing Practice, 19*(5), 217–221.

Food and Drug Administration. (2004). Lasik eye surgery. Retrieved April 1, 2013, from http://www.fda.gov/MedicalDevices/ProductsandMedicalProcedures/SurgeryandLifeSupport/LASIK/default.htm.

Haider, M., & Kreps, G. (2004). Forty years of Diffusion of Innovations: Utility and value in public health. *Journal of Health Communication, 9*, 3–11.

Hollander, D. (2004). Long–term use of female condom may hinge partly on depth of instruction. *International Family Planning Perspectives, 30*(1). Retrieved December 8, 2004, from http://www.agi-usa.org/pubs/journals/3004904b.html.

Inwood, S.M., Sharp, J.S., Moore, R.,H., & Stinner, D.H. (2009). Restaurants, chefs and local foods: insights drawn from application of a diffusion of innovation framework. *Agriculture and Human Values. 26*, 177–191.

Israel-Ballard, K., Chantry, C., Dewey, K., Lonnerdal, B., Sheppard, H., Donovan, R., Carlson, J., Sage, A., & Abrams, B. (2005). Viral, nutritional, and bacterial safety of flash-heated and pretoria-pasteurized breast milk to prevent mother-to-child transmission of HIV in resource-poor countries: A pilot study. *Journal of Acquired Immune Deficiency Syndromes, 40*(2), 175–181.

Janssen, P.A., Holt, V.L., & Sugg, N.K. (2002). Introducing domestic violence assessment in a postpartum clinical setting. *Maternal and Child Health Journal, 6*(3), 195–203.

Kane, M., & Mittman, R. (2002). *Diffusion of Innovation in Health Care.* Oakland, CA: California HealthCare Foundation. Retrieved April 1, 2013, from http://www.chcf .org/publications/2002/05/diffusion-of-innovation-in-health-care.

Lounsbury, B. (2006). Why don't we do it in our sleeves? Retrieved March 17, 2007, from http://www.coughsafe.com/index.html.

Lynam, D.R., Milich, R., Zimmerman, R., Novak, S.P., Logan, T.K., Martin, C., Leuke feld, C., & Clayton, R. (1999). Project DARE: No effects at ten year follow-up. *Journal of Consulting and Clinical Psychology, 67*(4), 590–593.

McCarthy, K.A., & Milus, T. (2000). Patient education viewed through the lens of Diffusion of Innovations research. *Topics in Clinical Chiropractic, 7*(4), 15–24.

National Cancer Institute. (2005). *Theory at a Glance: A Guide for Health Promotion Practice.* Washington, DC: U.S. Department of Health and Human Services.

Nguygen, H.Q., Carrieri-Kohlman, V., Rankin, S.H., Slaughter, R., & Stubarg, M.S. (2004). Supporting cardiac recovery through health technology. *Journal of Cardiac Nursing, 19,* 200–208.

O'Malley, K. (2006, June 13). Merck & Co: The marketing machine behind Gardasil. *Pharmaceutical Business Review.* Retrieved May 25, 2007, from http://www.pharmaceutical -business-review.com/article_feature.asp?guid=463AB18E-B911-4CC6-BD44- FB9CC69C6561.

Pemberton, H.E. (1936). The curve of culture diffusion rate. *American Sociological Review, 1*(4), 547–556.

Piot, P. (1998). *The Female Condom and AIDS: UNAIDS Point of View.* Geneva: UNAIDS. Retrieved April 1, 2013, from http://www.unaids.org/en/media/unaids/contentassets/ dataimport/publications/irc-pub03/fcondompv_en.pdf.

Rogers, E.M. (2003). *Diffusion of Innovation.* New York: Free Press.

Rogers, E.M. (2004). A prospective and retrospective look at the diffusion model. *Journal of Health Communication, 9,* 13–19.

Rogers, E.M., & Scott, K.L. (1997). The Diffusion of Innovations model and outreach from the National Network of Libraries of Medicine to Native American communities. Retrieved October 30, 2004, from http://nnlm.gov/pnr/eval/rogers.html.

Ryan, B., & Gross, N. (1943). The diffusion of hybrid seed corn in two Iowa communities. *Rural Sociology, 8,* 15–24.

Smerecnik, K.R. & Andersen, P.A. (2011). The diffusion of environmental sustainability innovations in North American hotels and ski resorts. *Journal of Sustainable Tourism, 19*(2), 171–196.

Valente, T.W. & Rogers, E.M. (1995). The origins and development of the diffusion of innovation paradigm as an example of scientific growth. *Science Communication, 16*(3), 243–273.

Wilson, M.C. (1927). *Influence of bulletins news stories and circular letters upon farm practice adoption with particular reference to methods of bulletin distribution.* Washington, DC: U.S. Department of Agriculture, Federal Extension Circular No. 57.

Yee, D. (2007). Hand sanitizers becoming popular. Retrieved March 17, 2007, from http:// www.abqtrib.com/news/2007/jan/05/hand-sanitizer-becoming-popular.

# Ecological Models

## THEORY ESSENCE SENTENCE

Factors at many levels influence health behavior.

## IN THE BEGINNING

Explaining behavior using ecological models has its origins in Germany in the 1870s, when two researchers, Schwabe and Bartholomai, studied how neighborhoods affect the development of the children who live in them (Bronfenbenner, 1974, 1994). However, it wasn't until the mid-1970s when a developmental psychologist, Urie Bronfenbrenner, put this approach on the map, so to speak (Bronfenbrenner, 1974). From Bronfenbrenner's extensive review of the literature, he found that the context in which child development research was conducted, in unfamiliar surroundings, with people the child didn't know, for a short period of time without any of the things or people the child is used to, provided a partial picture because there was a stark contrast between the research environment and the reality in which the child lived. Thus, an often used quote of his is "American developmental psychology is the science of behavior of children in strange situations with strange adults" (Bronfenbrenner, 1974, p. 3).

To address this, Bronfenbrenner (1974, 1994) developed a theoretical model based on two propositions. The first is that human development occurs through a process of complex back and forth interactions between those things in a person's immediate environment and that in order for these interactions to effect development, they must occur fairly regularly over time. He called these proximal or close processes. Examples of these processes are found in the parent-child relationship, child-child relationships, group or solitary play. The second proposition is that the effect of these back-and-forth interactions vary depending on the personal characteristics of the child, the environment in which they take place, and the developmental outcome being studied (Bronfenbrenner, 1974, 1994).

Additionally, the ecological model viewed the environment as a critical component of behavior and differentiated it into a set of concentric systems or levels. Each level of the environment is inside the other, like nesting dolls, starting with the one in which relationships are closest to the person (family, school, friends) to the one in which the relationships are most distant (the effects of time). The different concentric organizations of the environment were originally labeled: microsystem, mesosystem, exosystem, macrosystems, and chronosystems, with each having its own characteristics and interaction with the others to affect human development and behavior (Bronfenbrenner, 1994).

## THEORY CONCEPT

There are many ways in which health behavior can be explained. The explanations are based on many factors that are categorized as internal, such as beliefs, attitudes, skills, perceptions, and expectations, or external in the social environment, such as social supports, significant others, models, and rewards or consequences. Similar to the other theories and models, ecological models also explain behavior using these same factors. The difference is that ecological models use both internal and external factors, rather than one or the other. In addition, ecological models view the external environment as being composed of not only the social but also the physical environment (Sallis & Owen, 1997), focusing on environmental causes of behavior. Therefore, when ecological models are used in health promotion, the intent is to change the environment (social or physical), since changes in the environment change individual behavior (McLeroy et al., 1988).

Because ecological models are a point of view or perspective, they do not have constructs per se, unlike the other theories and models (Sallis & Owen, 2002). The internal and external factors that underpin behavior are presented as levels (McLeroy et al., 1988). Perceptually, these levels are like concentric circles (**Figure 9–1**), with the smallest at the center representing the internal or intrapersonal level; moving to the external levels, which include the interpersonal level; and widening to the community, institutional, and finally the societal level. The basis of ecological models is the recognition that the dynamic interplay among the various factors at different levels affects behavior (Stokols, 1992). Because of this interplay between and among the many levels of influence, changing one

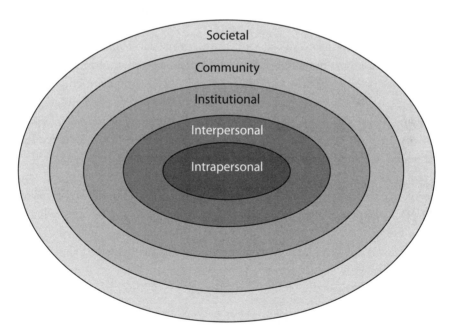

**FIGURE 9–1**  An Ecological Model

*Source:* World Health Organization. Violence Prevention Alliance. http://www.who.int/ violenceprevention/en/. Accessed February 12, 2013.

can have an impact on them all (Spence & Lee, 2003). This concept is similar to reciprocal determinism in the Social Cognitive Theory.

Although this multilevel perspective is consistent in all ecological models, the specific terms used to describe the levels or factors may differ slightly. The level designations presented here are those commonly used in health education and health promotion.

## INTRAPERSONAL LEVEL

All ecological models recognize the contribution intrapersonal-level factors make to health behavior. The impact of intrapersonal-level factors cannot be understated. In fact, historically, they have been the foundation for explaining health behavior and the basis for health promotion interventions (Novilla et al., 2006). Intrapersonal-level factors include knowledge, attitudes, beliefs, personality traits (McLeroy et al., 1988), skills, perceptions (Novilla et al., 2006), personal history (World Health Organization [WHO], 2006), self-efficacy, and perceptions (Sallis & Owen, 1999), to name but a few of the more common ones.

An example of how individual factors, or those at the intrapersonal level, affect health is seen in violent behavior. The intrapersonal factors in this case may include the personality trait of impulsivity, a personal history of being a victim of child abuse, or alcohol or drug abuse (WHO, 2006). Another example of an intrapersonal factor affecting health behavior is the impact of gender on physical exercise. When girls reach puberty, there is a 50% reduction in their physical activity levels. The reason for this may be physiological, in that a simultaneous reduction in energy expenditure occurs at this time (Goran et al., 1998).

Intrapersonal factors were found to be the most influential in explaining why people got vaccinated against H1N1 (Swine flu) in 2009. People who perceived the N1N1 vaccine as an effective way of preventing the disease were more likely to be vaccinated. Surprising though, the perception of susceptibility to H1N1 infection was not a factor that contributed to vaccination (Kumar et al., 2012).

## INTERPERSONAL LEVEL

The next set of factors in ecological models is at the interpersonal or relationship level. These are external factors included in the relationships we have with our relatives, friends, and peers. These people provide our social identity, make up our support systems, and define our role within the social structure (McLeroy et al., 1988; WHO, 2006).

Our relationships with others at this level influence our health behavior (see **Figure 9–2a–b**). For example, in the case of smoking, the strongest predictor of this behavior is having parents, siblings, or peers who smoke. Thus, if your friends and parents smoke, it is more likely that you will too (von Bothmer et al., 2002). The same is true of drug-taking behavior. The peer group and family have a major influence on whether or not someone will engage in this behavior (Eddy et al., 2002).

As seems apparent, interpersonal relationships can influence physical activity. Interpersonal relationships with people who are physically active enable people to connect to one another and support each other in being physically active. For example, parents of young children can support one another by providing child care for each other, people who already have a personal trainer can provide access to one for someone who doesn't have a personal trainer (McNeil et al., 2006), and someone who belongs to a health club can bring a friend as a guest. Think about this in the context of your own interpersonal relationships on campus. If your friends use the recreation facilities on campus, isn't there a better likelihood that you will too?

Also important is that when people engage in physical activity with others in their social network, physical activity can be established as a social norm (Stahl et al., 2001). When a behavior becomes a social norm, it is acceptable and often expected that members of the social network engage in the behavior. If the behavior is a health enhancing one, everyone benefits.

## INSTITUTIONAL LEVEL

In some ecological models, there are factors at the institutional level that constrain or promote certain behaviors. These are the rules, regulations, and policies of informal structures (McLeroy et al., 1988; Eddy et al., 2002) that are often associated with the workplace environment. Examples of institutional-level factors include policies providing flex time to enable employees to attend health programs, healthy food selections in the cafeteria (Eddy et al., 2002), corporate sponsorship of health initiatives, incentives for participation in health activities, and use of worksite communication networks (Watt et al., 2001), and recommendations from the medical establishment (Kumar et al., 2011).

(a)

(b)

**FIGURE 9–2** Our relationships influence our behavior for better or worse

Institutional factors, in the form of recommendations from healthcare providers, were found to be significant for people who chose to receive the H1N1 vaccine in 2009. There was a greater chance of people getting vaccinated if they received information from healthcare providers about the vaccine and if they believed the healthcare providers wanted them to be vaccinated (Kumar et al., 2011).

## COMMUNITY LEVEL

At the community level, factors influencing behavior include social networks, norms, or standards of behavior that exist formally or informally among individuals, groups, or organizations (Eddy et al., 2002; McLeroy et al., 1988; WHO, 2006). The norms of the community are associated with specific behaviors, some health enhancing, some not. For instance, they might include involvement in health initiatives such as the Great American Smoke-out (Watt et al., 2001), participation in organized sports, volunteering at the local fire department, not cutting your lawn on Sunday morning, or, driving children to school rather than allowing them to walk, allowing underage youngsters to drink in your home.

Looking at violent behavior again, associated factors at this level include high population density, people frequently moving in and out, and great diversity relative to age and income. These factors result in a community with little social glue holding it together. Violence is more likely to occur in a community with these characteristics. It is also more likely in communities where there is drug trafficking, a high level of unemployment, and where people do not know their neighbors and are not involved in local community activities (WHO, 2006).

Other factors, such as access to full-service supermarkets and fresh fruits and vegetables, affect behavior relative to dietary intake (see **Figure 9–3**). If the only food available in a community is poor quality and high calorie—think fast food—then it is only logical for the people in that community to have diets predominately composed of those foods.

## SOCIETAL LEVEL

At the societal level we find broader factors that encourage or discourage specific behaviors. These include economics, social policies, social or cultural norms of behavior, and attitudes. Going back to the violence example, factors at the societal level would be the cultural acceptability of resolving conflicts through violent

©Lisa S./Shutterstock, Inc.

**FIGURE 9–3**  Community-level factors influence health behavior

means, parental rights overriding child welfare, and male dominance over women and children (WHO, 2006).

If we look at smoking behavior from the societal level, laws are now in effect in many states banning indoor smoking in public places and making the sale of cigarettes to minors illegal. These laws affect behavior and ultimately health. Another example of factors at the policy or societal level that change behavior at the individual level are the May 2006 federal guidelines aimed at addressing childhood obesity. The guidelines restrict the types of beverages that can be sold in schools to water, certain juices with no added sweeteners, and fat-free or low-fat regular and flavored milks (American Heart Association, 2006).

The 2012 ban on sugary drinks of more than 16 oz. in NYC is an example of a society-level change in policy that affects behavior. This policy changes the behavior of everyone who lives, works, or visits NYC!

Another example is the 2012 change in the school lunch program. With this policy change, schools are required to increase availability of fruits and vegetables, whole grains, and fat-free or low-fat milk; reduce sodium, saturated and trans fats, and do this within children's calorie requirements (Nutrition Standards in the National School Lunch and Breakfast Program, 2012). With this one change in policy, the dietary intake of every child in the country who purchases (or is eligible for free) breakfast or lunch at school, changes!

In summary, ecological models explain behavior as the result of an interplay between internal and external factors.

## THEORY IN ACTION—CLASS ACTIVITY

Using the ecological model as the structure, brainstorm the kinds of activities and the people or agencies at each of the levels you would expect to see in a program aimed at increasing physical activity in your community. Then, read the following article and answer the questions at the end.

# Chapter 9 Article: An Ecological Model Using Promotores de Salud to Prevent Cardiovascular Disease on the US-Mexico Border: The HEART Project[1]

Hector Balcázar, PhD, Sherrie Wise, MPH, E. Lee Rosenthal, PhD, MPH, Cecilia Ochoa, Maria Duarte-Gardea, PhD, RD, Jose Rodriguez, Diana Hastings, Leticia Flores, MPH, and Lorraine Hernandez, MS
Hector Balcázar, University of Texas, School of Public Health, El Paso Regional Campus; 500 West University CH 400, El Paso, Texas 79968, Phone: (915)747-8507, Email: hector.g.balcazar@uth.tmc.edu.
Contributor Information.
Corresponding author.

## Background

To address cardiovascular disease risk factors among Hispanics, a community model of prevention requires a comprehensive approach to community engagement. The objectives of our intervention were to reduce cardiovascular disease risk factors in Hispanics living in 2 low-income areas of El Paso, Texas, and to engage the community in a physical activity and nutrition intervention.

## Methods

Drawing on lessons learned in phase 1 (years 2005–2008) of the HEART Project, we used an iterative, community-based process to develop an intervention based on an ecological framework. New community partners were introduced and community health workers delivered several elements of the intervention, including the curriculum entitled "Mi Corazón, Mi Comunidad" ("MiCMiC" [My Heart, My Community]). We received feedback from the project's Community Health Academy and Leadership Council throughout the development process and established a policy agenda that promotes integration of community health workers into the local and state workforce.

---

[1] Reproduced from Balcazar, H., Wise, S., Rosenthal, E. L., Ochoa, C., Duante-Gardea, M., Rodriguez, J., Hastings, D., et al. (2012). An ecological model using promotores de salud to prevent cardiovascular disease on the US-Mexico border: The HEART project. *Preventing Chronic Disease, 9*, available at: www.ncbi.nlm.nih.gov/pmc/articles/PMC3310145.

## Outcome

Collaboration with 2 new community partners, the YWCA and the Department of Parks and Recreation, were instrumental in the process of community-based participatory research. We enrolled 113 participants in the first cohort; 78% were female, and the mean age was 41 years. More than 50% reported having no health insurance coverage. Seventy-two (60%) participants attended 1 or more promotora-led Su Corazón, Su Vida sessions, and 74 (62%) participants attended 1 or more of the 15 exercise classes.

## Interpretation

HEART phase 2 includes a multilevel ecological model to address cardiovascular disease risk among Hispanics. Future similarly targeted initiatives can benefit from an ecological approach that also embraces the promotora model.

# BACKGROUND

The increasing rates of cardiovascular disease (CVD) among Hispanics, particularly those living in US-Mexico border communities, are of great public health concern (1). Obesity, diabetes, and hypertension contribute to poor health in this region, where much of the population is Hispanic or of Mexican origin. Community health promotion and disease prevention models are needed to compensate for the large number of uninsured, underinsured, and disadvantaged people living in these communities.

Moving from a clinical model of care to a community model of prevention requires a comprehensive approach to community engagement (2–5). The National Institute for Minority Health and Health Disparities has invested in an 8-year initiative introducing community-based participatory research (CBPR) to engage academia and communities in setting up programs with an ecological approach to health promotion and disease prevention. HEART (Health Education Awareness Research Team) is an example of one such collaborative effort; this program uses community health workers (promotoras de salud) in Hispanic communities along the US-Mexico border.

HEART has completed a 3-year pilot test (phase 1) using promotoras in a community randomized trial with participants from 2 underserved areas of El Paso, Texas. The pilot test resulted in more awareness of CVD risk factors among Hispanics, greater confidence in the control of these factors, and improved dietary habits (4,6) among trial participants. HEART phase 2 (2009–2013) will serve the same communities served by phase 1 (3,4,7–14). The objectives of phase 2 are 1) to reduce CVD risk factors among Hispanics, and 2) to engage the community in an environmental restructuring initiative that focuses on nutrition and exercise. The environmental restructuring is designed to promote community use of existing physical activity and nutrition facilities and to integrate promotores into public-sector settings such as public parks, to address cardiovascular health promotion and CVD prevention.

# METHODS

## ECOLOGICAL FRAMEWORK FOR HEART PHASE 2

The conceptual framework for HEART phase 2 incorporates an ecological approach, whereby the environment of communities is enhanced and restructured (14–17). Our decision to incorporate the ecological approach was guided by empirical evidence for using parks and recreation facilities to implement physical activity and nutrition programming (17,18). The National Heart, Lung, and Blood Institute's Hearts N' Parks Y2K program—which integrated nutrition and physical activities into the North Carolina parks and recreation departments—also supports this approach (19).

We identified change agents at 5 levels: individual, interpersonal, organizational, community, and policy (**Figure 1**). At the individual level, the change agents are HEART participants who engage in the MiCMiC family of programs. The interpersonal level is represented by the HEART promotoras, and the participant's family, friends, and social networks. At the organizational level, we engaged new partners: the YWCA, and the Parks and Recreation Department of the City of El Paso (Parks and Recreation). The Community Health Advisory Council (CHAC) developed during phase 1 represents the policy agenda.

## WORKING WITH PARTNERS

The Community Health Advisory Council was renamed the Community Health Academy and Leadership Council and was expanded to include members of the YWCA and the Parks and Recreation Department. It also included long-standing council members and Mexican American community members. We recruited new members through informal meetings. We established a Leadership Academy to support the Leadership Council and the promotoras hired to serve the intervention.

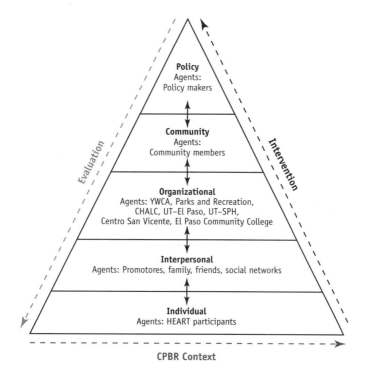

**FIGURE 1**

The University of Texas at El Paso initiated institutional agreements describing terms and responsibilities for each partner institution, which were signed by the designated officer at each institution. The research team held monthly meetings with the Leadership Council throughout the planning period and the intervention.

Parks and Recreation was instrumental in the coordination of park use, sound amplification, and other required city permits or reservations necessary for conducting MiCMiC activities outdoors and within recreation centers. We made arrangements with the Centro San Vicente clinic partner to use its teaching kitchen facility and with a popular grocery store chain to conduct heart-healthy grocery store tours.

## PROMOTORAS TRAINING AND PREPARATION

We hired 3 certified promotoras through the YWCA. In addition to a high school diploma or equivalent, each promotora was required to possess or obtain Texas state community health worker certification within 30 days of employment. Additional requirements were a minimum of 2 years' experience in community project work, health-related service, cardiovascular health, or CBPR. Computer skills, ability to exercise, and training in CPR and first aid were also required.

Promotoras participated in a 2-week Basic Skills Leveling course developed by the El Paso Community College Community Health Worker/Promotores de Salud program for 45 credit hours. Learning modules focused on basic skills for reducing and preventing CVD in Hispanics, capacity-building strategies, tools for identifying community resources, and advocacy. Evaluation methods were pretests and posttests, assignments, student presentations, and an exit exam.

Additionally, a bilingual curriculum development specialist from HEART phase 2 trained the promotoras to conduct each activity of the MiCMiC curriculum, including heart-healthy cooking demonstrations. Parks and Recreation provided training and certification in proper food-handling techniques, and promotoras participated in in-house training on the YWCA regulations as full-time employees. All promotoras were also thoroughly trained in preintervention and postintervention data collection techniques.

## MiCMiC PROGRAM PLANNING

Assembly of the final set of MiCMiC programs was based on the approach proposed by Stokols (14,16) and using social cognitive theory (20) to highlight a multicomponent conceptual model emphasizing the influence of social ecology on individual behavior. We engaged the Community Health Academy and Leadership Council in a discussion of these constructs.

The curriculum development specialist conducted a cross-sectional inventory at the YWCA and Parks and Recreation locations in the community to assess human and physical resources and current use of services and community programs. The inventory included facility tours and interviews with administrators and staff, and site visits to 3 recreation centers, 1 senior center, 4 city parks, 1 YWCA branch location, and 6 elementary schools housing partner after-school programs. Patron and staff satisfaction with programming and perceived barriers to use were also assessed. We selected locations and programs for phase 2 on the basis of recommendations from YWCA and Parks and Recreation administrators, taking into consideration the following factors: availability (selection of locations receiving low to moderate use, staff willingness to participate), accessibility to participants (additional costs to participants, safety, location), and applicability to the intervention (heart health-related programming, relevance to targeted domains).

MiCMiC integrated several best practice methods identified by the CDC Task Force on Community Preventive Services, specifically the following: 1) providing self-management education in community meeting places for adults with type 2 diabetes (21), 2) creating highly visible community-wide campaigns that encourage physical activity (18), 3) providing access to existing local exercise facilities (18), 4) setting up walking groups to offer social support and fellowship (18), 5) using interventions individually tailored to participants' preferences and physical ability (18), and 6) improving participants' goal-setting and self-monitoring skills (18). These best practices matched recommendations from HEART phase 1 (4,6).

MiCMiC included the Su Corazón, Su Vida classroom-based curriculum from phase 1 (6), as well as new community partner activities selected by the curriculum development specialist, mainly instructor-led land and water aerobics classes at the YWCA. Each program type was categorized as focusing on nutrition or exercise. In addition, supplemental activities included 1) coffee talks (charlas), 2) heart-healthy cooking demonstrations, 3) heart-healthy grocery shopping tours, 4) Latin dance aerobics in the parks, 5) family soccer games, 6) family swim, and 7) walking groups in city parks that emphasize peer support and the "buddy system."

## DEVELOPMENT OF PARTICIPANT MINIMUM EXPECTATIONS

The HEART phase 2 research team developed a minimum expectation of what constitutes a 4-month intervention for participants once they are enrolled in MiCMiC (**Box 1**). An incentives schedule listed awards for completing the minimum expectations as well as intermediate milestones.

We developed a "passport" tool in English and Spanish that outlines the MiCMiC activities to be accomplished by participants during a 4-month period of intervention, in addition to the minimum expectations for the nutrition and physical activities. Participants record their activities in the passport. The passport also includes a section for recording clinical measures. Promotoras encourage participants to bring their passports to the MiCMiC activities.

MiCMiC consists of 5 cohorts of 100 participants each. Each cohort participates in a 4-month intervention based on a pre-post design with 3 data collection points: baseline, 4 months, and 10 months (6 months post-intervention). Hispanic adults aged 18 years or older who resided in the 2 selected zip codes, were not planning to move from the area in the next 10 months, and were able to participate in the physical activities of MiCMiC were eligible. Recruitment was conducted by promotoras at community health fairs, the YWCA, recreation centers, Centro San Vicente, through personal contacts and referrals, and radio and TV Spanish programming.

---

**BOX 1** *Minimum Expectations for Participation*

| Activity | Expectations per Month | Total per Intervention (4 months) |
|---|---|---|
| **Lifestyle—Nutrition** Su Corazón, Su Vida | 1 session | 4 sessions |
| **Environment—Nutrition** | 1 session | 4 sessions |
| Coffee talks (charlas) | | |
| Heart-healthy cooking demonstrations | | |
| Heart-healthy shopping—grocery store tours | | |
| **Lifestyle and Environment—Exercise**[a] | 4 sessions | 16 sessions |
| YWCA aerobics classes | | |
| Family soccer | | |
| Latin dance aerobics in the parks | | |
| Walking groups in the parks | | |
| Swimming in the parks | | |
| **Free Choice (choose any activities from above)** | 1 session | 4 sessions |
| **TOTAL** | 7 sessions | 28 sessions |

[a]Beginner, intermediate, and advanced levels of difficulty available.

---

HEART policy makers aim to integrate promotores into the local and state workforce. HEART's vision statement reflects this aim: *"An El Paso where both community health workers and members of the community work together to promote wellness and a heart-healthy environment."* HEART held several focus workshops with local employers and promotoras to identify key issues related to building the workforce. Among issues identified were building understanding of promotoras by employers, increasing unity among promotoras, and developing the promotora network. An ad hoc HEART-led group was established, including representatives of the HEART Community Health Academy and Leadership Council, promotora networks, and other area stakeholders who are working together to develop the promotora workforce. This group is taking the lead on hosting a community stakeholders' meeting to develop a 5-year strategic plan for promotora workforce development in the El Paso area.

We are using several methods to evaluate HEART phase 2 (**Box 2**).

Box 2 *Change Strategies and Evaluation Methods, by Ecological Level*

| Level of HEART Intervention | Evaluation Method |
|---|---|
| 1. Individual: HEART participant | Pre- and postparticipant survey questionnaire to evaluate the impact of the MiCMiC 4-month intervention for the different study cohorts. Survey covers various heart-health domains including knowledge, beliefs, attitudes, perceptions and intentions, self-efficacy, social norms and outcomes such as blood pressure, BMI, waist circumference, dietary behaviors and 3-minute step test for heart rate. |
| 2. Interpersonal: promotoras, family, friends, social networks | Pre- and postsurvey questionnaire as in level 1.<br><br>Reflection notes and focus groups with the promotoras during pilot and cohort intervention. |
| 3. Organizational: HEART Partners: Community Health Academy and Leadership Council, YWCA, Parks and Recreation Department, University of Texas-El Paso, University of Texas School of Public Health, Centro San Vicente, El Paso Community College | HEART partnership self-assessment instrument[a] to assess effectiveness of Community Health Academy and Leadership Council meetings, outreach, trainings, and relationship with elected officials, as well as satisfaction with Community Health Academy and Leadership Council partnership development and strategic planning.<br><br>Reflection notes and discussion session for YWCA and Department of Parks and Recreation.<br><br>Community Health Academy and Leadership Council strategic planning and development of vision and mission statements.<br><br>Community Health Academy and Leadership Council meetings' minutes discussion and self-reflection. |

*(Continued)*

<table>
</table>

| Level of HEART Intervention | Evaluation Method |
| --- | --- |
| 4. Community | Community telephone survey to test the impact of MiCMiC at the community level. Pre- and postintervention telephone survey to be conducted in intervention community and a control community. The survey evaluates perception and use of community health workers, perception of community resources for exercise and healthy living, dietary behavior, diabetes, hypertension, drinking, smoking, and basic demographics. |
| | HEART participant sign-up sheet available at final ceremony to identify leaders to continue heart-healthy activities in the community, post-intervention (ie, walking groups, aerobics activities, cooking clubs). |
| 5. Policy: policy makers | Development of a policy agenda for HEART and documentation of actions carried out on that agenda. |

**Box 2** (CONTINUED)

[a]Adapted from the instrument developed by Butterfoss (22).

# OUTCOME

In the spring of 2010, we conducted a 6-week pilot among 37 participants for HEART phase 2. The purpose of this pilot was to test the MiCMiC schedule of activities at partner locations, promotora readiness, and preparation for participant enrollment and data collection. Participants were given 4 months of free access to the YWCA where the Su Corazón, Su Vida classes and most of the exercise activities were delivered. Enrollment consisted of completing consent, the HEART participant questionnaire (administered by promotoras), clinical measures, a tour of the YWCA facility, and a kick-off meeting with the research team.

A total of 18 participants completed the HEART questionnaire at the conclusion of the pilot. Ten of those also participated in postpilot focus groups and exit surveys. Feedback was obtained regarding satisfaction with MiCMiC activities, schedule, and the usefulness of the HEART passport. Overall, we received positive reviews of the program; all the participants stated that they would recommend this program to a family member or friend.

The HEART Community Health Academy and Leadership Council was instrumental in providing community involvement and facilitating feedback in the planning and implementation of MiCMiC. Monthly Community Health Academy and Leadership Council meetings allow continued dialogue between the research team and other partners. Also, the research team developed a quarterly newsletter that reports progress to HEART participants.

Postintervention data collection is currently under way for the first cohort intervention. For cohort 1, a total of 113 participants from our target intervention area were enrolled and successfully completed consent, the participant survey questionnaire, and baseline clinical measures throughout May and June of 2010. At baseline, 78% of participants were female, and the mean age was 41 years (**Table 1**). More than 60% of participants reported Mexico as their birthplace, and 38% reported their birthplace as the United States. Mean length of US residence was 24 years, and most participants reported Spanish as their preferred language (92%). More than 50% reported having no health insurance coverage, and only 36% reported being employed. Mean years of education attained was 12, and more than 40% of participants reported an annual family income of less than $10,000, and another 30% reported an income of $10,000 to $20,000.

More than 20% reported never having had their cholesterol checked. Approximately 72% of participants reported they had had their blood pressure checked within the past year. Approximately 27% reported never having been screened for diabetes.

More than 60% of participants reported they do not exercise at least 30 minutes, 3 times per week (Table 1). More than 70% reported not consuming at least 5 fruits and vegetables per day. Most participants (88%) did not smoke.

Approximately 25% of participants reported they have received a positive diagnosis of hyperlipidemia by a health care provider at some time in the past; 19% have been told they have high blood pressure; and 13% had been diagnosed with diabetes.

MiCMiC activities were offered throughout the 4-month schedule. Seventy-two (60%) participants attended 1 or more (of 11 modules offered) promotora-led Su Corazón, Su Vida sessions, and 74 (62%) participants attended 1 or more of the 15 hour-long exercise classes offered at the YWCA partner location or used the YWCA gym or indoor pool for a workout. Physical activity events held at city park locations were attended by 59 participants at least once. These include Latin dance aerobics in

**Table 1** Baseline Demographic Characteristics of Participants in the HEART Project, El Paso, Texas, 2010

| Characteristic | Cohort 1, n (%), (n = 113)[a] |
|---|---|
| Female sex | 84 (78) |
| Age, mean (SD), y | 41 (12) |
| Birthplace | |
| Mexico | 70 (62) |
| United States | 43 (38) |
| Years of residence in United States, mean (SD) | 24 (15.5) |
| Language preference | |
| English | 9 (8) |
| Spanish | 104 (92) |
| Years of educational attainment, mean (SD) | 12 (3.7) |
| Employed | 40 (36) |
| Financial status | |
| Very well off | 0 |
| Well off | 6 (5.5) |
| Getting by | 71 (64.5) |
| Not getting by | 33 (30) |
| Annual family income, $ | |
| <10,000 | 46 (41.8) |
| 10,000 to <20,000 | 33 (30) |
| ≥20,000 | 31 (28.2) |
| No health insurance | 62 (55) |
| Marital status | |
| Married/living with a partner | 57 (50.9) |
| Widowed/separated/divorced | 23 (20.5) |
| Never married | 32 (28.6) |
| No. of people in household, mean (SD) | |
| Adults | 2.25 (.7) |
| Children | 2.02 (1.4) |
| Ever diagnosed with hyperlipidemia | 28 (24.8) |
| Ever diagnosed with hypertension | 23 (19.5) |
| Ever diagnosed with diabetes | 15 (13.4) |
| Screened for hyperlipidemia | |
| Never | 27 (23.9) |
| Within the past year | 62 (54.9) |
| Within the past 2 years | 12 (10.6) |
| 3 or more years ago | 12 (10.6) |
| Had blood pressure checked | |
| Never | 18 (15.9) |
| Within the past year | 81 (71.7) |
| Within the past 2 years | 7 (6.2) |
| Within the past 3 years | 7 (6.2) |

**Table 1** (*Continued*)

| Characteristic | Cohort 1, n (%), (n = 113)[a] |
|---|---|
| **Screened for diabetes** | |
| Never | 31 (27.4) |
| Within the past year | 64 (56.6) |
| Within the past 2 years | 6 (5.3) |
| 3 or more years ago | 12 (10.6) |
| **Exercising 30 min 3 times/wk** | 42 (37.8) |
| **Eating 5 fruits and vegetables/d** | 33 (29.7) |
| **Smoking** | |
| Never | 73 (64.6) |
| Currently smoking | 13 (11.9) |
| Within the past 30 days | 14 (13) |

Abbreviation: SD, standard deviation.

[a] All values are reported as n (%) unless otherwise indicated. Values for each variable may not correspond to the cohort total n because of missing responses. Percentages may not total 100 because of rounding.

the park, family sports, and walking groups. Supplemental nutrition activities such as the 5 charlas, heart-healthy grocery store tours, and 8 cooking demonstrations were attended by 35 (29%), 32 (26%), and 54 (45%) participants, respectively.

# INTERPRETATION

The ecological model for prevention of CVD is the future of public health promotion. This ecological model must be culturally competent and must be a good fit for the community. HEART phase 2 embraces the promotora model as an important component of this ecological model. The model addresses each level, which is important, as others may concentrate only on one. Building such a comprehensive model is a challenge.

# ACKNOWLEDGMENTS

This research was supported by National Institutes of Health/National Center for Minority Health Disparities grant no. R24 MD001785-01.

# FOOTNOTES

Content source: National Center for Chronic Disease Prevention and Health Promotion.

*Suggested citation for this article:* Balcázar H, Wise S, Rosenthal EL, Ochoa C, Rodriguez J, Hastings D, et al. An ecological model using promotores de salud to prevent cardiovascular disease on the US-Mexico border: the HEART Project. Prev Chronic Dis 2012;9:110100. DOI: http://dx.doi.org/10.5888/pcd9.110100.

## CONTRIBUTOR INFORMATION

Hector Balcázar, University of Texas, School of Public Health, El Paso Regional Campus. 500 West University CH 400, El Paso, Texas 79968, Phone: (915)747-8507, Email: hector.g.balcazar@uth.tmc.edu.

Sherrie Wise, University of Texas, School of Public Health, El Paso Regional Campus, El Paso, Texas.

E. Lee Rosenthal, University of Texas at El Paso, Department of Public Health Sciences, El Paso, Texas.

Cecilia Ochoa, University of Texas at El Paso, Department of Public Health Sciences, El Paso, Texas.

Maria Duarte-Gardea, University of Texas at El Paso, Department of Public Health Sciences, El Paso, Texas.

Jose Rodriguez, City of El Paso Department of Parks and Recreation, El Paso, Texas.

Diana Hastings, YWCA El Paso Del Norte Region, El Paso, Texas.

Leticia Flores, El Paso Community College, El Paso, Texas.

Lorraine Hernandez, Centro San Vicente Clinic, El Paso, Texas.

## REFERENCES

1. Border lives: health status in the United States-Mexico border region. United States-Mexico Border Health Commission, 2010. [Accessed October 12, 2011]. http://www.borderhealth.org/extranet/files/file_1689.pdf.

2. Staten L, Scheu L, Bronson D, Pena V, Elenes J. Pasos Adelante: the effectiveness of a community-based chronic disease prevention program. *Prev Chronic Dis.* 2005; 2(1): Icon indicating a special focus article A18. http://www.cdc.gov/pcd/issues/2005/jan/04_0075.htm.

3. Balcázar H, Alvarado M, Hollen ML, Gonzalez-Cruz Y, Hughes O, Vazquez E, Lykens K. Salud Para Su Corazón-NCLR: a comprehensive promotora outreach program to promote heart healthy behaviors among Hispanics. *Health Promot Pract.* 2006;7(1):68–77.

4. Balcázar H, Rosenthal L, De Heer H, Aguirre M, Flores L, Vasquez E, et al. Use of community-based participatory research to disseminate baseline results for building a cardiovascular disease randomized community trial for Mexican Americans living in a US-Mexico border community. *Educ Health* (Abingdon) 2009;22(3):279.

5. Balcázar H, Alvarado M, Cantu F, Pedregon V, Fulwood R. A promotora de salud model for addressing cardiovascular disease risk factors in the US-Mexico border

region. *Prev Chronic Dis.* 2009;*6*(1):A02. http://www.cdc.gov/pcd/issues/2009/jan/08_0020.htm.

6. Balcázar HG, De Heer, H, Rosenthal L, Aguirre M, Flores L, Puentes FA, et al. A promotores de salud intervention to reduce cardiovascular disease risk in a high-risk Hispanic border population, 2005–2008. *Prev Chronic Dis.* 2010;*7*(2):A28. http://www.cdc.gov/pcd/issues/2010/mar/09_0106.htm.

7. Balcázar H, Alvarado M, Hollen ML, Gonzalez-Cruz Y, Pedregon V. Evaluation of Salud Para Su Corazón (Health for Your Heart)—National Council of La Raza promotora outreach program. *Prev Chronic Dis.* 2005;*2*(3):A09. http://www.cdc.gov/pcd/issues/2005/jul/04_0130.htm.

8. Medina A, Balcázar H, Hollen ML, Nkoma E, Mas FS. Promotores de salud: educating Hispanic communities on heart-healthy living. *Am J Health Educ.* 2007;*38*(4):194–202.

9. Anders RL, Balcázar H, Paez L. Hispanic community-based participatory research using a promotores de salud model. *Hisp Health Care Int.* 2006;*4*(2):71–78.

10. Butterfoss FD, Goodman RM, Wandersman A. Community coalitions for prevention and health promotion. *Health Educ Res.* 1993;*8*(3):315–330.

11. Brownstein JN, Bone LR, Dennison CR, Hill MN, Kim MN, Levine DM. Community health workers as interventionists in the prevention and control of heart disease and stroke. *Am J Prev Med.* 2005;*29*(5 Suppl 1):128–133.

12. Eng E, Young R. Lay health advisors as community change agents. *Fam Community Health.* 1992;*15*(1):24–40.

13. Andrews JO, Felton G, Wewers ME, Heath J. Use of community health workers in research with ethnic minority women. *J Nurs Scholarsh.* 2004;*36*(4):358–365.

14. Stokols D. Translating social ecological theory into guidelines for community health promotion. *Am J Health Promot.* 1996;*10*(4):282–298.

15. Bartholomew LK, Parcel GS, Kok G, Gottlieb NH. *Planning health promotion programs: an intervention mapping approach.* San Francisco (CA): Jossey-Bass; 2006.

16. Stokols D, Allen J, Bellingham RL. The social ecology of health promotion: implications for research and practice. *Am J Health Promot.* 1996;*10*(4):247–251.[PubMed]

17. Moody JS, Prochaska JJ, Sallis JF, McKenzie TL, Brown M, Conway TL. Viability of parks and recreation centers as sites for youth physical activity promotion. *Health Promot Pract.* 2004;*5*(4):438–443.

18. Task Force on Community Preventive Services Recommendations to increase physical activity in communities. *Am J Prev Med.* 2002;*22*(4 Suppl):67–72.

19. Hearts N' Parks Y2K: research and evaluation report. National Heart, Lung, and Blood Institute; 2000. [Accessed November 10, 2011]. http://www.nhlbi.nih.gov/health/prof/heart/obesity/hrt_n_pk/fnlrpt.pdf.

20. Bandura A. *Social foundations of thought and action: a social cognitive theory.* Englewood Cliffs (NJ): Prentice-Hall; 1986.

21. Task Force on Community Preventive Services Recommendations for healthcare system and self-management education interventions to reduce morbidity and mortality from diabetes. *Am J Prev Med.* 2002;*22*(4S):10–14.

22. Butterfoss FD. *Coalitions and partnerships in community health.* San Francisco (CA): Wiley and Sons; 2007.

# CLASS ACTIVITY QUESTIONS

1. What people or agencies were represented at each of the levels and what did they contribute to the program?
2. How were these people or agencies at each level similar or different than those you identified during your brainstorming session?

# CHAPTER REFERENCES

American Heart Association. (2006). Alliance for a Healthier Generation and industry leaders set healthy school beverage guidelines for U.S. schools. Retrieved May 8, 2006, from http://www.americanheart.org/presenter.jhtml?identifier=3039339.

Berkman, L., Glass, T., Brissette, I., & Seeman, T. (2000). From social integration to health: Durkheim in the new millennium. *Social Science & Medicine*, 51, 843–857.

Bronfenbrenner, U. (1974). Developmental research, public policy, and the ecology of childhood. *Child Development, 45*, 1–5.

Bronfenbrenner, U. (1994). Ecological models of human development. In *International Encyclopedia of Education* (2nd ed., *3*, pp. 1643–1647). Oxford: Elsevier Sciences Ltd.

Eddy, J.M., Donahue, R.E., Webster, R.D., & Bjornstad, E. (2002). Application of an ecological perspective in worksite health promotion: A review. *American Journal of Health Studies, 17*(4), 197–202.

Goran, M.I., Gower, B.A., Nagy, T.R., & Johnson, R.K. (1998). Developmental changes in energy expenditure and physical activity in children: Evidence for a decline in physical activity in girls before puberty. *Pediatrics, 101*(5), 887–891.

Kumar, S., Quinn, S.C., Kim, K.H., Musa, D., Hilyard, K.M., Freimuth, V.S. (2012). The social ecological model as a framework for determinants of the 2009 H1N1 influenza vaccine uptake in the United States. *Health Education and Behavior, 39*(2), 229–243.

McLeroy, K.R., Bibeau, D., Steckler, A., & Glanz, K. (1988). An ecological perspective on health promotion programs. *Health Education Quarterly, 15*, 351–377.

National School Lunch and Breakfast Program, 77 Federal Register, 4088 (2012) (to be codified at 7 C.F.R. pts 210 and 220).

McNeil, L.H., Kreuter, M., & Subramanian, S.V. (2006). Social environment and physical activity: A review of concepts and evidence. *Social Science & Medicine, 63*, 1011–1022.

Novilla, M.L.B., Barnes, M.D., DeLaCruz, N.G., Williams, P.N., & Rogers, J. (2006). Public health perspectives on the family: An ecological approach to promoting health in the family and community. *Family and Community Health, 29*(1), 28–42.

Sallis, J.F., & Owen, N. (1997). Ecological models of health behavior. In K. Glanz, B.K. Rimer, & F.M. Lewis (Eds.), *Health Behavior and Health Education* (2nd ed., pp. 403–424). San Francisco: Jossey-Bass.

Sallis, J.F., & Owen, N. (1999). *Physical Activity and Behavioral Medicine*. Thousand Oaks, CA: Sage Publications.

Sallis, J.F., & Owen, N. (2002). Ecological models of health behavior. In K. Glanz, B.K. Rimer, & F.M. Lewis (Eds.), *Health Behavior and Health Education* (3rd ed., pp. 462–484). San Francisco: Jossey-Bass.

Stahl, T., Rutten, A. Nutbeam, D., Bauman, A. Kannas, L., Abel, T., et al. (2001). The importance of social environment for physically active lifestyle results from an international study. *Social Science and Medicine, 52*(1), 1–10.

Spence, J.C., & Lee, R.E. (2003). Toward a comprehensive model of physical activity. *Psychology of Sport and Exercise, 4,* 7–24.

Stokols, D. (1992). Establishing and maintaining healthy environments: Toward a social ecology of health promotion. *American Psychologist, 47*(1), 6–22.

von Bothmer, M.I.K., Mattsson, B., & Fridlund, B. (2002). Influences on adolescent smoking behaviour: Siblings' smoking and norms in the social environment do matter. *Health and Social Care in the Community, 10*(4), 213–220

Watt, G.F., Donahue, R.E., Eddy, J.M., & Wallace, E.V. (2001). Use of an ecological approach to worksite health promotion. *American Journal of Health Studies, 17*(3), 144–147.

World Health Organization. (2006). Ecological framework. Retrieved April 9, 2013 from http://www.who.int/violenceprevention/approach/ecology/en.

# Social Capital Theory

## THEORY ESSENCE SENTENCE

Behavior is influenced by who we know and how we know them.

## Constructs Chart

| | |
|---|---|
| Networks | The connections or associations we have with other people and through them, the connections with the people in their networks. |
| Relationships | The strength of the association with other people. |

# IN THE BEGINNING

Although not called "social capital" at the time, the underlying concept of social capital was used in the 1970s to challenge the equal opportunity and affirmative action policies of the 1960s (Loury, 1976). These were based on the belief that— if everyone with the same ability is given the same opportunity, they will all rise to their potential and achieve. Loury's argument against this was that affirmative action and equal opportunity ignore the whole social context that influences achievement or success regardless of ability or potential (Loury, 1976).

The term "social capital" was introduced a few years later in the 1980s by the French sociologist Pierre Bourdieu. Social capital, as Bourdieu saw it, was made up of social obligations or relationships that can be converted into economic capital (money) in certain situations (Bourdieu, 1986). Stated another way, being part of a group gives each individual in the group access to the resources (social capital) of all the other people in the group (Bourdieu, 1986; Portes, 1998) and in this way affects behavior.

## THEORETICAL CONCEPT

From a public health or community perspective, the concept of *social capital* refers to the networks, relationships, norms, and trust people need to cooperate with each other, in a reciprocal fashion, for the benefit of all (Putnam, 2000; Putnam et al., 1993). Social capital includes the resources (monetary and otherwise) we have available to us by virtue of our connections with others.

## CONSTRUCTS

The constructs of Social Capital Theory are networks and relationships. The extent (or amount, if you will) of our social capital depends on the "richness" of the people we know in terms of their connections and their resources (money, education, clout, etc.) (Carpiano, 2006) and our relationship with them.

### Networks

Networks are the connections or associations we have with other people and through them, the connections with the people in their networks. However, before network resources (i.e., the social capital) can be used or accessed, there must be trust and reciprocity between the members of the social network (Carpiano, 2006). Trust and reciprocity are at the very core of Social Capital Theory. They lead to the expectations and obligations that come with being part of a particular network (Hawe & Shiell, 2000). Without trust and reciprocity, there is no social capital. Perhaps it is in this way that social capital influences health behavior.

The networks of social capital are diverse: they are what make up our social environment. They may be whole societies, communities, neighborhoods, civic associations, organizations, schools, religious affiliations, or families, to name but a few. Think of all the groups to which you belong and the resources (connections, clout, money, jobs) available to you as a result of your relationships with the people in these networks.

Social capital can also include one's social skills or ability to negotiate and work with others to find solutions to common problems (Szreter & Woolcock, 2004). It may refer to styles and forms of leadership, structure of service delivery, and social unity among communities (Szreter & Woolcock, 2004).

As you can see, social capital can be many things. Consequently, it is often used as an umbrella term that takes into account social cohesion (which includes trust and reciprocity), support, and integration or participation (Almedon, 2005) in social networks. It is the connectedness that people have to the people around them (Carpiano, 2006). When people feel connected to each other, they develop behaviors and attitudes that benefit themselves and their society as a whole (Putnam, 2000).

A community in which people are more connected to each other, where everyone knows everyone else and they each watch out for each other, is better able to support positive health behaviors and dissuade negative ones (Berkman & Kawachi, 2000; Ross & Jang, 2000), organize itself, and is better positioned to fight with one voice in one direction (Veenstra et al., 2005). In this type of neighborhood, there may be lower tolerance for illegal behavior, drug use, or crime (**Figure 10–1**) (Berkman & Kawachi, 2000; Ross & Jang, 2000); improved child development and adolescent well-being; better mental health, less youth delinquency; overall reduced mortality; lower susceptibility to binge drinking, depression, and loneliness; and higher perceptions of well-being and health (Szreter & Woolcock, 2004).

Unfortunately, the number of Americans who live in these types of neighborhoods and socialize with their neighbors has steadily declined along with the

© carolyn brule/Shutterstock, Inc.

**FIGURE 10–1**  Neighbors watching out for each other

extent to which people trust each other (Putnam, 1995). This does not bode well for the health of a community or the health of the people living in it. There are higher rates of stress and isolation and lower rates of child well-being, ability to respond to environmental health hazards, and likelihood of receiving effective health interventions (Szreter & Woolcock, 2004).

## RELATIONSHIPS

The more people you know, the more relationships you have, the more connected you are to a variety of others in a number of ways, the more resources you have at your disposal (see **Figure 10–2**). This is akin to the old saying, "It's not what you know but who you know that counts." There are three different types of relationships that affect social capital, each defined by the strength of the association

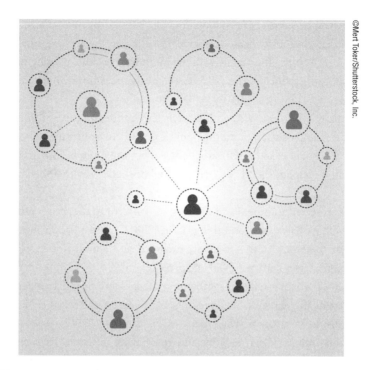

©Mert Toker/Shutterstock, Inc.

**FIGURE 10–2**  Networks are the connections we have with other people and their connections

between the people who make up the social network. They are bonding, bridging, and linking social capital.

## BONDING SOCIAL CAPITAL

*Bonding social capital* refers to those relationships between people who see themselves as being similar in terms of their shared social identity (Szreter, 2002; Szreter & Woolcock, 2004; Woolcock, 2001), origin, or status or position in society (Szreter, 2002). An example of this is the network of ties that holds families and groups together (Wakefield & Poland, 2005). Think about the behaviors, attitudes, expectations, and obligations that come with being part of your family. How do these things impact your health behavior?

Social networks, in general, facilitate and support bonding between people. This support may directly or indirectly, positively or negatively affect health. This occurs directly by their impact on self-esteem, exercise, sexual activity, the utilization of health services, or stress levels (Berkman et al., 2000). To cope with the stress of an HIV/AIDS diagnosis, people in rural Canada use the social capital of their bonding relationships. The people with whom they have close, trusting ties are the ones to whom they disclose their diagnosis and the ones from whom they obtain emotional support (Veinat, 2010).

Bonding relationships also influence health more indirectly through their effects on the larger social, economic, political, and environmental determinants of health (Berkman et al., 2000). They may affect the types of jobs and housing available in a neighborhood, as well as neighborhood wealth (Veenstra et al., 2005).

Being connected to others and needing to conform to the group norm is not always possible or always a good thing (Crow, 2002). When people don't or can't conform to the group norms, they are excluded and barred from accessing the social capital of the network (Wakefield & Poland, 2005). Think of the social network of a particular religious affiliation. When some people in a community are not part of the network, they are not able to access the social capital of that church, mosque, temple, or synagogue.

Exclusion from a social network and not having access to its social capital are important in terms of understanding health behaviors. Unless people can be "named, blamed and shamed" (Rose, 2000, p. 1407) for unacceptable behavior (health or otherwise), there is little incentive to conform or behave in acceptable ways (Wakefield & Poland, 2005). People with higher levels of social capital tend to be healthier than those with lower levels of social capital (Bolin et al., 2003) because greater social capital is linked to lower rates of overall mortality. It is specifically linked to reduced mortality from cardiovascular disease and cancers (Kawachi et al., 1997).

Needing to conform to the group norms, and in so doing remaining part of the network, does not always result in positive health outcomes. In fact, conformity with the group norms may support unhealthy or inappropriate behaviors. Take the case of a woman enduring sexual harassment in the workplace. She may be reluctant to report it for fear of losing her job, being blacklisted within the network, and consequently becoming unemployable (Wakefield & Poland, 2005). Similarly, in cultures where spousal abuse is considered the norm, women tolerate repeated beatings because it is the norm of the group not to complain about such treatment. Complaining may result in a divorce. Although bringing relief from the beatings, a divorce may also mean losing her children to her ex-husband and his family and being an outcast in her society.

## BRIDGING SOCIAL CAPITAL

*Bridging social capital* refers to networks of people who come together as acquaintances. They are from different social groups and differ in some sociodemographic sense, be it age, ethnicity, education, or self-esteem (Wakefield & Poland, 2005). People become part of these networks to engage in an activity with mutually beneficial outcomes that were not possible within their bonded relationships. Examples of this type of relationship are those among sports team members, a choir, people working on a group project, students in a class, and tenants in an apartment building (Szreter, 2002). These relationships may affect health behavior by virtue of a desire to do what the group does, or to be a "team player," in order to have access to the resources of the group.

Bridging relationships among college students, through participation in a community or service organization, affects their alcohol use. Students who have these types of relationships are less likely to abuse alcohol or engage in risky drinking behaviors (Theall et al., 2009).

## LINKING SOCIAL CAPITAL

The weakest social capital relationships are *linking* relationships. In these, we have norms of respect and networks of trusting relationships, but they are between people who interact across power or authority gradients representing formal institutions (see **Figure 10–3**). These are the relationships seen between teacher and student, police officer and crime victim, physician and patient (Szreter & Woolcock, 2004).

For the rural Canadians living with HIV/AIDS discussed above, linking relationships with their healthcare providers also helps them cope with stress and stigmatization. In addition, these network relationships provide much needed information about their health status and treatment (Veinat, 2010), thereby affecting their health decisions and health behavior.

In summary, according to Social Capital Theory, trust impacts norms, expectations, and relationships and, therefore, affects behavior (see **Figure 10–4**).

# THEORY IN ACTION—CLASS ACTIVITY

In a small group, discuss the characteristics of the neighborhood or community in which you live that fosters or hinders trusting relationships. Then, discuss how these characteristics might foster or hinder HIV outreach education or services in the area.

FIGURE 10–3  Relationship across power gradient

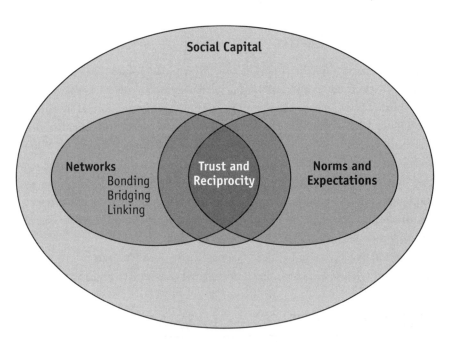

FIGURE 10–4  Social Capital

Finally, share your thoughts with the others in your group about the role you believe the linking relationships with religious leaders would play in HIV prevention or education services in your community. Now read the following article and answer the questions at the end.

# Chapter 10 Article: Understanding Social Capital and HIV Risk in Rural African American Communities[1]

*Crystal W. Cené[1], Aletha Y. Akers[2], Stacey W. Lloyd[3], Tashuna Albritton[4], Wizdom Powell Hammond[5] and Giselle Corbie-Smith[6]*

[1]Department of Medicine, UNC Division of General Medicine, The University of North Carolina at Chapel Hill, Chapel Hill, NC, USA;
[2]Department of Obstetrics, Gynecology and Reproductive Science, Magee-Women's Hospital, Pittsburgh, PA, USA;
[3]RTI International, Research Triangle Park, NC, USA;
[4]School of Social Work, The University of North Carolina at Chapel Hill, Chapel Hill, NC, USA;
[5]Department of Health Behavior and Health Education, The University of North Carolina at Chapel Hill, Chapel Hill, NC, USA;
[6]Departments of Social Medicine, Medicine and Epidemiology, The University of North Carolina at Chapel Hill, Chapel Hill, NC, USA.

**Background:** African Americans (AA) and rural communities often suffer disproportionately from poorer health. Theory-guided research examining how individual- and community-level factors influence health behaviors and contribute to disparities is needed.

**Objective:** To understand how a social network model that captures the interplay between individual and community factors might inform community-based interventions to reduce HIV risk in rural AA communities.

**Design:** Qualitative study.

**Setting and Participants:** Eleven focus groups with 38 AA 16–24 year olds, 42 adults over age 25, and 13 formerly incarcerated individuals held in community settings in two rural, predominantly AA counties in North Carolina. Thirty-seven semi-structured interviews with multiethnic key informants.

**Approach:** Semi-structured interviews and focus groups with open-ended questions assessed a) perceptions of multi-level HIV risk determinants from a social

---

[1] Reproduced from Cene, C.W., Akers, A.Y., Lloyd, S.W., Albritton, T., Hammond, W.P., Corbie-Smith, G. (2011). Understanding Social Capital and HIV Risk in Rural African American Communities. *Journal Of General Internal Medicine, 26*(7), 737–744, DOI: 10.1007/S11606-011-1646-4.

network model (individual, interpersonal, social, economic, political and structural) identified through literature review and b) community needs and assets affecting local HIV rates. Qualitative data was analyzed using directive content analysis guided by a social network model.

**Results:** We identified four themes regarding the interaction between individuals and their communities that mediate HIV risk: interpersonal processes, community structural environment, social disorder, and civic engagement. Communities were characterized as having a high degree of cohesiveness, tension, and HIV-related stigma. The community structural environment—characterized by neighborhood poverty, lack of skilled jobs, segregation, political disenfranchisement and institutional racism—was felt to reduce the availability and accessibility of resources to combat HIV. Adults noted an inability to combat social problems due to social disorder, which fuels HIV risk behaviors. Civic engagement as a means of identifying community concerns and developing solutions is limited by churches' reluctance to address HIV-related issues.

**Conclusion:** To combat HIV-related stigma, physicians should follow recommendations for universal HIV testing. Besides asking about individual health behaviors, physicians should ask about the availability of support and local community resources. Physicians might consider tailoring their treatment recommendations based on available community resources. This strategy may potentially improve patient adherence and clinical outcomes.

**Key words:** social capital, HIV prevention, rural communities, African Americans, community-based participatory research

## INTRODUCTION

Racial disparities in health are well-documented.[1] African Americans and individuals living in rural communities are often disproportionately affected by poor health and suboptimal health care. Extant literature largely focuses on individual-level factors which contribute to health disparities, with less emphasis on the contextual factors within communities that often underlie and perpetuate disparities.[2,3]

Social capital is a potentially useful construct for understanding health disparities because it acknowledges the contribution of individual- and community-level factors that impact health care and outcomes. Social capital has various definitions, ranging from the strength of connections within and between groups (i.e. social cohesion) to the resources (e.g., economic, political, or material) available to groups.[4-6] Social capital theories suggest that individuals embedded in social networks can access and benefit from group resources.[7] Thus, individuals belonging to groups possessing a greater amount of social capital are expected to exhibit lower disease rates.[2]

Social capital has been examined in relation to a variety of health-related outcomes, including mortality,[8] health status,[9] sexually transmitted diseases,[10,11] mental health,[12-15] health care access,[16] and health behaviors.[17,18] Findings from studies examining social capital as a contributor to racial disparities have been inconclusive.[19] The ambiguity stems from variations in the definitions and measures used to assess social capital.[4-6] Measures of social capital that fail to understand the dynamic interplay between individuals and their communities produce only partial accounts of individuals' lived experiences and little insight into why disparities persist or how to eliminate them.[20,21]

Therefore, the goals of our study were twofold: 1) to understand, using qualitative methods, how a social network model that emphasizes the impact of differential social capital on health disparities and outcomes can be used to understand disparities in HIV risk by examining the reciprocal relationship between rural AAs and their communities, and 2) to use this information to develop a community-based HIV risk reduction intervention.

# METHODS

## DESCRIPTION OF SOCIAL NETWORK MODEL

This model (**Figure 1**) incorporates aspects of an individual's interpersonal environment, as well as broader neighborhood factors that influence health behaviors, health outcomes, and health disparities.[22] It is based on a definition of social capital as "the aggregate of actual or potential resources linked to possession of a durable network available to group members for pursuing action in the absence of, or in conjunction with their own economic capital."[4] This model proposes three critical conceptual domains: (1) social cohesion which leads to social capital, (2) social capital, or the actual or potential group resources that can be leveraged by individuals for their benefit, and (3) the influence of the broader neighborhood environment on the exercise of capital. Social cohesion represents trust, familiarity, and shared values among neighborhood residents. Social capital takes four forms: support (assistance coping with daily life issues and stressors),

**Content removed due to copyright restrictions**

**FIGURE 1** Proposed Conceptual Model of Neighborhood Social Capital Processes on Individual Health Outcomes.

leverage (providing access to information and social advancement), control (collective maintenance of order and neighborhood safety), and civic participation (engagement in organized groups or structured activities to address community issues).[22] The neighborhood environment influences both the degree of cohesion that can develop between individuals and the availability and accessibility of community resources.

## STUDY DESIGN AND SETTING

Our work was conducted through an academic-community partnership which uses community-based participatory research (CBPR) approaches to develop HIV prevention interventions.[23] Data were collected through focus groups (FG) and key informant (KI) interviews conducted in 2006–2007 as part of a community needs and assets assessment to guide intervention development. The study took place in two counties in northeast North Carolina (NC) with some of the highest rates and most significant disparities in HIV/AIDS in the state (**Table 1**).[24,25] These counties rank 3rd and 16th among NC's 100 counties in the three-year average rate of new HIV cases for 2005–2007. In 2006, the majority of each county's HIV/AIDS cases were among AAs (86% and 82%). Participants aged 18 and older provided verbal informed consent; those under age 18 provided verbal assent and their parents provided written informed consent. This

**Table 1** Descriptive Statistics by County

| Characteristic | County A | County B |
|---|---|---|
| Population size | 55,606 | 87,420 |
| % African American | 58 | 34 |
| State ranking in 3-year average rate of new HIV cases* | 3rd | 16th |
| % of HIV/AIDS cases per county among African Americans† | 86 | 82 |
| $ Median Household Income | 30,983 | 37,147 |
| % with less than a High School Education | 34.4 | 24.4 |
| % with a High School Diploma | 36.9 | 33.9 |
| % with a Bachelor's Degree or higher | 8.5 | 17.2 |

*For years 2005–2007
†For year 2006

study was approved by the Institutional Review Board at The University of North Carolina at Chapel Hill.

## FOCUS GROUPS

We recruited individuals from three populations that our community partners felt were at greatest risk for HIV infection: youth/young adults aged 16–24, formerly incarcerated (FI) individuals, and adults over age 25. Together with community-based organizations in both counties, our team posted flyers, used print and radio advertising, and person-to-person sampling. Eleven gender-stratified FG were held: four with youth/young adults, five with general adults, and two with FI individuals. Groups were held at local youth centers, a church, and a community administration facility. Each lasted approximately two hours and was led by an experienced moderator, matched to participants' race and gender.

The semi-structured discussion guide assessed three topic areas: 1) perceptions about local HIV determinants based on literature review, 2) community needs, assets and resources affecting local HIV rates and 3) key considerations for intervention development. We asked two general questions about factors contributing to the spread of HIV locally: 1) "Why do you think rates are higher among AAs than Whites in this community?", and 2) "If our goal is to reduce high rates of HIV/AIDS among AA around here, list everything that gets in the way of achieving that goal"; interviewees were asked to consider individual, interpersonal, social, economic, political, and structural barriers, as well as physical surroundings. To ensure that all FG and KI interviews covered these topics, probes were used if participants' responses did not fit within at least one of the aforementioned categories. To identify community needs, assets, resources, and key considerations for intervention development, we asked, "What can you and your community do to address these (e.g. cultural) issues to help reduce HIV/AIDS among AA in this community?" Each participant completed a demographic questionnaire and received a $20 incentive for their participation.

## KEY INFORMANT INTERVIEWS

Community partners were asked to identify influential individuals in each county whose opinions about HIV risk, disparities, and potential solutions would be valuable. We sought individuals from the following sectors: political, economic, health, law enforcement, media, recreation, community groups, education, religious, social welfare, and leaders of grassroots organizations. Project staff contacted nominees about participating. Nominees were asked to identify other KI using these same criteria. Semi-structured interviews were conducted in private offices, lasted approximately 2 hours, and used a 12-question discussion guide that paralleled the FG guide.

## ANALYSIS

FG and KI interviews were audio-recorded, transcribed and entered into Atlas. ti version 5.2, a qualitative data management program. Since we used an existing framework to guide the data coding process, we conducted directive content analysis (DCA). DCA is performed when the analytic goal is to validate or extend prior theoretical frameworks.[26] Coders reviewed transcripts line-by-line to identify passages supporting the three domains from the social network model.[22] Coders considered whether a comment explicitly addressed a domain in a general sense (e.g., descriptions of social cohesion), as well as whether narratives linked one of the models' domains specifically to HIV risk or prevention (e.g., how dilapidated houses foster engagement in HIV risk behaviors). Finally, coders considered the relevance of participants' comments for developing an HIV prevention intervention.

Transcripts were coded by two independent coders. The team organized coded passages into major and sub-themes and explored theoretical links between themes. When there was ambiguity or coders differed in their assignment of a thematic category, coders met with a third party to discuss the issue and reach consensus. We compared thematic content within and across FG and interviews. For FG, we also compared themes across participant gender and type. Reported themes were consistent across study participant types, unless otherwise specified, and consistent across coders.

# RESULTS

## SAMPLE CHARACTERISTICS

We interviewed 93 FG participants and 37 KIs. All FG participants and 23 (62%) of KI were AA. Eighteen (47%) of the youth/young adult, 24 (57%) of general adults, and 4 (31%) of the FI FG participants were female. Mean ages for youth/young adult, general adult, and FI participants was 18, 35, and 37 years, respectively. The mean age of KIs was 49 years. More KIs reported having a graduate degree (n = 14, 38%) than general adult FG participants (n = 1, 2%) (**Table 2**).

**Table 2** Characteristics of Study Sample

Focus Group Participants

| Characteristic | Youth/ Youths (N=38) | General Adults (n=42) | Formerly Incarcerated (n=37) | Key Informants (n=13) |
|---|---|---|---|---|
| African American, N (%) | 38 (100) | 42 (100) | 13 (100) | 23 (62) |
| Female gender, N (%) | 18 (47) | 24 (57) | 4 (31) | 16 (43) |
| Mean age, years (range) | 18 (16-24) | 35 (22-46) | 37 (25-53) | 49 (32-64) |
| Education, N (%)* | | | | |
| Less than high school grad | 32 (84) | 8 (19) | 7 (54) | 0 (0) |
| Graduate high school/ GED | 3 (8) | 8 (19) | 5 (15) | 2 (5) |
| Some college | 2 (5) | 8 (19) | 1 (8) | 6 (16) |
| Graduate degree | 1 (3) | 1 (2) | 0 (0) | 14 (38) |
| Family receiving Public Assistance, % | 13 (34) | 5 (12) | 3 (23) | N/A |

*Numbers may not add up to 100% since not all possible categories are represented
N/A = not asked

## THEMATIC OVERVIEW

We identified 4 main themes as important for understanding racial disparities in local HIV rates: Interpersonal processes, community structural environment, social disorder, and civic engagement (**Table 3**).

## INTERPERSONAL PROCESSES

Adults described strong cohesion and a deep-seated sense of community resulting from small population size, population stability, long-standing intergenerational connections, and shared values between residents. In contrast, youth and FI individuals believed that social tension (i.e. lack of cohesion), largely related to segregation and poverty, overshadowed their sense of belonging and restricted access to beneficial resources outside their personal networks. They described racial tensions between AA and Whites, conflicts based on neighborhood boundaries, and socio-economic class differences among AAs as fostering this tension.

**Table 3** Four Main Themes, Subthemes and Representative Quotes

**Interpersonal Processes***

Social cohesion    "I like the ability that we have to work on various problems in the community. I like the cohesiveness that exists among our community . . . Wanting to make sure that what I do is in the best interest of everybody in the community."

*—AA female KI*

Social tensions    "We are so in that 'crab attitude'. We're so scared one will get higher than the other that instead of trying to take both of them and move up, we'd rather pull somebody down instead of try to lift them up."

*—AA adult male FG*

HIV-related stigma    "Everybody is so secretive about it. [HIV] is like a disease that you don't want to talk about. It's a disease that you don't want in your neighborhood."

*—AA female KI*

People don't know about HIV and the people don't want to talk about it . . . it's a fear of stigma for one of the reasons that stand in the way for HIV AIDS.

*—AA adult female FG*

**Community Structural Forces**

Availability of resources    "If I don't have a job to go to and I'm sitting around all day, the only thing that I'm thinking about doing is something to make me feel better. I'm going to get high or I'm gonna have sex."

*—AA adult male FG*

"[County Name] is one of the poorest counties . . . having one of the highest . . . AIDS rates and highest drugs and alcohol activity it makes you wonder why . . . It's not that we don't have jobs, we don't have resources. Folk are depressed and oppressed and, and therefore we're turning to other things . . ."

*—AA male KI*

Accessibility of resources    "A lot of people have a hard time getting to different functions and community things because they don't have transportation or a way to get there . . ."

*—AA youth/young adult female FG*

"Most men that could be role models are either working and do not have that time, accessibility to come out and be role models for the children. And those that do, the few that has the ability to do that are overworked . . ."

*—AA male KI*

**Table 3** (*Continued*)

| | |
|---|---|
| Segregation, political forces and institutional racism | "We still have some racial tension here in this county . . . I think a lot of it is in government, not so much the people in the community . . . Some of that carries over to the school where students sometimes are not treated fairly I think. Also it carries over to the job market where certain people of certain races may not be promoted in this county because of the close-mindedness."<br>*—AA female KI* |

**Social Disorder**

"Either you don't have enough police presence there or if you do have the police presence there, you have a lot of community people who don't trust them . . . And to me that, that prevents them [police and community members] from working together and trying to control the neighborhood."

*—AA male KI*

**Civic Engagement**

"When a person is more involved in their church, they have often times a greater sense of purpose and they have a support network that helps with their mental health and helps with so many other things."

*—White male KI*

"I'm not sure that there is a support network through the churches because . . . I think that religion . . . often times people who are in that 'at risk' category for HIV AIDS are probably not viewed positively in a religious setting . . ."

*—White female KI*

Features of these communities, which made them desirable for some participants (e.g., small size and familiarity between individuals) also served to foster HIV-related stigma. Individuals living with or presumed to be at risk for HIV were unable to draw upon support of others in the community. As illustrated by an AA female KI, "individuals who test positive are outcasts...no longer a part of the community." HIV-related stigma also adversely affected outreach and prevention efforts. Community members were less willing to be tested for HIV for fear that doing so may cause others to assume they were homosexual or engaging in high-risk behaviors.

## COMMUNITY STRUCTURAL ENVIRONMENT

### Availability of Resources

Adult respondents remarked that tight connections between individuals engendered a high degree of perceived support. Yet, the ability of social networks to provide tangible support was reportedly reduced by a combination of neighbor-hood poverty, lack of skilled jobs, lack of transportation, and segregation by race and socio-economic status. These factors concentrated AAs into communities lacking crucial resources necessary for self-sufficiency. For some, this adversity led to engagement in criminal activities, such as selling drugs or prostitution. Others responded by leaving the community to seek better opportunities for economic and social advancement. Those remaining often worked multiple jobs or long shifts and had little time for civic engagement. Thus, individuals capable of pro-viding tangible support or mentorship were often inaccessible or overextended. Material and psychological effects of poverty fostered feelings of hopelessness and isolation. Participants' narratives suggested that many AAs in these communities have a sense of 'fatalism' about their futures, which reportedly led to engagement in high-risk behaviors as an escape mechanism.

## Accessibility to Resources

Our respondents reported an inability to fully utilize information and other health-promoting community resources. Concentrated poverty in these commu-nities meant AAs primarily utilized public health departments or "free clinics" as primary sources of care. Participants perceived that shame surrounding the use of these facilities combined with fear of confidentiality breeches, common in small communities, led many to avoid seeking health care or HIV testing services. Such avoidance was thought to indirectly facilitate HIV transmission. Youth and adult participants articulated barriers to accessing certain health services to reduce HIV transmission. A female FI participant noted:

> "...the people who use drugs they don't go to the health department... speaking from being on that life, living in that life. You won't come up and take care of yourself like you should. And at any given time, you don't have condoms. You won't use condoms."

## Segregation, Political Forces and Institutional Racism

Participants attributed AAs collective inability to capitalize on resources external to their personal networks to historical and continued racial segregation at the county level and a lack of AA representation in social welfare and political institutions. As one female KI noted: [African Americans] are outnumbered ... on [the] school board…These decision makers at the hospital level, at the political level, at where something can be done about this issue [HIV], is generally led and financed by Whites. And they are more concerned about their race than they are [about] Blacks.

Despite the HIV burden in the target counties, participants felt county-level funding for prevention remained inadequate. Participants blamed institutional racism for AAs inability to translate their growing political power into lower HIV risk. One white male KI commented: If this was an epidemic in the White, middle-class high school students, all the resources of the town and county would be diverted immediately to address it. But it's predominantly seen as an African-American issue and I think that racism, the institutional racism of our community, is what keeps us inactive.

## SOCIAL DISORDER

Many respondents noted a lack of informal control over the criminal activity and violence perpetuated by local gangs. Some participants attributed this inability to maintain control as both a product and consequence of a lack of community cohesiveness and downward spiraling community norms. Many feared retaliation from perpetrators if they spoke out. This fear was compounded by their perception that police ignored criminal activity in AA communities and, therefore, were not a resource that could be utilized to help maintain order. In addition, dilapidated and abandoned houses and buildings, remnants of a hurricane seven years prior, served as visible symbols of community disorder. These structures became venues where individuals could engage unabated in drug use and prostitution—behaviors which increased HIV risk.

## CIVIC ENGAGEMENT

Participants noted that the expression of community concerns and the utilization of informal networks to address important issues traditionally occur in religious settings, particularly AA churches. However, participants perceived that churches are not good sources of support or activism for HIV prevention due to their reluctance to talk about or participate in HIV-related activities. HIV is considered to be a 'gay disease' by many religious leaders who preach against homosexuality and pre-marital sex. Such sentiments served to alienate some individuals and make it harder to access the myriad resources inherent within churches.

# DISCUSSION

In this study, FG participants and KIs described four main themes relevant to how a social network model emphasizing the impact of differential social capital on health disparities and outcomes can be used when considering community-based interventions to address disparities in HIV risk—interpersonal processes, community structural environment, social disorder and civic engagement. Our findings have several implications for how social network models and community participation in research might inform HIV risk reduction interventions in rural AA communities.

Emergent themes from our data suggest several considerations and targets for community-based interventions to reduce HIV risk in rural AA communities. Small rural communities may offer the advantage of strong networks between individuals, which may facilitate sharing of knowledge and other health-related resources. However, these same networks may serve to marginalize and exclude certain individuals (i.e. those considered 'at risk' for HIV). Insufficient numbers of positive role models and constructive social outlets were felt to increase HIV risk indirectly through engagement in risky behaviors to combat feelings of isolation. These dynamics suggest that interventions to reduce HIV risk behaviors which capitalize on network cohesion and include peer education and mentoring may be efficacious.

HIV-related stigma in rural predominantly AA communities is rampant and perpetuated by some religious organizations and leaders. This finding has implications for whom researchers can partner and the approach that must be taken when designing interventions to improve access to HIV-related services. Novel strategies are needed to lessen the stigma associated with attending certain types of health facilities in order to reduce access-related barriers. For example, mobile units which provide various health- and non-health-related services (e.g., HIV testing and counseling, education and testing for other health conditions, and information on social services) may be beneficial.

Our findings related to the effect of community structural forces on the development and exercise of social capital is illustrative of the dynamic interplay between individuals and their communities. Neighborhood poverty, lack of skilled jobs, poor housing conditions, segregation, and political disenfranchisement were perceived by respondents to contribute to higher rates of HIV among AAs through their influence on individuals' health behaviors and on the availability and accessibility of community resources. Consistent with other studies, these suggest that variability in social determinants of health is a significant source of health disparities among AAs and inequities in contextual factors must be eliminated if health disparities are to be effectively addressed.[27–29] Therefore, interventions to reduce HIV risk in AAs should target factors operant outside the health care system. Concentrated and sustained efforts may be required to address neighborhood segregation and institutionalized racism that fuel HIV risk. Individuals designing HIV prevention interventions should consider using CBPR approaches whereby community and academic partners work together to identify problems and design solutions. Interventions employing these approaches might be more successful and sustainable because they are informed by those most affected and are more likely to address context-specific influences on risk.

We focused on how social capital influences HIV risk in two rural U.S. counties. Previous studies examined the role of social capital in HIV.[10,30–32] However, these studies relied on social capital measures that reflect only social cohesion, civic participation, norms of reciprocity, and trust between individuals. These measures have limited relevance for understanding how the social environment influences health disparities because they only tap relational aspects of social capital without considering the material and political aspects. Furthermore, few of these studies emphasize how social capital unfolds to influence risk in U.S. rural communities. Although we applied a specific model to explain disparities in HIV, this model and our qualitative approach can be successfully applied to understand disparities in other conditions and inform community-based intervention development.

Our study illustrates how different conceptualizations of social capital examined in isolation can yield contradictory results. Had we only considered social cohesion as our measure of social capital, we might surmise that high social capital was related to HIV risk. Likewise, had we only examined social capital resources, we would have found that low levels of social capital were associated with HIV risk. However, by simultaneously considering the influence of community structural features, we see that complex forces act synergistically to negate the positive effects of social cohesion and limit individuals' ability to develop or exercise social capital. Our findings are consistent with theory and empiric research suggesting that social capital can have negative as well as positive consequences.[4,33]

Our findings have implications for clinical practice and patient education. In clinical settings, providers generally focus on individual-level HIV risk behaviors, such as not using condoms, intravenous drug use, or having concurrent sexual partners. In taking a "social history," physicians should question the availability of support and local community resources, since communities may differ in their capacity to support individuals in avoiding high-risk behaviors. Physicians should consider using this information to tailor patients' treatment recommendations. Such an approach may potentially improve patient adherence and clinical outcomes. Integration of case management services into primary care practices may help patients identify and access various health-promoting community resources, thereby potentially improving care delivery and health outcomes. To combat HIV-related stigma, physicians should follow the Centers for Disease Control recommendations for universal HIV testing of all individuals aged 13–64 who visit health care settings.[34] Patient education about HIV prevention should extend to non-traditional settings, such as prisons and jails, and continue through re-entry into the community since immediate release from these facilities represents one of the greatest risk periods for injection drug use and risky sexual behavior.[35,36]

This study has notable limitations. We sampled participants from two rural counties in one state and only included AAs in our FGs, thereby limiting external validity to other groups and settings. We did not query respondents about their specific HIV risk behaviors or objectively measure their HIV status.

Our study has several strengths. A large sample size and triangulation of data from FG participants and KIs provide a rich understanding of how social capital influences HIV risk in the target communities. Use of a qualitative approach guided by a strong theoretical model for examining this issue is novel. We examined the interface between communities which provide the structure that positively or negatively influences disease risk and individuals who are bound by and help shape that structure. Consequently, we have a better understanding of how individual and community level factors interact to influence health behaviors which fuel HIV-related disparities. This work can inform the development of effective interventions which target multi-level HIV determinants to lower HIV risk among AAs in rural communities.

## CONCLUSION

We used qualitative methods to understand how a specific social network model, which captures the dynamic interplay between individual and community factors, might inform community-based interventions to reduce HIV risk in rural AA communities. Cohesiveness between individuals may help mitigate HIV risk (e.g. through sharing of resources). However, it may not be sufficient for lowering HIV risk when coupled with community-level disadvantage, neighborhood segregation and institutionalized racism—factors which may constrain individuals' rational choices and facilitate engagement in high risk behaviors. Although clinicians may have little direct control over the community-level factors that influence an individual patient's HIV risk, they should have a multi-faceted understanding of factors which influence HIV risk from the patient's perspective. Such understanding may result in the delivery of more "patient-centered care"—care which considers patients' illness experiences within a broader biopsychosocial framework.

## ACKNOWLEDGEMENTS

We would like to acknowledge the contributions of all steering committee members in the development of Project GRACE Consortium: Larry Auld, Reuben Blackwell, Hank Boyd, III, John Braswell, Angela Bryant, Cheryl Bryant, Don Cavellini, Trinette Cooper, Dana Courtney, Eugenia Eng, Jerome Garner, Vernetta Gupton, Davita Harrell, Shannon Hayes-Peaden, Stacey Henderson, Doris Howington, Clara Knight, Gwendolyn Knight, Taro Knight, Patricia Oxendine-Pitt, Donald Parker, Reginald Silver, Doris Stith, Jevita Terry, and Cynthia Worthy. We would also like to thank the three anonymous reviewers, Dr. Amina Chaudhry, Dr. Karran Phillips, and Mr. R.H. Wright for their helpful comments on this manuscript. We would especially like to thank the assigned Deputy Editor for her very detailed and thoughtful comments which strengthened this manuscript tremendously.

This work was funded by grants from the National Center on Minority Health and Health Disparities (R24MD001671) and The University of North Carolina Center for AIDS Research (UNC CFAR P30 AI50410). Dr. Corbie-Smith is a Health Disparities Scholar with the National Center on Minority Health and Health Disparities. Drs. Cené and Akers received support as funded scholars through the Clinical Translational Science Award-K12 Scholars Program (KL2). The CTSA is a national consortium with the goal of transforming how clinical and translational research is conducted, ultimately enabling researchers to provide new treatments more efficiently and quickly to patients. Drs. Cené and Akers' work on this project was supported by award number KL2RR025746 and KL2 RR024154-0, respectively from the National Center for Research Resources, a component of the National Institutes of Health (NIH) and NIH Roadmap for Medical Research. Dr. Powell Hammond is supported by the National Center for Minority Health and Health Disparities (Award # 1L60MD002605-01), National Cancer Institute (Grant # 3U01CA114629-04 S2) and a developmental award from the UNC Center for Aids Research Award (CFAR P30 AI50410).

The content is solely the responsibility of the authors and does not necessarily represent the official views of any of the funding agencies. This paper was presented at the 32th Annual Meeting of the Society of General Internal Medicine, May 14, 2009, Miami, Florida.

Conflicts of Interest

None disclosed.

# REFERENCES

1. Institute of Medicine, Committee on Understanding and Eliminating Racial and Ethnic Disparities in Health Care. Unequal treatment: Confronting racial and ethnic disparities in health care. 2002.
2. Shaw M, Dorling D, Smith GD. Poverty, social exclusion, and minorities. In: Marmot M, Wilkinson RG, eds. *Social determinants of health*. 2nd ed. Oxford: Oxford University Press; 2006:196–223.
3. Nazroo JY, Williams DR. The social determination of ethnic/racial inequalities in health. In: Marmot M, Wilkinson RG, eds. *Social determinants of health*. 2nd ed. Great Britain: Oxford University Press; 2006:238–66.
4. Bourdieu P. The handbook of theory and research for the sociology of education. In: Richardson JG, ed. *The forms of capital*. New York: Greenwood Press; 1986:241–58.
5. Coleman JS. Social Capital in the Creation of Human Capital. *AJS*. 1988; *94*(Supplement):S95–S120.
6. Putnam RD. Bowling alone: America's declining social capital. JOD. 1995;6(1):65–78.
7. Hsieh CH. A concept analysis of social capital within a health context. *Nurs Forum*. 2008;*43*(3):151–59.
8. Kawachi I, Kennedy BP, Lochner K, Prothrow-Stith D. Social capital, income inequality, and mortality. *Am J Public Health*. 1997;*87*(9):1491–8.
9. Kawachi I, Kennedy BP, Glass R. Social capital and self-rated health: a contextual analysis. *Am J Public Health*. 1999;*89*(8):1187–93.
10. Holtgrave DR, Crosby RA. Social capital, poverty, and income inequality as predictors of gonorrhea, syphilis, chlamydia and AIDS case rates in the United States. *Sex Transm Infect*. 2003;*79*(1):62–4
11. Semaan S, Sternberg M, Zaidi A, Aral SO. Social capital and rates of gonorrhea and syphilis in the United States: spatial regression analyses of state-level associations. *Soc Sci Med*. 2007;*64*(11):2324–41.
12. Almedom AM. Social capital and mental health: an interdisciplinary review of primary evidence. *Soc Sci Med*. 2005;*61*(5):943–64.
13. De Silva MJ, McKenzie K, Harpham T, Huttly SR. Social capital and mental illness: a systematic review. *J Epidemiol Community Health*. 2005;*59*(8):619–27.
14. Islam MK, Merlo J, Kawachi I, Lindstrom M, Gerdtham UG. Social capital and health: does egalitarianism matter? A literature review. *Int J Equity Health*. 2006;*5*:3.
15. Macinko J, Starfield B. The utility of social capital in research on health determinants. *Milbank Q*. 2001;*79*(3):387–427, IV.
16. Pitkin Derose K, Varda DM. Social capital and health care access: a systematic review. *Med Care Res Rev*. 2009;*66*(3):272–306.
17. Holtgrave DR, Crosby R. Is social capital a protective factor against obesity and diabetes? Findings from an exploratory study. *Ann Epidemiol*. 2006;*16*(5):406–8.
18. Crosby RA, Holtgrave DR, DiClemente RJ, Wingood GM, Gayle JA. Social capital as a predictor of adolescents' sexual risk behavior: a state-level exploratory study. *AIDS Behav*. 2003;*7*(3):245–52.

19. Carlson ED, Chamberlain RM. Social capital, health, and health disparities. *J Nurs Scholarsh*. 2003;*35*(4):325–31.

20. Carpiano RM. Neighborhood social capital and adult health: an empirical test of a Bourdieu-based model. *Health Place*. 2007;*13*(3):639–55.

21. Baum F, Palmer C. 'Opportunity structures': urban landscape, social capital and health promotion in Australia. *Health Promot Int*. 2002;*17*(4):351–61.

22. Carpiano RM. Toward a neighborhood resource-based theory of social capital for health: can Bourdieu and sociology help? *Soc Sci Med*. 2006;*62*(1):165–75.

23. Corbie-Smith G, Adimora A, Youmans S, Muhammad M, Blumenthal C, Ellison A, Akers A, Council B, Thigpen Y, Wynn M, Lloyd S. "Project GRACE: A Staged Approach to Development of a Community-Academic Partnership to address HIV in Rural African American Communities." Health Promotion and Practice.

24. Edgecombe County Health Department/Nash County Health Department. Edgecombe County Health Department/Nash County Statistical Analysis Query Report. Retrieved on April 1, 2007.

25. NC Rural Economic Development Center. North Carolina Rural Data Bank. http://www.ncruralcenter.org/databank/index.html. Updated 2009. Accessed July, 2010.

26. Hsieh HF, Shannon SE. Three approaches to qualitative content analysis. *Qual Health Res*. 2005;*15*(9):1277–88.

27. Lynch JW, Kaplan GA, Salonen JT. Why do poor people behave poorly? Variation in adult health behaviours and psychosocial characteristics by stages of the socioeconomic lifecourse. *Soc Sci Med*. 1997;*44*(6):809–19.

28. American College of Physicians. Racial and ethnic disparities in health care, updated 2010.

29. Buffardi AL, Thomas KK, Holmes KK, Manhart LE. Moving upstream: ecosocial and psychosocial correlates of sexually transmitted infections among young adults in the United States. *Am J Public Health*. 2008;*98*(6):1128–36.

30. Gregson S, Terceira N, Mushati P, Nyamukapa C, Campbell C. Community group participation: can it help young women to avoid HIV? An exploratory study of social capital and school education in rural Zimbabwe. *Soc Sci Med*. 2004;*58*(11):2119–32.

31. Pronyk PM, Harpham T, Morison LA, et al. Is social capital associated with HIV risk in rural South Africa? *Soc Sci Med*. 2008;*66*(9):1999–2010.

32. Campbell C, Williams B, Gilgen D. Is social capital a useful conceptual tool for exploring community level influences on HIV infection? An exploratory case study from South Africa. *AIDS Care*. 2002;*14*(1):41–54.

33. Takahashi LM, Magalong MG. Disruptive social capital: (un)healthy socio-spatial interactions among Filipino men living with HIV/AIDS. *Health Place*. 2008;*14*(2):182–97.

34. Branson BM, Handsfield HH, Lampe MA, Janssen RS, Taylor AW, Lyss SB, Clark JE. *Revised recommendations for HIV testing of adults, adolescents, and pregnant women in health-care settings*. 2006:592–7.

35. Khan MR, Wohl DA, Weir SS, et al. Incarceration and risky sexual partnerships in a southern US city. *J Urban Health*. 2008;*85*(1):100–13.

36. MacGowan RJ, Margolis A, Gaiter J, et al. Predictors of risky sex of young men after release from prison. *Int J STD AIDS*. 2003;*14*(8):519–23.

# CHAPTER ACTIVITY QUESTIONS

1. What were the four main themes identified as contributing to disparities in HIV rates?
2. What were the community characteristics identified by the "adults" that foster trusting relationships? Were these among the characteristics your groups identified?
3. How did these characteristics hinder or foster HIV outreach and access to community resources according to the youth?
4. What part did the linking relationships of religious leaders play in access to HIV-related services and prevention activities?
5. What were some of the strategies that might be used to address these issues?
6. What were the community forces that contributed to the increased HIV rates?

# CHAPTER REFERENCES

Almedon, A. (2005). Social capital and mental health: An interdisciplinary review of primary evidence. *Social Science & Medicine, 61*(5), 943–964.

Berkman, L., Glass, T., Brissette, I., & Seeman, T. (2000). From social integration to health: Durkheim in the new millennium. *Social Science & Medicine, 51*, 843–857.

Berkman, L., & Kawachi, I. (2000). *Social Epidemiology.* New York: Oxford University Press.

Bolin, K., Lindgren, B., Lindstrom, M., & Nystedt, P. (2003). Investments in social capital—implications of social interactions for the production of health. *Social Science & Medicine, 56*(12), 2379–2390.

Bourdieu, P. (1986). The forms of capital. In J.G. Richardson (Ed.), *Handbook of Theory and Research for the Sociology of Education* (pp. 241–258). New York: Greenwood.

Carpiano, R.M. (2006). Toward a neighborhood resource-based theory of social capital for health: Can Bourdieu and sociology help? *Social Science and Medicine, 62*, 165–175.

Crow, G. (2002). The relationship between trust, social capital and organizational success. *Nursing Administration Quarterly, 26*(3), 1–11.

Hawe, P., & Shiell, A. (2000). Social capital and health promotion. A review. *Social Science & Medicine, 51*, 871–885.

Kawachi, I., Kennedy, B.P., Lochner, K., & Prothrow-Stith, D. (1997). Social capital, income inequality and mortality. *American Journal of Public Health, 87*, 1491–1498.

Loury, G.C. (1976) A dymanic theory of racial income differences. Discussion Paper 225. Retrieved July 20, 2012 from http://www.kellogg.northwestern.edu/research/math/papers/225.pdf.

Portes, A. (1998). Social capital: Its origins and applications in modern sociology. *Annual Review of Sociology, 24*(1), 1–24.

Putnam, R.D. (1995). Bowling alone: America's declining social capital. *Journal of Democracy, 6*(1), 65–78.

Putnam, R.D. (2000). *Bowling Alone: The Collapse and Revival of American Community.* New York: Simon and Schuster.

Putnam, R.D., Leonardi, R., & Nanetti, R.Y. (1993). *Making Democracy Work: Civic Traditions in Modern Italy.* Princeton, NJ: Princeton University Press.

Rose, N. (2000). Citizenship and the third way. *American Behavioral Scientist, 43,* 1395–1411.

Ross, C.E., & Jang, S.J. (2000). Neighborhood disorder, fear, and mistrust: The buffering role of social ties with neighbors. *American Journal of Community Psychology, 28*(4), 401–420.

Szreter, S. (2002). The state of social capital: Bringing back in power, politics, and history. *Theory and Society, 31*(2), 573–621.

Szreter, S., & Woolcock, M. (2004). Health by association? Social capital, social theory and the political economy of public health. *International Journal of Epidemiology, 33*(4), 650–667.

Theall, K.R., DeJong, W., Scribner, R. Mason, K., Schneider, S.K., Simonsen, N. (2009). Social capital in the college setting: The impact of participation in campus activities on drinking and alcohol related harms. *Journal of American College Health, 58*(1), 15–23.

Veenstra, G., Luginaah, L., Wakefield, S., Birch, S., Eyles, J., & Elliott, S. (2005). Who you know, where you live: Social capital, neighborhood and health. *Social Science & Medicine, 60,* 2799–2818.

Veinat, T. (2010). A multi-level model of HIV/AIDS information/help network development. *Journal of Documentation, 66*(6), 85–905.

Wakefield, S.E.L., & Poland, B. (2005). Family, friend or foe? Critical reflections on the relevance and role of social capital in health promotion and community development. *Social Science & Medicine, 60,* 2819–2832.

Woolcock, M. (2001). The place of social capital in understanding social and economic outcomes. *Canadian Journal of Policy Research, 2*(1), 1–17.

# Choosing a Theory

## GUIDELINES FOR CHOOSING A THEORY

Knowing some of the many different theories and models that can be used to explain health behavior is one thing—knowing which theory to use when is another. Unfortunately, there is no magic formula or chart to tell you which theory is just right for a given situation, because there are no right or wrong theories. Some may work better than others in a particular situation, with a certain population, to address a specific health problem, or to produce a desired result.

With this said, the following guidelines may help you narrow down the choices:

1. Identify the health issue or problem and the population affected.
2. Gather information about the issue or population or both.
3. Identify possible reasons or causes for the problem.

4. Identify the level of interaction (intrapersonal, interpersonal, or community) under which the reasons or causes most logically fit.

5. Identify the theory or theories that best match the level and the reasons or causes.

## IDENTIFY THE HEALTH ISSUE AND THE POPULATION AFFECTED

The first and most logical step in identifying a theory is to identify the health issues you are trying to address and the population affected. Is the issue alcohol use at the high school, a head lice outbreak at the local day care center, or falls among the elderly? Each problem and population may require a different theory. The same problem in different populations may also require different theories.

## GATHER INFORMATION

Next, do a literature search to learn what others have found and done about the issue. A literature search is not limited to a search of the Internet (**Figure 11–1**). You need to search the professional literature using an appropriate database. Ones commonly used for health education and health promotion include the following:

- CINAHL (Cumulative Index to Nursing and Allied Health Literature): Available through a university or college library or a public library
- Academic Search Complete: Accessed through a university or college library
- PubMed: Maintained by the National Library of Medicine and National Institutes of Health; accessed directly at http://www.pubmed.gov
- ERIC (Education Resource Information Center): The database for school health information; accessed directly at http://www.eric.ed.gov

## IDENTIFY POSSIBLE REASONS OR CAUSES FOR THE PROBLEM

Third, take the information you found in the literature and combine it with the information you have from your community. This will enable you to identify possible causes for the problem, that is, to answer the question "Why does this problem exist?" Remember, theories help explain the *why* of health behavior, that is, why people do what they do. Why is it that some people fall, use alcohol, get head lice, go for mammograms, or do self testicular exams, and others do not?

**FIGURE 11-1** Conduct a literature search

## IDENTIFY THE LEVEL OF INTERACTION

Once you have determined possible causes or reasons why the health issue exists, it is time to determine under which level of interaction these reasons fall—intrapersonal, interpersonal, community, or all three. Identifying the level helps you determine which theories would most likely explain the behavior and therefore would best serve as the basis for change.

## IDENTIFY THE THEORY OR THEORIES THAT MATCH BEST

Use the Theory Chart that accompanies this chapter to help you identify which theories would most likely explain the behavior and enable you to plan an intervention to change the behaviors you have identified. Remember, for a theory to be most effective, all of it should be used (Hochbaum et al., 1992), although sometimes health educators do mix and match aspects from the different theories.

Let's say that the health issue is a high rate of influenza among the elderly in your community. After assessing the situation, you find that the reasons for this are poor compliance with influenza vaccination, lack of transportation to the health department, and inadequate parking facilities. An ecological approach would be appropriate in this situation to explain the poor compliance behavior, but it might also be explained by the perceived barriers construct of the Health Belief Model.

When you think you have determined which theory would fit best, see how it answers the following questions (National Cancer Institute [NCI], 2003):

- Is it logical given the situation you are trying to address?
- Is it similar to the theories others have used successfully in similar situations, as you found in the literature?
- Is it supported by research?

Choosing a theory is a lot like choosing your clothes. All of your clothes do the same thing—they cover your body—but they do so in different ways. You choose which clothes to wear depending on a host of factors, such as time of day, climate, occasion, and what your friends are wearing (if you're female, it may depend on whether you have the right shoes to wear). For example, you wouldn't wear a bathing suit to shovel snow. Once you have decided on which clothes to wear, you need to try them on to see whether they fit.

Theories, just like clothes, all do the same thing. They all help explain why people do what they do, but they do it in different ways. You choose a theory depending on a host of factors such as behavioral causes of the health issue or problem, the level of interaction (intrapersonal, interpersonal, or community), the target population, and the desired outcomes or change. Once you decide on which theory to use, you need to apply it to see whether it fits (**Table 11–1**).

# THEORY IN ACTION—CLASS ACTIVITY

In small groups, brainstorm possible causes for the low level of physical activity among female students on your campus. In your discussion, take into account the ethnic diversity of your small group, as well as that of the student population on your campus in general. List the possible causes or reasons for the lack of physical activity. Based on this (limited) information, use the theory chart in this

**Table 11–1** Theory Chart

| Level | Theory | Constructs |
|---|---|---|
| Intrapersonal | *Self-Efficacy Theory:* People will only try to do what they think they can do, and people won't try what they think they can't do. | Mastery experience<br>Vicarious experience<br>Verbal persuasion<br>Emotional state |
| | *Theory of Reasoned Action and Theory of Planned Behavior:* Health behavior results from intention influenced by attitude, norms, and control. | Attitudes<br>Subjective norms<br>Behavioral control<br>Volitional control |
| | *Health Belief Model:* Personal beliefs influence health behavior. | Perceived seriousness<br>Perceived susceptibility<br>Perceived benefits<br>Perceived barriers<br>Cues to action<br>Modifying variables<br>Self-efficacy |
| | *Attribution Theory:* There is a cause or explanation for things that happen. | Locus of control<br>Stability<br>Controllability |
| | *Transtheoretical Model or Stages of Change:* Behavior change is a process that occurs in stages. | Stages of change<br>Processes of change<br>Self-efficacy |
| Interpersonal | *Social Cognitive Theory:* Behavior, personal factors, and environmental factors interact with each other, and changing one changes them all. | Self-efficacy<br>Observational learning<br>Expectations<br>Expectancies<br>Emotional arousal<br>Behavioral capability<br>Reinforcement<br>Locus of control |
| Community | *Diffusion of Innovation:* Behavior changes as innovations are adopted. | Innovation<br>Communication channels<br>Time<br>Social system |
| | *Ecological Models:* Factors at many levels influence health behavior. | Intrapersonal level<br>Interpersonal level<br>Community level<br>Institution level<br>Societal level |
| | *Social Capital Theory:* Behavior is influenced by who we know and how we know them. | Bonding relationships<br>Bridging relationships<br>Linking relationships |

chapter to identify a theory or theories that may be appropriate to explain the behavior and which can then be used as the basis for an intervention to increase their physical activity level. Provide a rationale for why you made this choice.

Now read the following article and answer the questions at the end.

# Chapter 11 Article: *Camine con Nosotros*: Connecting Theory and Practice for Promoting Physical Activity Among Hispanic Women[1]

*Francisco G. Soto Mas, MD, MPH, William M. Kane, PhD, Scott Going, PhD, Earl S. Ford, MD, PhD, James R. Marshall, PhD, Lisa K. Staten, PhD, Joan E. Smith, BSN, MBA*

Francisco G. Soto Mas, MD, MPH, is at the University of New Mexico College of Education, Albuquerque, NM.
William M. Kane, PhD, is an associate professor in the health education program at the University of New Mexico College of Education, Albuquerque, NM.
Scott Going, PhD, is an associate research scientist in the Department of Nutritional Sciences, at the University of Arizona, Tucson, AZ.
Earl S. Ford, MD, PhD, is in the Division of Nutrition and Physical Activity at the Centers for Disease Control and Prevention.
James R. Marshall, PhD, is a professor of public health at the Arizona Cancer Center, Tucson, AZ.
Lisa K. Staten, PhD, is a research assistant professor of public health at the Arizona Cancer Center, Tucson, AZ.
Joan E. Smith, BSN, MBA, is an adult program operations administrator in the Office of Chronic Disease Prevention, Bureau of Prevention and Health Promotion, Arizona Department of Health Services, Phoenix, AZ.

## Abstract

Despite the popularity and widespread use of theory in health education, practitioners still find it difficult to design and implement theory-based interventions. This is especially true when working with ethnic/racial minority groups, including Hispanic groups. Practitioners working with Hispanic communities face additional barriers that may often discourage them from using theories when planning interventions. These barriers include the diversity that exists within the Hispanic population, lack of reliable data, and issues related to cross-cultural applicability of current behavior theories. However, the use of theory constitutes a valuable tool for developing more effective programs, and theorist researchers should be more sensitive to practitioners' needs. By explaining the processes for

[1] Reproduced from Soto Mas, F.G., Kane, W.M., Going, S., Ford, E.S., Marshall, J.R., Staten, L.K., & Smith, J.E. (2000). *Camine con Nosotros*: Connecting theory and practice for promoting physical activity among Hispanic women. *Health Promotion Practice, 1*(2), 178–187.

selecting and applying theory in the same detail as outcome results, researchers will contribute to increasing practitioners' interest in theory. This article describes *Camine con Nosotros*, a theory-based physical activity program for Hispanic women, and explains the process of selecting the theoretical framework of the program and connecting theory and practice.

Over the past 30 years, the fields of health education and health promotion have shown significant development, particularly in program planning and evaluation. A considerable contributing factor has been the application of behavioral and social science theory, which facilitates the planning and evaluation of programs. However, practical explanation of the processes by which theories are selected and applied is lacking in the literature. As a consequence, practitioners find it difficult to connect theory and practice and to design and implement theory-based programs. The recognition of the difficulties faced in applying theory in everyday practice is not new: In the 1980s and early 1990s, theorist researchers made some effort to address the issue (D'Onofrio, 1992; Turner, 1987; van Ryn & Heaney, 1992). Nevertheless, there is still a recognized need for bridging the gap between theory and practice (Bartholomew, Parcel, & Kok, 1998; Glanz, Lewis, & Rimer, 1997), and innovative models to facilitate the process of selecting and applying theories are being proposed (Bartholomew et al., 1998).

Despite efforts to overcome utilization barriers, connecting theory and practice is, in many cases, a challenge for health educators, especially for those working with Hispanic populations. Lack of familiarity with cultural and psychosocial issues can lead practitioners to choose theories that are inconsistent with the particular characteristics of the participant population or to inappropriately predict the relationship between their key variables. It is the responsibility of the program planner to understand the cultural and psychological contexts of the population subject to intervention, and to select theories that properly address the factors related to the behavior to be studied. From this perspective, it has been suggested that researchers who belong to the same ethnic group being studied are better able to understand and analyze the cultural and psychosocial realities of that group (Marín & VanOss, 1991; Rogler, Malgady, & Rodríguez, 1989). Other researchers argue that some of the differences between Hispanics and non-Hispanics in epidemiological studies can, in part, be explained by the misinterpretation of data by professionals who are not familiar with Hispanic cultural issues (Good & Good, 1986). The recognized lack of Hispanic public health professionals, including researchers (Cantor, Bergeisen, & Baker, 1998; Palepu et al., 1998; Soto Mas & Papenfuss, 1997), may constitute a considerable barrier to the use of theory with Hispanic communities.

Practitioners working with Hispanics face additional barriers that may discourage them from considering the use of theory. First, the Hispanic population is composed of a variety of groups, with different national origins, acculturation levels, language skills, races, and life experiences. Second, the health status of Hispanics is still imprecisely known and insufficiently analyzed; contradictions exist not only in reported mortality and morbidity but also in risk factors and behavior data (Soto Mas, Papenfuss, & Guerrero, 1997). This makes it more difficult for practitioners to find the resources for developing a sound theoretical framework for a particular Hispanic group and to understand the circumstances that influence the health behaviors of the participant population. It may also be the reason why some authors point out that, in planning and delivering health education and promotion programs, practitioners usually depend on models that have not been developed to meet the needs of Hispanic communities (National Coalition of Hispanic Health and Human Services Organization [COSSMHO], 1995).

Practitioners working with Hispanics may have other reasons to be confused about the appropriateness of using theory. Generalization across populations is considered by some authors to be a characteristic of formal theory (Green, 1991; van Ryn & Heaney, 1992), and studies have found that the combination of elements from different models has broad applicability across ethnic groups (Pasick, 1997). On the other hand, the lack of cultural sensitivity has been cited as a main weakness of current health behavior theories (Pasick, 1997; Pasick, D'Onofrio, & Otero-Sabogal, 1996). The literature also alerts researchers to the danger of assuming universality of theoretical concepts or constructs, and recommends the distention between what is ethnic or universal and what is emic or group specific (Marín & VanOss, 1991). Although teasing apart these conflicting views and agreeing on the cross-cultural applicability of theory are essential to research in social and behavioral sciences and health education, the discourse confuses practitioners and discourages them from using theory.

Nevertheless, we should insist on the benefits of developing theory-based interventions for Hispanic populations. Although using theories and models cannot guarantee the success of a program, they provide a framework in which programmers can better plan, implement, and evaluate an intervention. They also contribute to the understanding of conditions affecting specific behaviors and help us identify factors and circumstances that are most likely to produce particular results (D'Onofrio, 1992). Therefore, we should commit to building practitioners' confidence in theory and to providing them with the resources to select and apply theory in a rational way. *Camine con Nosotros* (Come Walk with

Us), the program described here, is an example of a theory-based intervention that was developed following a rational process that facilitates the selection and practical application of a theoretical framework.

# CAMINE CON NOSOTROS

## BACKGROUND

The first surgeon general's report on physical activity and health (U.S. Department of Health and Human Services, 1996) declares the need for promoting physical activity among minority populations and developing theory-based strategies that facilitate the planning, implementation, and evaluation of physical activity interventions. One group in need of effective programs promoting regular physical activity is the Hispanic adult population. Regional and national data demonstrate that Hispanic adults have lower levels of physical activity than Whites (Burchfield et al., 1990; Centers for Disease Control and Prevention [CDC], 1992, 1994; Crespo, Keteyian, Heath, & Sempos, 1996; Hovell et al., 1991; Perez-Stable, Marín, & Marín, 1994). In addition, the *Healthy People 2000 Review, 1997* (National Center for Health Statistics [NCHS], 1997) shows that Hispanics are far from reaching the year 2000 physical activity objectives: 34% of Hispanics age 18 years and older are sedentary (year 2000 target = 25%), and only 13.6% engage in vigorous physical activity and 20% in moderate physical activity (year 2000 target = 17% and 25%, respectively). Within the Hispanic population, adult women merit particular attention. The prevalence of physical inactivity is higher among Hispanic women than among Hispanic men. In comparison with White women, Hispanic women have been shown to have lower levels of leisure-time physical activity and lower levels of light to moderate and vigorous physical activity (CDC, 1991a, 1991b). Sixty-one percent of Hispanic women report a sedentary lifestyle (defined as less than 3 sessions of leisure-time physical activity a week), compared with 56.4% of White women ("Prevalence of Selected Risk Factors," 1994).

Given the demonstrated relationship between physical activity and health, the promotion of physical activity among Hispanic women should become a public health priority. Although health promotion programs aimed at Hispanic women have traditionally focused on maternal health (CDC, 1994), the prevalence of chronic diseases among this group calls for a different approach. Coronary heart disease, stroke, breast and colorectal cancer, diabetes, and hypertension are the leading causes of morbidity and mortality among Hispanic women (CDC, 1994), all of which point to physical activity as a particularly effective prevention strategy. In addition, the impact of chronic conditions on this group is expected to increase during the next two decades. As more Hispanics move into an older age group, more women will be living with chronic disease and disability for longer periods of time (Soto Mas, 1999).

*Camine con Nosotros* is a theory-based physical activity program for Hispanic women age 50 years and older in Maricopa County, Arizona. The program selected a theoretical framework through a step-by-step process that began with the identification of the goals and objectives of the intervention (see **Figure 1**).

## IDENTIFYING GOALS AND OBJECTIVES

The goal of *Camine con Nosotros* was to decrease risk factors for cardiovascular disease by increasing participants' daily physical activity level. Because the qualifying requirements for participation included not having medical insurance or not qualifying for state medical assistance, it was expected that the participating population would include mainly low-income women from underserved communities. Because of the region's proximity to the border, a high percentage of Mexican-descendent participants were expected.

Focus groups and a review of the literature assisted in the identification of the measurable objectives of the program. Several studies have demonstrated that the level of intensity is related to participation in physical activities. Low to moderate intensity, home-based activities are more likely to be adopted (King, Haskell, Young, Oka, & Stefanick, 1995; Pollock, 1998), especially if cognitive-behavioral strategies and regular follow-up support are included (e.g., self-monitoring,

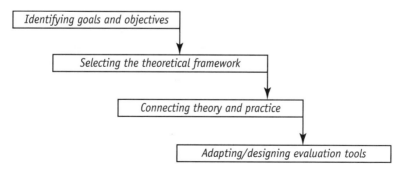

**FIGURE 1** From Theory to Practice

personal contact, and feedback) (King et al., 1997). In addition, walking is one of the preferred types of leisure-time physical activity of U.S. adults, including Mexican Americans (Crespo et al., 1996), and it is well suited to the population in this study, which faces limited availability of and access to exercise facilities. Therefore, a home-based program was identified as the most feasible approach for this group. To be consistent with current recommendations for physical activity in healthy adults, the objective of the program was established as engaging participants in 30 minutes of walking, 5 days a week, during the period of the intervention (1 year). A moderate intensity level was adopted (between 50% and 70% of the age-predicted maximum heart rate, defined as 220 minus age).

## SELECTING THE THEORETICAL FRAMEWORK

Through focus groups made up of community lay health advisers (*promotoras*), prospective participants, and health education specialists, key issues related to physical activity in the population studied by *Camine con Nosotros* were identified. Although the idea of exercising appealed to focus group participants, program planners found three main issues of concern: (a) lack of knowledge of the relationship between moderate physical activity and health, (b) perceived lack of personal resources for engaging in regular physical activity, and (c) lack of environmental support (family, friends, and community) for performing the intended behavior. Three theoretical frameworks were selected to address these factors: the Health Belief Model (HBM), self-efficacy (SE), and the Social Learning Theory (SLT) (see **Figure 2**).

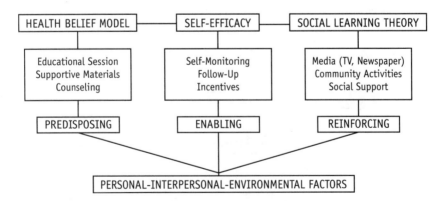

**FIGURE 2**  *Camine con Nosotros* Theoretical Design

*HBM.* According to the HBM, a person's health-related behavior depends on his or her perception of (a) the severity of the problem or illness, (b) his or her vulnerability to that problem, and (c) the benefits and barriers to taking preventive action (Houchbaum, 1958). Although the model focuses on cognitive-perceptive variables, which have been questioned as predictors of physical activity behaviors (Dishman & Sallis, 1994; Mirotznik, Feldman, & Stein, 1995; Oldridge & Streiner, 1990), researchers recommended the use of the HBM for a number of reasons. It is known that knowledge and information vary across populations (Finnegan, Viswanath, Kahn, & Hannan, 1993; Tichenor, Donohue, & Olien, 1970), and due to language and cultural barriers, Hispanics may have less access than other groups to quality health information (Jacobson, 1999). This may influence their health-related knowledge, perceptions, attitudes, and behaviors. The San Antonio Heart Study found that Mexicans were significantly less informed than non-Hispanic Whites on how to prevent heart attacks and on the benefits of regular exercise (Hazuda, Stern, Gaskill, Haffner, & Gardner, 1983). Other studies have found that Hispanics have more misconceptions about the health consequences of certain risk behaviors than Anglos (Ford & Jones, 1991; Perez-Stable, Sabogal, Otero-Sabogal, Hiatt, & McPhee, 1992). Therefore, a theoretical model such as the HBM, which emphasizes knowledge and perception, seemed appropriate for a population to which the health outcome of a preventive behavior (e.g., physical activity) may never have been properly presented. Other studies have shown an association between the knowledge of and belief in the health benefits of physical activity and the adoption and maintenance of an exercise program in men and women (Dishman & Gettman, 1980; Dishman & Steinhardt, 1990; Sallis et al., 1986). In addition, positive (benefits) and negative (barriers) behavioral outcome expectations, both principal constructs of the HBM, have been associated with physical activity among adults (Ali & Twibell, 1995; Neuberger, Kasal, Smith, Hassanein, & DeViney, 1994). It has been proposed that decreasing the perceived barriers to exercise may facilitate walking among healthy middle-class Hispanic adults (Hovell et al., 1991). All of these issues can be addressed through an educational component based on the HBM.

*SE.* SE is the confidence that people have in performing a behavior in a specific situation (Bandura, 1977). SE has been found to be significantly associated with the adoption and maintenance of an exercise program (Caspersen, Christenson, & Pollard, 1986; Sallis, Hovell, & Hofstetter, 1992; Sallis et al., 1989). It has also been positively correlated with physical activity among older adults, women (Sallis et al., 1989), and Hispanics (Hovell et al., 1991). SE is a major construct in SLT, and Bandura (1986) considers SE to be the most important prerequisite for behavioral change. Performance accomplishments, vicarious experiences, verbal persuasion, and physiological feedback are factors influencing SE (Bandura, 1977). It has been suggested that feelings of low SE may be more common among racial/ethnic minority groups, including Hispanics. Some authors relate this lower SE among Hispanics to misconceptions about the relationship between certain risk behaviors and disease, given that misconceptions can give a false perception of the need for change (Jackson, Proulx, & Pelican, 1991).

*SLT.* Finally, Bandura's (1986) SLT depicts human behavior as an interactive model between environmental, personal, and behavioral factors. Reinforcement, observational learning, self-control, expectations, behavioral capability, and emotional coping responses, together with SE, are principal constructs in SLT (Bandura, 1977). Another construct is the environment, or the external factors that affect behavior. These factors can be particularly important for promoting physical activity among Hispanic women for several reasons. First, the term *environment* includes the social environment, such as family members, friends, and peers, who are part of the cultural legacy of Hispanics. In Hispanic culture, the family constitutes an emotional support system that includes both immediate and extended members. This broad conception includes the community, which generally serves as a support network (COSSMHO, 1995). Second, environment also refers to factors such as place, time, or facilities, which are also crucial in health promotion programs for underserved Hispanic communities. More than 26% of Hispanic families live in poverty (U.S. Bureau of the Census, 1993) and in neighborhoods that are likely to be lacking in available spaces for exercise and recreational activities. They may also live in areas with critical social problems and safety concerns. All of these factors influence the adoption and maintenance of a physical activity program.

The three theories discussed above were deemed appropriate for this program, given the particular characteristics of the problem to be addressed, the population, and the identified socioeconomic and environmental factors.

## CONNECTING THEORY AND PRACTICE

The next question that a program planner confronts after deciding on a theoretical framework is how to connect theory and practice, that is, how to develop an intervention that is consistent with the concepts and variables of the selected theory or theories. *Camine con Nosotros* took a comprehensive approach to addressing the modifiable determinants of physical activity. The intervention considered individual, interpersonal, and environmental approaches.

To be consistent with the HBM, an educational session based on the three key variables of the model was developed. This included a lesson plan with goals and measurable learning objectives. The leading causes of mortality and morbidity within the Hispanic female adult population and their relation to physical inactivity served as a basis for addressing perceived susceptibility. Perceived severity was addressed by presenting the most common illnesses among this population for which a sedentary lifestyle constitutes a risk factor. Preventive action to be taken (increasing daily physical activity through walking) and specific instructions on how, where, and when were included for developing a positive effect on expectations (perceived benefits). Perceived barriers, such as the identification of an appropriate location, safety issues, and walking equipment, were also addressed. Activities for SE, such as assessing the heart rate while walking, preventing injury, and self-monitoring, were included as part of the educational component. In addition to the educational session, a bilingual booklet containing information learned during the session was developed and distributed to participants.

Other intervention components included a mail-delivered packet that was sent to participants monthly during the yearlong intervention (see **Table 1**). The packet included three items.

The first item was a self-monitoring daily activity log that participants were instructed to fill out and return by mail at the end of each month. The number of minutes walked and whether the target heart rate was reached were the two main sections that participants were asked to complete. Self-monitoring is considered an effective behavioral management technique for starting a physical activity program (Weber & Wertheim, 1989), and it provides internal reinforcement.

**Table 1** Program Components

Educational session

Booklet

Mail-delivered monthly packet

Daily activity log

Contest

Newsletter

Staff telephone calls

A space for comments was provided on this form, which allowed participants to provide feedback on the program.

The second item was a component to provide incentive for participation and maintenance, and it consisted of a contest in which participants responded to monthly questions related to well-known Hispanic people and cultural and historical events. Incentives have been identified as a way of reducing perceived barriers and motivating people to act (Bandura, 1986). In addition, the questions allowed family members and friends to be involved, promoting a positive social environment.

The third item was a newsletter to provide information about the program and to help participants maintain motivation and a positive attitude toward behavior, both of which have been positively correlated with physical activity (Dishman & Steinhardt, 1990; Kimiecik, 1992). Other topics that were expected to appeal to family members and friends (e.g., child development) were included to contribute to a positive social environment.

These components of the intervention focused on perception and SE, the core constructs within the theoretical framework chosen by *Camine con Nosotros*. Knowledge, attitudes, and skills, which are also predisposing and enabling factors that facilitate the initiation and adoption of health behaviors, were crucial factors addressed in these activities and materials.

An additional environmental component was developed to create positive social support related to community, family, friends, and peers. Social support is a core component of SLT and an important reinforcing factor that has been positively related to adult physical activity (Felton & Parson, 1994; Minor & Brown, 1993). Instrumental in this effort was the involvement of *promotoras de salud* or lay health advisers. The use of lay workers has gained recognition as a valuable health promotion strategy (Eng, 1993; Eng & Young, 1992; Israel, 1985; Meister, Warrick, Zapién, & Wood, 1992). This approach has been proposed as a way of overcoming cultural and linguistic barriers between health providers and community groups (Baker et al., 1997). As active community members, *promotoras* were involved in television and radio promotional activities, community health fairs, school and church meetings, and clinical activities that were organized for recruitment, promotion, and retention purposes. They assisted participants in filling out recruitment forms and evaluation questionnaires, and they served as facilitators for the educational session and follow-up activities, which included regular phone contacts and personal one-to-one interaction. As peers, many *promotoras* participated in the walking program and provided vicarious support and modeling for participants. The *promotora* activities and the family involvement pursued through the contest and newsletter were directed toward creating a positive neighborhood and family climate for the promotion of physical activity.

Finally, a main concern of program planners should always be the cultural and linguistic competence of the intervention. Focus groups and *promotoras* provided continuous feedback during the assessment and preparation stages of the program, and a Hispanic health promotion specialist was involved in the planning stage and contributed to the development of the intervention and evaluation protocols. Materials were initially developed in Spanish by a Hispanic health education specialist and translated into English by a professional translator. The final version was then revised by a bilingual staff (*promotoras* and health professionals) to ensure appropriate language level and health information accuracy. All written materials were bilingual, and the educational session was offered in both Spanish and English.

## EVALUATION

The overall project included three levels of evaluation: process, impact, and outcome. The study involved a control group that received standard provider interaction with no specific walking message. However, given that the purpose of this article is to describe and justify the theoretical design of the intervention, only process and impact evaluation protocols will be described here. Outcome protocols and results will be subsequently reported.

As previously discussed, the heterogeneous characteristics of Hispanic populations and the lack of agreement as to the cross-cultural sensitivity of health behavior theories represent special concerns for practitioners when considering the use of theory. An additional barrier is the lack of available evaluation tools (Green, 1991), including social behavior instruments. Evaluation tools are particularly problematic when dealing with Hispanic groups because existing instruments must often be culturally and/or linguistically adapted, which changes their internal structure and compromises their validity and reliability (VanOss & Marín, 1991). In many cases, researchers working with minority groups have to choose an instrument, adapt it, and use it, because validating an instrument requires additional time and resources that are often unavailable.

For *Camine con Nosotros*, we developed an evaluation protocol that included the implementation of existing instruments, the adaptation of existing instruments, and the development of new instruments by the investigators. The Arizona

Activity Frequency Questionnaire was used for assessing physical activity levels (related to the goal and general objectives of the program). This questionnaire is a bilingual instrument developed by the University of Arizona, and it is in the process of being validated. The instrument measures the total daily energy expenditure, amount of time spent on various activities, and metabolic-equivalent threshold (MET) levels. The instrument was not modified in this project. SE and attitudes-perceptions questionnaires were used to assess the overall impact of the intervention. The SE questionnaire was adapted from the Exercise Efficacy Instrument developed by Sallis, Pinski, Grossman, Patterson, and Nader (1988), and it consisted of a bilingual, seven-item protocol (e.g., "How confident are you that you could increase your physical activity without it interfering with things you like to do?"), using a 5-point Likert-type scale ranging from *I am sure I could* to *I can't*. The attitudes-perceptions questionnaire was developed by the investigators, and it is composed of a bilingual, five-item protocol (e.g., "I believe that simply walking can provide me with health benefits"), using a 5-point Likert-type scale ranging from *strongly agree* to *strongly disagree*. These three assessments were used in a pretest-posttest protocol over a 1-year period.

The impact of the educational session on knowledge and skills was also assessed using a pretest-posttest design. Two different questionnaires were developed by the investigators. These questionnaires were also bilingual, and the contents were based on the lesson plan and consistent with the learning objectives established for the educational session. Knowledge was assessed using a 10-item protocol (e.g., "Daily walking can prevent diabetes") and a true-false scale. Skills were assessed using a five-item protocol (e.g., "One thing I can do to stick to this program is") and a multiple five-choice scale.

The process evaluation focused not only on assessing participation but also on receiving feedback from participants and *promotoras* regarding the feasibility of the program, quality of materials and information, and their personal evaluation of the program. Three bilingual questionnaires were developed by the investigators, two for collecting participants' feedback and one for collecting *promotoras'* feedback. Five process evaluation activities were scheduled over the 12-month intervention period.

## CONCLUSIONS

Although, traditionally, the Hispanic population has been concentrated in certain areas of the United States, the growth of this group is projected to increase in every region throughout the country. It has been estimated that, by the year 2020, persons of Hispanic origin will comprise 29% of the population in the west, 14% in the south, 12% in the northeast, and 6% in the Midwest (Campbell, 1994). This demographic change is already having a great impact at the community level. Latino students make up more than 13% of the public school population, although they sit in about half of the desks in many urban schools (Soto Mas, 1999). In terms of labor force participation, the number of Hispanic workers will increase to more than 16 million by the year 2005, up from 10 million in 1992 (Soto Mas et al., 1997).

It is essential that health promotion programs be sensitive to these facts and develop programs that meet the needs of this growing population. Health behavior theories are a recommended resource for practitioners working with Hispanic communities, although it is the responsibility of researchers to provide constructs and evaluation tools that are consistent with the social, cultural, and linguistic characteristics of different Hispanic groups. In the meantime, existing theories constitute a valuable tool for practitioners who understand how to justify the selection of a theory and properly connect theory and practice.

Health behavior researchers can make a significant contribution toward this effort by focusing more on the process. Describing the rationale for program design, defining intervention components in detail, and providing accurate information on process and impact evaluation protocols are as important as the outcome and should be given equal importance in reporting. This is particularly critical for studies involving Hispanics and other ethnic/racial minority groups, because it will facilitate the use of theory and the design of more effective programs.

# REFERENCES

Ali, N. S., & Twibell, R. K. (1995). Health promotion and osteoporosis prevention among postmenopausal women. *Preventive Medicine, 24,* 528–534.

Baker, E. A., Boulding, N., Durham, M., Escobar Lowell, M., González, M., Jodaitis, N., Negrón Cruz, L., Torres, I., Torres, M., & Trillio Adams, S. (1997). The Latino health advocacy program: A collaborative lay health advisor approach. *Health Education and Behavior, 24,* 495–509.

Bandura, A. (1977). *Social Learning Theory.* Englewood Cliffs, NJ: Prentice Hall.

Bandura, A. (1986). *Social foundations of thought and action: A social-cognitive theory.* Englewood Cliffs, NJ: Prentice Hall.

Bartholomew, L. K., Parcel, G. S., & Kok, G. (1998). Intervention mapping: A process for developing theory- and evidence-based health education programs. *Health Education and Behavior, 25,* 545–563.

Burchfield, C. M., Hamman, R. F., Marshall, J. A., Baxter, J., Kahn, L. B., & Amirani, J. J. (1990). Cardiovascular risk factors and impaired glucose tolerance: The San Luis Valley Diabetes Study. *American Journal of Epidemiology, 131*, 57–70.

Campbell, P. (1994). *Population projections of the United States, by age, race, and sex: 1993 to 2020* (Current Population Reports Series P25-1111). Washington, DC: Bureau of the Census.

Cantor, J. C., Bergeisen, L., & Baker, L. C. (1998). Effect of an intensive educational program for minority college students and recent graduates on the probability of acceptance to medical school. *Journal of the American Medical Association, 280*, 772–776.

Caspersen, C. J., Christenson, G. M., & Pollard, R. A. (1986). Status of the 1990 physical fitness and exercise objectives—evidence from NHIS 1985. *Public Health Reports, 101*, 587–592.

Centers for Disease Control and Prevention. (1991a). *National Health Interview Survey, 1991* [Public use data tapes]. Atlanta, GA: National Center for Health Statistics, Centers for Disease Control and Prevention.

Centers for Disease Control and Prevention. (1991b). *National Health and Nutrition Examination Survey (NHNES III) (1988–1991)* [Public use data tapes]. Atlanta, GA: National Center for Health Statistics, Centers for Disease Control and Prevention.

Centers for Disease Control and Prevention. (1992). *1992 BRFSS summary prevalence report*. Atlanta, GA: Department of Health and Human Services, Public Health Service, National Center for Chronic Disease Prevention and Health Promotion, Centers for Disease Control and Prevention.

Centers for Disease Control and Prevention. (1994). *Chronic disease in minority populations*. Atlanta, GA: Author.

Crespo, C. J., Keteyian, S. J., Heath, G. W., & Sempos, C. T. (1996). Leisure-time physical activity among U.S. adults: Results from the Third National Health and Nutrition Examination Survey. *Archives of Internal Medicine, 156*, 93–98.

Dishman, R. K., & Gettman, L. R. (1980). Psychobiologic influences on exercise adherence. *Journal of Sport and Exercise Psychology, 2*, 295–310.

Dishman, R. K., & Sallis, J. F. (1994). Determinants and interventions for physical activity and exercise. In C. Bouchard, R. J. Shephard, & T. Stephens (Eds.), *Physical activity, fitness, and health: International proceeding and consensus statement*. Champaign, IL: Human Kinetics.

Dishman, R. K., & Steinhardt, M. (1990). Health locus of control predicts free-living, but not supervised, physical activity: A test of exercise-specific control and outcome-expectancy hypotheses. *Research Quarterly for Exercise and Sport, 61*, 383–394.

D'Onofrio, C. N. (1992). Theory and the empowerment of health education practitioners. *Health Education Quarterly, 19*, 385–403.

Eng, E. (1993). The Save our Sisters Project: A social network strategy for reaching rural Black women. *Cancer, 72*, 1071–1077.

Eng, E., & Young, R. (1992). Lay health advisors and community change agents. *Family and Community Health, 15*, 24–40.

Felton, G. M., & Parson, M. A. (1994). Factors influencing physical activity in average-weight and overweight young women. *Journal of Community Health Nursing, 11*, 109–119.

Finnegan, J. R., Viswanath, K., Kahn, E., & Hannan, P. (1993). Exposure to sources of heart disease prevention information: Community type and social group differences. *Journalism Quarterly, 70,* 569–584.

Ford, E. S., & Jones, D. H. (1991). Cardiovascular health knowledge in the United States: Findings from the National Health Interview Survey, 1985. *Preventive Medicine, 20,* 725–736.

Glanz, K., Lewis, F. M., & Rimer, B. (Eds.). (1997). *Health behavior and health education: Theory, research, and practice.* San Francisco, CA: Jossey-Bass.

Good, B. J., & Good, M. J. (1986). The cultural context of diagnosis and therapy: A view from medical anthropology. In M. R. Miranda & H. Kitano (Eds.), *Mental health research and practice in minority communities: Development of culturally sensitive training programs* (pp. 1–27). Washington, DC: National Institute of Mental Health.

Green, L. W. (1991). Everyone has a theory, few have measurement. *Health Education Research, 6,* 249–250.

Hazuda, J. P., Stern, M. P., Gaskill, S. P., Haffner, S. M., & Gardner, L. I. (1983). Ethnic differences in health knowledge and behaviors related to the prevention and treatment of coronary heart disease: The San Antonio Heart Study. *American Journal of Epidemiology, 117,* 717–728.

Houchbaum, G. M. (1958). *Public participation in medical screening programs: A sociopsychological study* (USPHS Publication No. 572). Washington, DC: Public Health Service.

Hovell, M., Sallis, J., Hofstetter, R., Barrington, E., Hackley, M., Elder, J., Castro, F., & Kilbourne, K. (1991). Identification of correlates of physical activity among Latino adults. *Journal of Community Health, 16,* 23–36.

Israel, B. (1985). Social network and social support: Implications for natural helper and community level interventions. *Health Education Quarterly, 12,* 65–80.

Jackson, M. Y., Proulx, J. M., & Pelican, S. (1991). Obesity prevention. *American Journal of Clinical Nutrition, 53,* 1625S–1630S.

Jacobson, H. (1999). La comunicación con pacientes hispanohablantes [Communicating with Spanish-speaking patients]. *Médico Interamericano, 18,* 12–16. Available: http://www.users.interport.net/~icps/medico/medico99/january/

Kimiecik, J. (1992). Predicting vigorous physical activity of corporate employees: Comparing the theories of reasoned action and planned behavior. *Journal of Sport and Exercise Psychology, 14,* 192–206.

King, A. C., Blair, S. N., Bild, D. E., Dishman, R. K., Dubbert, P. M., Marcus, B. H., Oldridge, N. B., Paffenbarger, R. S., Powell, K. E., & Yeager, K. K. (1997). Determinants of physical activity and interventions in adults. *Medicine and Science in Sports and Exercise, 24,* S221–S236.

King, A. C., Haskell, W. L., Young, D. R., Oka, R. K., & Stefanick, M. L. (1995). Long-term effects of varying intensities and formats of physical activity on participation rates, fitness, and lipoproteins in men and women aged 50 to 65 years. *Circulation, 91,* 2596–2604.

Marín, G., & VanOss Marín, B. (1991). *Research with Hispanic populations.* Newbury Park, CA: Sage.

Meister, J., Warrick, L. L., Zapién, J., & Wood, A. (1992). Using lay health workers: Case study of a community-based prenatal intervention. *Journal of Community Health, 17,* 37–51.

Minor, M. A., & Brown, J. D. (1993). Exercise maintenance of persons with arthritis after participation in a class experience. *Health Education Quarterly, 20,* 83–95.

Mirotznik, J., Feldman, L., & Stein, R. (1995). The Health Belief Model and adherence with a community center-based, supervised coronary heart disease exercise program. *Journal of Community Health, 20,* 233–247.

National Center for Health Statistics. (1997). *Healthy people 2000 review, 1997* (DHHS Publication No. PHS 98-1256). Hyattsville, MD: Department of Health and Human Services.

National Coalition of Hispanic Health and Human Services Organizations (COSSMHO). (1995). Meeting the health promotion needs of Hispanic communities. *American Journal of Health Promotion, 9,* 300–311.

Neuberger, G. B., Kasal, S., Smith, K. V., Hassanein, R., & DeViney, S. (1994). Determinants of exercise and aerobic fitness in outpatients with arthritis. *Nursing Research, 43,* 11–17.

Oldridge, N. B., & Streiner, D. L. (1990). The Health Belief Model: Predicting compliance and dropout in cardiac rehabilitation. *Medicine and Science in Sports and Exercise, 22,* 678–683.

Palepu, A., Carr, P. L., Friedman, R. H., Amos, H., Ash, A. S., & Moskowitz, M. A. (1998). Minority faculty and academic rank in medicine. *Journal of the American Medical Association, 280,* 767–771.

Pasick, R. J. (1997). Socioeconomic and cultural factors in the development and use of theory. In K. Glanz, F. M. Lewis, & B. K. Rimer (Eds.), *Health behavior and health education: Theory, research, and practice* (pp. 425–440). San Francisco, CA: Jossey-Bass.

Pasick, R. J., D'Onofrio, C. N., & Otero-Sabogal, R. (1996). Similarities and differences across cultures: Questions to inform a third generation for health promotion research. *Health Education Quarterly, 23,* S142–S161.

Perez-Stable, E. J., Marín, G., & Marín, B. V. (1994). Behavioral risk factors: A comparison of Latinos and non-Latino whites in San Francisco. *American Journal of Public Health, 84,* 971–976.

Perez-Stable, E. J., Sabogal, F., Otero-Sabogal, R., Hiatt, R. A., & McPhee, S. J. (1992). Misconceptions about cancer among Latinos and Anglos. *Journal of the American Medical Association, 268,* 3219–3223.

Pollock, M. L. (1998). Prescribing exercise for fitness and adherence. In R. K. Dishman (Ed.), *Exercise adherence* (pp. 259–277). Champaign, IL: Human Kinetics.

Prevalence of selected risk factors for chronic disease by education level in racial/ethnic populations—United States, 1991–1992. (1994). *Morbidity and Mortality Weekly Report, 43,* 894–899.

Rogler, L. H., Malgady, R. G., & Rodríguez, O. (1989). *Hispanics and mental health: A framework for research.* Malabar, IL: Robert E. Krieger.

Sallis, J. F., Haskell, W. L., Fortmann, S. P., Vranizan, K. M., Taylor, C. B., & Solomon, D. S. (1986). Predictors of adoption and maintenance of physical activity in a community sample. *Preventive Medicine, 15,* 331–341.

Sallis, J. F., Hovell, M. F., & Hofstetter, C. R. (1992). Explanation of vigorous activity during two years using social learning variables. *Social Science and Medicine, 34,* 25–32.

Sallis, J. F., Hovell, M. F., Hofstetter, C. R., Faucher, P., Elder, J. P., Blanchard, J., Carpensen, C. J., Powell, K. E., & Christenson, G. M. (1989). A multivariate study of determinants of vigorous exercise in a community sample. *Preventive Medicine*, *18*, 20–34.

Sallis, J. F., Pinski, R. B., Grossman, R. M., Patterson, T. L., & Nader, P. R. (1988). The development of self-efficacy scales for health-related diet and exercise behaviors. *Health Education Research*, *3*, 283–292.

Soto Mas, F. (1999). Salud para todos en el año 2000: Una agenda de salud pœblica hispana para el siglo XXI [Health for all by the year 2000: A Hispanic public health agenda for the 21st century]. *Médico Interamericano*, *18*, 6–10. Available: http://www.users.interport.net/~icps/ medico/medico99/january/

Soto Mas, F., & Papenfuss, R. (1997). El médico hispano y la promoción de la salud [The role of the Hispanic physician in health promotion]. *Médico Interamericano*, *16*, 206–209.

Soto Mas, F., Papenfuss, R. L., & Guerrero, J. J. (1997). Hispanics and worksite health promotion: Review of the past, demands for the future. *Journal of Community Health*, *22*, 361–371.

Tichenor, P. J., Donohue, G. A., & Olien, C. N. (1970). Mass media flow and differential growth in knowledge. *Public Opinion Quarterly*, *34*, 159–170.

Turner, B. S. (1987). *Medical power and social knowledge*. Newbury Park, CA: Sage.

U.S. Bureau of the Census. (1993). *Income, poverty and health insurance, 1992*. Washington, DC: Author.

U.S. Department of Health and Human Services. (1996). *Physical activity and health: A report of the surgeon general*. Atlanta, GA: Department of Health and Human Services, Centers for Disease Control and Prevention, National Center for Chronic Disease Prevention and Health Promotion.

van Ryn, M., & Heaney, C. A. (1992). What's the use of theory? *Health Education Quarterly*, *19*, 315–330.

Weber, J., & Wertheim, E. H. (1989). Relationships of self-monitoring, special attention, body fat percent, and self-motivation to attendance at a community gymnasium. *Journal of Sport and Exercise Psychology*, 11, 105–114.

## CLASS ACTIVITY QUESTIONS

1. What were the three main causes or reasons for low physical activity identified by the authors?
2. How were these similar or different from what your group identified?
3. What theories were chosen as the basis for the program, and what was the rationale the authors gave for choosing these theories?
4. How similar or different were these from yours?
5. How did the authors use the constructs of the theories in practice?

# CHAPTER REFERENCES

Hochbaum, G.M., Sorenson, J.R., & Lorig, K. (1992). Theory in health education. *Health Education Quarterly*, *19*(3), 295–313.

National Cancer Institute. (2003). *Theory at a Glance: A Guide for Health Promotion Practice*. Washington, DC: U.S. Department of Health and Human Services.

# Index

Note: Page numbers followed by *b*, *f*, or *t* indicate material in boxes, figures, or tables, respectively.